Modern Standard Arabic Verbs

Conjugation Tables

(by Sample Verb)

Matthew Aldrich

lingualism

ISBN-10: 098581604X

website: www.lingualism.com

Contents

Preface

Modern Standard Arabic Verbs: Conjugation Tables of Sample Verbs aims to present Arabic verb morphology through easy to read tables, organized in a user-friendly manner. The model conjugations in the tables are meant to help learners see patterns, recognize similarities and differences between conjugations, and ultimately to enable learners to conjugate any verb with confidence.

This book is the companion to the *Lingualism Arabic Learner's Dictionary* (ISBN 0985816023), which contains references to the conjugation tables. Every verb appearing in the dictionary falls into one of the conjugation patterns presented in this book. The following pages show how to use the book in conjunction with the dictionary.

Users of this book are expected to have a working background of Arabic verbs from their studies. Although some information is presented in regards to the differences in form and meaning between the measures, a full grammatical explanation of the tenses, moods, methods of negation, etc., is currently beyond the scope of the book.

There are two versions of this book available. The version you are now reading contains **sample verbs**. That is, each conjugation table uses a common verb that belongs to the table's conjugation pattern. The other version of this book (ISBN 0985816031) uses hypothetical verbs with the root ف ع ل in all tables.

Using the Book

Although there are only 120 conjugation tables presented in this book, the patterns found in these tables can be applied to all Arabic verbs. If you give the index at the back of the book a quick look, you will see that thousands of verbs each fit into a certain conjugation table. Very common verbs were chosen to exemplify each pattern. Table 1s3, for example, uses the verb درس (to study) to model the conjugation of all sound measure I verbs which have fatha (a) in the perfect tense and Damma (u) in the imperfect tense.

Each conjugated verb appears above a transcription of the word's pronunciation. The radicals appear gray.

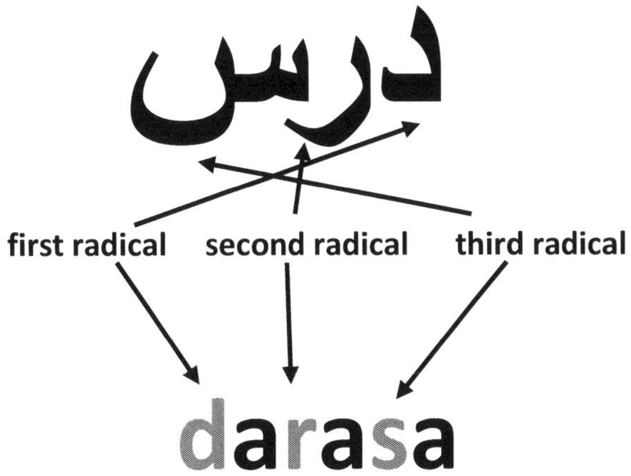

All occurences of the consonants which make up the radical of the model verb in the tables should be swapped out for the radicals in the verb you wish to conjugate. Let's take the verb **كتب** (*kataba* – 'write') as an example. This verb belongs to table **1s3**. If you want to conjugate the verb in the first-person singular indicative (translating 'I write'), first locate this form in the table.

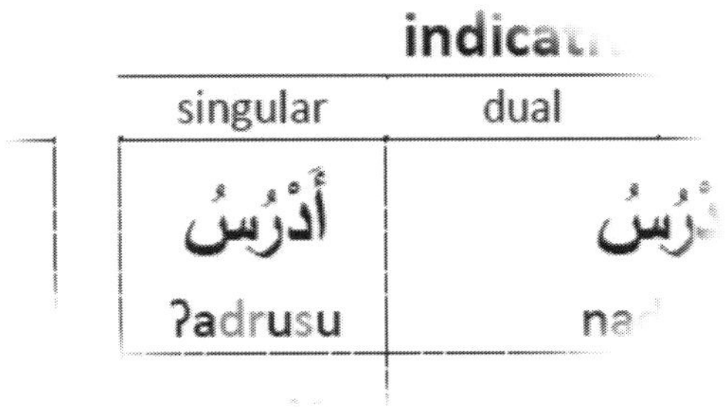

Next, swap out the model radicals for the actual radicals in our verb.

1st radical	د → ك	(d → k)
2nd radical	ر → ت	(r → t)
3rd radical	س → ب	(s → b)

We now have **أَكْتُبُ** (ʔaktubu).

In the *Lingualism Arabic Learner's Dictionary*, every verb entry contains a **reference** to its corresponding table in this book.

> **كتب** *kataba v.tr.* |*1s3* يكتب *yaktub*^{u} | كتابة *kitāba*^{t}|
> • write *sth* ◦ *to* لِـ, write down ◊ كتبت له رسالة طويلة. *I wrote him a long letter.* ▪ كتب بالحروف اللاتينية *kataba bi-lḫurūf*^{i} *-llātīnīya*^{ti} Romanize (lit. write in Latin letters) • write, author, compose, pen

The table name is followed by the third-person singular indicative form and the masdar (gerund).

The index in the back of this book lists all verbs from the dictionary, grouped according to table.

Measure I verbs have unpredictable, unique **masdars**. Verbs which otherwise follow identical patterns and belong to the same table will have different masdar patterns. However, non-measure I verbs have regular masdars, the patterns for which are found in the header for each table.

A unique feature of this book is the consolidation of tables into the minimal number required to model all Arabic verbs. Traditionally, all verbs which contain a weak radical (و or ي) are classified as weak, even when these radicals are treated as regular (sound) consonants. They are then assigned their own conjugation table. This is misleading to the learner, however, and tends to overcomplicate the rules of conjugation. For instance, if the first radical of a measure II verb, is never assimilated. It is treated as a regular consonants, and is thus grouped in table 2s (as a *sound* measure II verb); likewise, measure II verbs are never hollow, and so there is no separate table for those verbs which have a weak second radical. A quick look at the 'check box' in the header of the table 2s on p. 48 confirms that this table is valid for verbs which contain و, ي, as well as 'other' consonants.

Hamzated verbs (those containing ء as a radical) are also treated separately in traditional grammars. In reality, there is no need for this. Hamzated verbs only differ from sound verbs in that the spelling of the hamza is complicated.[1] (Otherwise, the only difference is that the first-person singular of the imperfect tense often takes a long vowel when the first radical is hamza.) Tables for hamzated verbs follow tables for their sound counterparts, taking a variation of the same table name.

Table names consist of two to four parts.

1) Measure number
2) **s** (sound), **g** (geminate), **a** (assimilated), **h** (hollow), **d** (defective)
3) Number showing variation. For example, there are six variations of sound measure I verbs, each with different voweling. These are tables 1s1, 1s2, 1s3, 1s4, 1s5, and 1s6.
4) A letter in parantheses shows a hamzated version of the previous table. Table 1s1(a) has the same voweling as table 1s1 but has a hamza as the second radical.

[1] A table on p. 1 of the *Lingualism Arabic Learner's Dictionary* aids in determining the spelling of hamza.

Pronunciation

Consonants

The following sounds are also found in English and should pose no difficulties for the learner:

			examples
b	ب	[b] as in **b**ed	بنت *bint* girl
d	د	[d̪] as in **d**og, but with the tongue touching the back of the upper teeth	درس *dars* lesson
đ	ذ	[ð] as in **th**at	ذرة *đura*[t] corn
f	ف	[f] as in **f**our	فم *fam* mouth
g	ج/غ	[g] as in **g**as (used for some foreign words; alternatively spelled ك or گ in some regions)	جولف *golf* golf غرام *grām* gram
h	ه	[h] as in **h**ouse	هو *huwa* he
j	ج	[ʤ] as in **j**am (commonly [ʒ] as in bei**g**e in the Levent and [g] as in **g**as in Egypt)	جد *jadd* grandfather
k	ك	[k] as in **k**id	كل *kull* every
l	ل	[l] as in **l**ove *(that is, a light **l**, and not a dark **l** as in yell)*	لبن *laban* milk
L	ل	[ɫ] as the dark ***l*** in ye**ll**, found only in the word الله *aLLāh*	الله *aLLāh* God
m	م	[m] as in **m**oon	مات *māta* die
n	ن	[n] as in **n**ice	نسي *nasiya* forget
p	ب	[p] as in **p**an (used for some foreign words and sometimes written as پ; pronounced [b] by some speakers)	بكين *pikīn* Beijing
s	س	[s] as in **s**un	سنة *sana*[t] year
š	ش	[ʃ] as in **sh**ow	شك *šakk* doubt
t	ت	[t̪] as in **t**ie, but with the tongue touching the back of the upper teeth	تل *tall* hill
ṯ	ث	[θ] as in **th**ink	ثلث *ṯulṯ* third
v	ف	[v] as in **v**alley (used for some foreign words and sometimes written as ڤ; pronounced [f] by some speakers)	فيروس *vayrūs* virus
w	و	[w] as in **w**ord	ود *wadd* wish
y	ي	[j] as in **y**es (when final, usually written without dots (ى) in Egypt)	يد *yad* hand
z	ز	[z] as in **z**oo	زار *zāra* visit

The following sounds have no equivalent in English and require special attention. However, some exist in other languages you may be familiar with.

r	ر	[ɾ] tapped (flapped) as in the Spanish ca**r**a or the Scottish pronunciation of t**r**ee	رجل *rajul* man
ɣ	غ	[ɣ] very similar to a guttural R as in the French Pa**r**is, or the German **r**ot	غرب *ɣarb* west
x	خ	[x] as in the German do**ch**, Spanish ro**j**o, or Scottish lo**ch**	خبر *xabar* news
q	ق	[q] like K but further back, almost in the throat, with the tongue touching the uvula	قدم *qadam* foot
ɦ	ح	[ħ] like a strong, breathy H, as if you were trying to fog up a window	حب *ɦubb* love
3	ع	[ʕ] a voiced glottal stop, as if you had opened your mouth under water and constricted your throat to prevent choking and then released the constriction with a sigh	عرف *3arafa* know
ʔ	ء	[ʔ] an unvoiced glottal stop, as [ʕ] above, but with a wispy, unvoiced sigh; or more simply put, like the constriction separating the vowels in uh-oh	أب *ʔab* father

The following sounds also have no equivalent in English but are emphatic versions of otherwise familiar sounds. An emphatic consonant is produced by pulling the tongue back toward the pharynx (throat), spreading the sides of the tongue wide, as if you wanted to bite down on both sides of your tongue, and producing a good puff of air from the lungs.

ḑ	ض	[dˤ] emphatic version of [d]	ضرب *ḑaraba* hit
ş	ص	[sˤ] emphatic version of [s]	صدر *şadr* chest
ţ	ط	[tˤ] emphatic version of [t]	طبيب *ţabīb* doctor
z̧	ظ	[ðˤ] or [zˤ] emphatic version of [ð] or [z]	ظن *z̧ann* thought

Vowels

			examples
a	ـَ	[æ] normally as in c**a**t (but with the jaw not quite as lowered as in English); [a] as in h**o**t when in the same syllable with ***ħ*** or **3** (with the tongue lower than [æ]); usually [ɑ] as in f**a**ther (but shorter) when in the same word as **q**, **ḍ**, **ṣ**, **ṭ**, **ẓ**, or, in most cases, **r**	كتب *kataba* write حمام *ħammām* bath ضرب *ḍaraba* hit
ā	ـَا/ـَى	[æ:] / [a:] / [ɑ:] as with **a** above but longer	نام *nāma* sleep جوع *jū3* hunger قاد *qāda* lead
i	ـِ	[ɪ] as in k**i**d; when in the same word as **q**, **ḍ**, **ṣ**, **ṭ**, or **ẓ**, [ɨ] with the tongue pulled back a bit	بنت *bint* girl علم *3ilm* knowledge قصة *qiṣṣa*^{t} story
ī	ـِي	[i:] as in sk**i**; when in the same word as **q**, **ḍ**, **ṣ**, **ṭ**, or **ẓ**, [ɨ:] as with **i** above (but longer)	جزيرة *jazīra*^{t} island الصين *aṣṣīn* China
u	ـُ	[ʊ] as in b**oo**k	بد *budd* option
ū	ـُو	[u:] as in m**oo**n	تونة *tūna*^{t} tuna
e		[ɛ] as in b**e**d (used for some foreign words)	إسبرسو *ʔespresō* espresso
o/ō		[o]/[o:] as is b**oa**t, but without the glide to [w] (used for some foreign words)	فودكا *vodka* vodka بروتين *brōtīn* protein
-a^t	ـَة	[a] or [ah] in pausal form; when pronounced in full form with i3rāb, the ^{t} is pronounced.	ذرة *đura*^{t} corn
-u/-a/-i *-un/-an/-in*		Transcription written in superscript (small and raised) represents vowels and nunation which belong to i3rāb (grammatical declension). These vowels are often omitted from relaxed speech or before a pause (end of a sentence, etc.).	

Measure I

Name(s)	non-augmented verb, non-derived verb, basic verb
	مجرد ثلاثي mujarrad ŧulāŧīy
Characteristics	• **triliteral** • the most basic forms of verbs, having no prefixes or doubled consonants • sub-categorized depending on the vowels present in the stem
Meaning(s)	• Measure I verbs are not limited to any particular usage or meaning • Some are transitive, while others are intransitive

Sound Measure I مجرد ثلاثي سالم mujarrad ŧulāŧīy sālim

		imperfect		
perfect		**a**	**i**	**u**
	a	1s1	1s2	1s3
	i	1s4	1s5	
	u			1s6

The perfect tense stem for sound measure I verbs follows the pattern fa3_l-. The vowel **a** always follows the first radical, while the second radical is followed by **a**, **i**, or **u**. The imperfect tense stem is -f3_l-, which also has a variable vowel. The table on the left references the conjugation tables which fit these patterns.

Geminate Measure I مجرد ثلاثي مضاعف mujarrad ŧulāŧīy muḍā3af

		imperfect		
perfect		**a**	**i**	**u**
	a	1g1	1g2	1g3
	i			
	u			

The perfect tense stem for geminate measure I verbs follows the pattern fa33-. The imperfect tense stem is -f_33-, which has a variable vowel.

Assimilated Measure I مجرد ثلاثي معتل الفاء mujarrad ŧulāŧīy mu3tall alfā?

		imperfect		
perfect		**a**	**i**	**u**
	a	1a1	1a2	
	i	1a3		
	u			

The perfect tense stem for assimilated measure I verbs follows the pattern wa3_l-. The first radical is always **w**, which is always followed by **a**. The second radical is followed by either **a** or **i**. The imperfect tense stem is -3_l-, and contains either **a** or **i**. Notice that the **w** is assimilated (disappears) in the imperfect tense.

Hollow Measure I مجرد ثلاثي معتل العين mujarrad ŧulāŧīy mu3tall al3ayn

		imperfect		
perfect		**a**	**i**	**u**
	a			
	i	1h1	1h2	
	u			1h3

The perfect tense stem for hollow measure I verbs follows the pattern fāl-. However, this long **ā** shortens to i or u in many forms. In the imperfect tense, the vowel can be a long or short **a**, **i**, or **u**.

Defective Measure I مجرد ثلاثي معتل اللام mujarrad ŧulāŧīy mu3tall allām

		imperfect		
perfect		**a**	**i**	**u**
	a	1d1	1d2	1d3
	i	1d4	1d5	
	u			

The perfect tense stem for defective measure I verbs follows the pattern fa3-. The vowel **a** always follows the first radical, both in the perfect and imperfect tenses. The vowel following the final radical varies by tense and form.

sound measure I *perfect vowel:* **a** *imperfect vowel:* **a**		و	ي	ء	*other*	**1s1** to go
	R1				✓	
	R2				✓	
	R3				✓	

perfect

	singular	dual	plural
1	ذَهَبْتُ đahabtu	ذَهَبْنَا đahabnā	
2m	ذَهَبْتَ đahabta	ذَهَبْتُمَا đahabtumā	ذَهَبْتُمْ đahabtum
2f	ذَهَبْتِ đahabti		ذَهَبْتُنَّ đahabtunna
3m	ذَهَبَ đahaba	ذَهَبَا đahabā	ذَهَبُوا đahabū
3f	ذَهَبَتْ đahabat	ذَهَبَتَا đahabatā	ذَهَبْنَ đahabna

indicative

	singular	dual	plural
1	أَذْهَبُ ʔađhabu	نَذْهَبُ nađhabu	
2m	تَذْهَبُ tađhabu	تَذْهَبَانِ tađhabāni	تَذْهَبُونَ tađhabūna
2f	تَذْهَبِينَ tađhabīna		تَذْهَبْنَ tađhabna
3m	يَذْهَبُ yađhabu	يَذْهَبَانِ yađhabāni	يَذْهَبُونَ yađhabūna
3f	تَذْهَبُ tađhabu	تَذْهَبَانِ tađhabāni	يَذْهَبْنَ yađhabna

subjunctive

	singular	dual	plural
1	أَذْهَبَ ʔađhaba	نَذْهَبَ nađhaba	
2m	تَذْهَبَ tađhaba	تَذْهَبَا tađhabā	تَذْهَبُوا tađhabū
2f	تَذْهَبِي tađhabī		تَذْهَبْنَ tađhabna
3m	يَذْهَبَ yađhaba	يَذْهَبَا yađhabā	يَذْهَبُوا yađhabū
3f	تَذْهَبَ tađhaba	تَذْهَبَا tađhabā	يَذْهَبْنَ yađhabna

jussive

	singular	dual	plural
1	أَذْهَبْ ʔađhab	نَذْهَبْ nađhab	
2m	تَذْهَبْ tađhab	تَذْهَبَا tađhabā	تَذْهَبُوا tađhabū
2f	تَذْهَبِي tađhabī		تَذْهَبْنَ tađhabna
3m	يَذْهَبْ yađhab	يَذْهَبَا yađhabā	يَذْهَبُوا yađhabū
3f	تَذْهَبْ tađhab	تَذْهَبَا tađhabā	يَذْهَبْنَ yađhabna

imperative

	singular	dual	plural
2m	اِذْهَبْ iđhab	اِذْهَبَا iđhabā	اِذْهَبُوا iđhabū
2f	اِذْهَبِي iđhabī		اِذْهَبْنَ iđhabna

participles

active	passive
ذَاهِب đāhib	مَذْهُوب mađhūb

passive

perfect	imperfect
ذُهِبَ đuhiba	يُذْهَبُ yuđhabu

hamzated measure I *perfect vowel:* **a** *imperfect vowel:* **a**		و	ي	ء	*other*
	R^1				✓
	R^2			✓	
	R^3				✓

1s1(a)
to ask

perfect

	singular	dual	plural
1	سَأَلْتُ saʔaltu	سَأَلْنَا saʔalnā	
2m	سَأَلْتَ saʔalta	سَأَلْتُمَا saʔaltumā	سَأَلْتُمْ saʔaltum
2f	سَأَلْتِ saʔalti		سَأَلْتُنَّ saʔaltunna
3m	سَأَلَ saʔala	سَأَلَا saʔalā	سَأَلُوا saʔalū
3f	سَأَلَتْ saʔalat	سَأَلَتَا saʔalatā	سَأَلْنَ saʔalna

indicative

	singular	dual	plural
1	أَسْأَلُ ʔasʔalu	نَسْأَلُ nasʔalu	
2m	تَسْأَلُ tasʔalu	تَسْأَلَانِ tasʔalāni	تَسْأَلُونَ tasʔalūna
2f	تَسْأَلِينَ tasʔalīna		تَسْأَلْنَ tasʔalna
3m	يَسْأَلُ yasʔalu	يَسْأَلَانِ yasʔalāni	يَسْأَلُونَ yasʔalūna
3f	تَسْأَلُ tasʔalu	تَسْأَلَانِ tasʔalāni	يَسْأَلْنَ yasʔalna

subjunctive

	singular	dual	plural
1	أَسْأَلَ ʔasʔala	نَسْأَلَ nasʔala	
2m	تَسْأَلَ tasʔala	تَسْأَلَا tasʔalā	تَسْأَلُوا tasʔalū
2f	تَسْأَلِي tasʔalī		تَسْأَلْنَ tasʔalna
3m	يَسْأَلَ yasʔala	يَسْأَلَا yasʔalā	يَسْأَلُوا yasʔalū
3f	تَسْأَلَ tasʔala	تَسْأَلَا tasʔalā	يَسْأَلْنَ yasʔalna

jussive

	singular	dual	plural
1	أَسْأَلْ ʔasʔal	نَسْأَلْ nasʔal	
2m	تَسْأَلْ tasʔal	تَسْأَلَا tasʔalā	تَسْأَلُوا tasʔalū
2f	تَسْأَلِي tasʔalī		تَسْأَلْنَ tasʔalna
3m	يَسْأَلْ yasʔal	يَسْأَلَا yasʔalā	يَسْأَلُوا yasʔalū
3f	تَسْأَلْ tasʔal	تَسْأَلَا tasʔalā	يَسْأَلْنَ yasʔalna

imperative

	singular	dual	plural
2m	اِسْأَلْ isʔal	اِسْأَلَا isʔalā	اِسْأَلُوا isʔalū
2f	اِسْأَلِي isʔalī		اِسْأَلْنَ isʔalna

participles

active	passive
سَائِل sāʔil	مَسْؤُول masʔūl

passive

perfect	imperfect
سُئِلَ suʔila	يُسْأَلُ yusʔalu

hamzated measure I *perfect vowel:* **a** *imperfect vowel:* **a**		و	ي	ء	*other*	**1s1(b)** **to begin**
	R¹				✓	
	R²				✓	
	R³			✓		

perfect

	singular	dual	plural
1	بَدَأْتُ badaʔtu	بَدَأْنَا badaʔnā	
2m	بَدَأْتَ badaʔta	بَدَأْتُمَا badaʔtumā	بَدَأْتُمْ badaʔtum
2f	بَدَأْتِ badaʔti		بَدَأْتُنَّ badaʔtunna
3m	بَدَأَ badaʔa	بَدَآ badaʔā	بَدَؤُوا badaʔū
3f	بَدَأَتْ badaʔat	بَدَأَتَا badaʔatā	بَدَأْنَ badaʔna

indicative

	singular	dual	plural
1	أَبْدَأُ ʔabdaʔu	نَبْدَأُ nabdaʔu	
2m	تَبْدَأُ tabdaʔu	تَبْدَآنِ tabdaʔāni	تَبْدَؤُونَ tabdaʔūna
2f	تَبْدَئِينَ tabdaʔīna		تَبْدَأْنَ tabdaʔna
3m	يَبْدَأُ yabdaʔu	يَبْدَآنِ yabdaʔāni	يَبْدَؤُونَ yabdaʔūna
3f	تَبْدَأُ tabdaʔu	تَبْدَآنِ tabdaʔāni	يَبْدَأْنَ yabdaʔna

subjunctive

	singular	dual	plural
1	أَبْدَأَ ʔabdaʔa	نَبْدَأَ nabdaʔa	
2m	تَبْدَأَ tabdaʔa	تَبْدَآ tabdaʔā	تَبْدَؤُوا tabdaʔū
2f	تَبْدَئِي tabdaʔī		تَبْدَأْنَ tabdaʔna
3m	يَبْدَأَ yabdaʔa	يَبْدَآ yabdaʔā	يَبْدَؤُوا yabdaʔū
3f	تَبْدَأَ tabdaʔa	تَبْدَآ tabdaʔā	يَبْدَأْنَ yabdaʔna

jussive

	singular	dual	plural
1	أَبْدَأْ ʔabdaʔ	نَبْدَأْ nabdaʔ	
2m	تَبْدَأْ tabdaʔ	تَبْدَآ tabdaʔā	تَبْدَؤُوا tabdaʔū
2f	تَبْدَئِي tabdaʔī		تَبْدَأْنَ tabdaʔna
3m	يَبْدَأْ yabdaʔ	يَبْدَآ yabdaʔā	يَبْدَؤُوا yabdaʔū
3f	تَبْدَأْ tabdaʔ	تَبْدَآ tabdaʔā	يَبْدَأْنَ yabdaʔna

imperative

	singular	dual	plural
2m	اِبْدَأْ ibdaʔ	اِبْدَآ ibdaʔā	اِبْدَؤُوا ibdaʔū
2f	اِبْدَئِي ibdaʔī		اِبْدَأْنَ ibdaʔna

participles

active	passive
بَادِئ bādiʔ	مَبْدُوء mabdūʔ

passive

perfect	imperfect
بُدِئَ budiʔa	يُبْدَأُ yubdaʔu

sound measure I *perfect vowel:* **a** *imperfect vowel:* **i**		و	ي	ء	*other*	**1s2** **to sit**
	R¹				✓	
	R²				✓	
	R³				✓	

perfect

	singular	dual	plural
1	جَلَسْتُ jalastu	جَلَسْنَا jalasnā	
2m	جَلَسْتَ jalasta	جَلَسْتُمَا jalastumā	جَلَسْتُمْ jalastum
2f	جَلَسْتِ jalasti		جَلَسْتُنَّ jalastunna
3m	جَلَسَ jalasa	جَلَسَا jalasā	جَلَسُوا jalasū
3f	جَلَسَتْ jalasat	جَلَسَتَا jalasatā	جَلَسْنَ jalasna

indicative

	singular	dual	plural
1	أَجْلِسُ ʔajlisu	نَجْلِسُ najlisu	
2m	تَجْلِسُ tajlisu	تَجْلِسَانِ tajlisāni	تَجْلِسُونَ tajlisūna
2f	تَجْلِسِينَ tajlisīna		تَجْلِسْنَ tajlisna
3m	يَجْلِسُ yajlisu	يَجْلِسَانِ yajlisāni	يَجْلِسُونَ yajlisūna
3f	تَجْلِسُ tajlisu	تَجْلِسَانِ tajlisāni	يَجْلِسْنَ yajlisna

subjunctive

	singular	dual	plural
1	أَجْلِسَ ʔajlisa	نَجْلِسَ najlisa	
2m	تَجْلِسَ tajlisa	تَجْلِسَا tajlisā	تَجْلِسُوا tajlisū
2f	تَجْلِسِي tajlisī		تَجْلِسْنَ tajlisna
3m	يَجْلِسَ yajlisa	يَجْلِسَا yajlisā	يَجْلِسُوا yajlisū
3f	تَجْلِسَ tajlisa	تَجْلِسَا tajlisā	يَجْلِسْنَ yajlisna

jussive

	singular	dual	plural
1	أَجْلِسْ ʔajlis	نَجْلِسْ najlis	
2m	تَجْلِسْ tajlis	تَجْلِسَا tajlisā	تَجْلِسُوا tajlisū
2f	تَجْلِسِي tajlisī		تَجْلِسْنَ tajlisna
3m	يَجْلِسْ yajlis	يَجْلِسَا yajlisā	يَجْلِسُوا yajlisū
3f	تَجْلِسْ tajlis	تَجْلِسَا tajlisā	يَجْلِسْنَ yajlisna

imperative

	singular	dual	plural
2m	اِجْلِسْ ijlis	اِجْلِسَا ijlisā	اِجْلِسُوا ijlisū
2f	اِجْلِسِي ijlisī		اِجْلِسْنَ ijlisna

participles

active	passive
جَالِس jālis	مَجْلُوس majlūs

passive

perfect	imperfect
جُلِسَ julisa	يُجْلَسُ yujlasu

hamzated measure I *perfect vowel:* **a** *imperfect vowel:* **i**		و	ي	ء	other	**1s2(a)** to capture
	R¹			✓		
	R²				✓	
	R³				✓	

perfect

	singular	dual	plural
1	أَسَرْتُ ʔasartu	أَسَرْنَا ʔasarnā	
2m	أَسَرْتَ ʔasarta	أَسَرْتُمَا ʔasartumā	أَسَرْتُمْ ʔasartum
2f	أَسَرْتِ ʔasarti		أَسَرْتُنَّ ʔasartunna
3m	أَسَرَ ʔasara	أَسَرَا ʔasarā	أَسَرُوا ʔasarū
3f	أَسَرَتْ ʔasarat	أَسَرَتَا ʔasaratā	أَسَرْنَ ʔasarna

indicative

	singular	dual	plural
1	آسِرُ ʔāsiru	نَأْسِرُ naʔsiru	
2m	تَأْسِرُ taʔsiru	تَأْسِرَانِ taʔsirāni	تَأْسِرُونَ taʔsirūna
2f	تَأْسِرِينَ taʔsirīna		تَأْسِرْنَ taʔsirna
3m	يَأْسِرُ yaʔsiru	يَأْسِرَانِ yaʔsirāni	يَأْسِرُونَ yaʔsirūna
3f	تَأْسِرُ taʔsiru	تَأْسِرَانِ taʔsirāni	يَأْسِرْنَ yaʔsirna

subjunctive

	singular	dual	plural
1	آسِرَ ʔāsira	نَأْسِرَ naʔsira	
2m	تَأْسِرَ taʔsira	تَأْسِرَا taʔsirā	تَأْسِرُوا taʔsirū
2f	تَأْسِرِي taʔsirī		تَأْسِرْنَ taʔsirna
3m	يَأْسِرَ yaʔsira	يَأْسِرَا yaʔsirā	يَأْسِرُوا yaʔsirū
3f	تَأْسِرَ taʔsira	تَأْسِرَا taʔsirā	يَأْسِرْنَ yaʔsirna

jussive

	singular	dual	plural
1	آسِرْ ʔāsir	نَأْسِرْ naʔsir	
2m	تَأْسِرْ taʔsir	تَأْسِرَا taʔsirā	تَأْسِرُوا taʔsirū
2f	تَأْسِرِي taʔsirī		تَأْسِرْنَ taʔsirna
3m	يَأْسِرْ yaʔsir	يَأْسِرَا yaʔsirā	يَأْسِرُوا yaʔsirū
3f	تَأْسِرْ taʔsir	تَأْسِرَا taʔsirā	يَأْسِرْنَ yaʔsirna

imperative

	singular	dual	plural
2m	اِئْسِرْ iʔsir	اِئْسِرَا iʔsirā	اِئْسِرُوا iʔsirū
2f	اِئْسِرِي iʔsirī		اِئْسِرْنَ iʔsirna

participles

active	passive
آسِر ʔāsir	مَأْسُور maʔsūr

passive

perfect	imperfect
أُسِرَ ʔusira	يُؤْسَرُ yuʔsaru

sound measure I *perfect vowel:* **a** *imperfect vowel:* **u**		و	ي	ء	*other*	**1s3** **to study**
	R[1]				✓	
	R[2]				✓	
	R[3]				✓	

perfect

	singular	dual	plural
1	دَرَسْتُ darastu	دَرَسْنَا darasnā	
2m	دَرَسْتَ darasta	دَرَسْتُمَا darastumā	دَرَسْتُمْ darastum
2f	دَرَسْتِ darasti		دَرَسْتُنَّ darastunna
3m	دَرَسَ darasa	دَرَسَا darasā	دَرَسُوا darasū
3f	دَرَسَتْ darasat	دَرَسَتَا darasatā	دَرَسْنَ darasna

indicative

	singular	dual	plural
1	أَدْرُسُ ʔadrusu	نَدْرُسُ nadrusu	
2m	تَدْرُسُ tadrusu	تَدْرُسَانِ tadrusāni	تَدْرُسُونَ tadrusūna
2f	تَدْرُسِينَ tadrusīna		تَدْرُسْنَ tadrusna
3m	يَدْرُسُ yadrusu	يَدْرُسَانِ yadrusāni	يَدْرُسُونَ yadrusūna
3f	تَدْرُسُ tadrusu	تَدْرُسَانِ tadrusāni	يَدْرُسْنَ yadrusna

subjunctive

	singular	dual	plural
1	أَدْرُسَ ʔadrusa	نَدْرُسَ nadrusa	
2m	تَدْرُسَ tadrusa	تَدْرُسَا tadrusā	تَدْرُسُوا tadrusū
2f	تَدْرُسِي tadrusī		تَدْرُسْنَ tadrusna
3m	يَدْرُسَ yadrusa	يَدْرُسَا yadrusā	يَدْرُسُوا yadrusū
3f	تَدْرُسَ tadrusa	تَدْرُسَا tadrusā	يَدْرُسْنَ yadrusna

jussive

	singular	dual	plural
1	أَدْرُسْ ʔadrus	نَدْرُسْ nadrus	
2m	تَدْرُسْ tadrus	تَدْرُسَا tadrusā	تَدْرُسُوا tadrusū
2f	تَدْرُسِي tadrusī		تَدْرُسْنَ tadrusna
3m	يَدْرُسْ yadrus	يَدْرُسَا yadrusā	يَدْرُسُوا yadrusū
3f	تَدْرُسْ tadrus	تَدْرُسَا tadrusā	يَدْرُسْنَ yadrusna

imperative

	singular	dual	plural
2m	أُدْرُسْ udrus	أُدْرُسَا udrusā	أُدْرُسُوا udrusū
2f	أُدْرُسِي udrusī		أُدْرُسْنَ udrusna

participles

active	passive
دَارِس dāris	مَدْرُوس madrūs

passive

perfect	imperfect
دُرِسَ durisa	يُدْرَسُ yadrasu

hamzated measure I *perfect vowel:* **a** *imperfect vowel:* **u**		و	ي	ء	*other*	**1s3(a)** **to order**
	R1			✓		
	R2				✓	
	R3				✓	

perfect

	singular	dual	plural
1	أَمَرْتُ ʔamartu	أَمَرْنَا ʔamarnā	
2m	أَمَرْتَ ʔamarta	أَمَرْتُمَا ʔamartumā	أَمَرْتُمْ ʔamartum
2f	أَمَرْتِ ʔamarti		أَمَرْتُنَّ ʔamartunna
3m	أَمَرَ ʔamara	أَمَرَا ʔamarā	أَمَرُوا ʔamarū
3f	أَمَرَتْ ʔamarat	أَمَرَتَا ʔamaratā	أَمَرْنَ ʔamarna

indicative

	singular	dual	plural
1	آمُرُ ʔāmuru	نَأْمُرُ naʔmuru	
2m	تَأْمُرُ taʔmuru	تَأْمُرَانِ taʔmurāni	تَأْمُرُونَ taʔmurūna
2f	تَأْمُرِينَ taʔmurīna		تَأْمُرْنَ taʔmurna
3m	يَأْمُرُ yaʔmuru	يَأْمُرَانِ yaʔmurāni	يَأْمُرُونَ yaʔmurūna
3f	تَأْمُرُ taʔmuru	تَأْمُرَانِ taʔmurāni	يَأْمُرْنَ yaʔmurna

subjunctive

	singular	dual	plural
1	آمُرَ ʔāmura	نَأْمُرَ naʔmura	
2m	تَأْمُرَ taʔmura	تَأْمُرَا taʔmurā	تَأْمُرُوا taʔmurū
2f	تَأْمُرِي taʔmurī		تَأْمُرْنَ taʔmurna
3m	يَأْمُرَ yaʔmura	يَأْمُرَا yaʔmurā	يَأْمُرُوا yaʔmurū
3f	تَأْمُرَ taʔmura	تَأْمُرَا taʔmurā	يَأْمُرْنَ yaʔmurna

jussive

	singular	dual	plural
1	آمُرْ ʔāmur	نَأْمُرْ naʔmur	
2m	تَأْمُرْ taʔmur	تَأْمُرَا taʔmurā	تَأْمُرُوا taʔmurū
2f	تَأْمُرِي taʔmurī		تَأْمُرْنَ taʔmurna
3m	يَأْمُرْ yaʔmur	يَأْمُرَا yaʔmurā	يَأْمُرُوا yaʔmurū
3f	تَأْمُرْ taʔmur	تَأْمُرَا taʔmurā	يَأْمُرْنَ yaʔmurna

imperative*

	singular	dual	plural
2m	أُؤْمُرْ uʔmur	أُؤْمُرَا uʔmurā	أُؤْمُرُوا uʔmurū
2f	أُؤْمُرِي uʔmurī		أُؤْمُرْنَ uʔmurna

participles

active	passive
آمِر ʔāmir	مَأْمُور maʔmūr

passive

perfect	imperfect
أُمِرَ ʔumira	يُؤْمَرُ yuʔmaru

* The verbs أَكَلَ ʔakala (*eat*) أَخَذَ ʔaxađa (*take*) have irregular imperative forms; they do not begin with أُؤْ: كُلْ, etc.

sound measure I *perfect vowel:* **i** *imperfect vowel:* **a**		و	ي	ء	*other*	**1s4** **to know**
	R¹	(✓)	✓		✓	
	R²				✓	
	R³				✓	

perfect

	singular	dual	plural
1	عَلِمْتُ 3alimtu	عَلِمْنَا 3alimnā	
2m	عَلِمْتَ 3alimta	عَلِمْتُمَا 3alimtumā	عَلِمْتُمْ 3alimtum
2f	عَلِمْتِ 3alimti		عَلِمْتُنَّ 3alimtunna
3m	عَلِمَ 3alima	عَلِمَا 3alimā	عَلِمُوا 3alimū
3f	عَلِمَتْ 3alimat	عَلِمَتَا 3alimatā	عَلِمْنَ 3alimna

indicative

	singular	dual	plural
1	أَعْلَمُ ʔa3lamu	نَعْلَمُ na3lamu	
2m	تَعْلَمُ ta3lamu	تَعْلَمَانِ ta3lamāni	تَعْلَمُونَ ta3lamūna
2f	تَعْلَمِينَ ta3lamīna		تَعْلَمْنَ ta3lamna
3m	يَعْلَمُ ya3lamu	يَعْلَمَانِ ya3lamāni	يَعْلَمُونَ ya3lamūna
3f	تَعْلَمُ ta3lamu	تَعْلَمَانِ ta3lamāni	يَعْلَمْنَ ya3lamna

subjunctive

	singular	dual	plural
1	أَعْلَمَ ʔa3lama	نَعْلَمَ na3lama	
2m	تَعْلَمَ ta3lama	تَعْلَمَا ta3lamā	تَعْلَمُوا ta3lamū
2f	تَعْلَمِي ta3lamī		تَعْلَمْنَ ta3lamna
3m	يَعْلَمَ ya3lama	يَعْلَمَا ya3lamā	يَعْلَمُوا ya3lamū
3f	تَعْلَمَ ta3lama	تَعْلَمَا ta3lamā	يَعْلَمْنَ ya3lamna

jussive

	singular	dual	plural
1	أَعْلَمْ ʔa3lam	نَعْلَمْ na3lam	
2m	تَعْلَمْ ta3lam	تَعْلَمَا ta3lamā	تَعْلَمُوا ta3lamū
2f	تَعْلَمِي ta3lamī		تَعْلَمْنَ ta3lamna
3m	يَعْلَمْ ya3lam	يَعْلَمَا ya3lamā	يَعْلَمُوا ya3lamū
3f	تَعْلَمْ ta3lam	تَعْلَمَا ta3lamā	يَعْلَمْنَ ya3lamna

imperative

	singular	dual	plural
2m	اِعْلَمْ i3lam	اِعْلَمَا i3lamā	اِعْلَمُوا i3lamū
2f	اِعْلَمِي i3lamī		اِعْلَمْنَ i3lamna

participles

active	passive
عَالِم 3ālim	مَعْلُوم ma3lūm

passive

perfect	imperfect
عُلِمَ 3ulima	يُعْلَمُ yu3lamu

hamzated measure I

perfect vowel: **i**
imperfect vowel: **a**

	و	ي	ء	*other*
R[1]			✓	
R[2]				✓
R[3]				✓

1s4(a)
to be sorry

perfect

	singular	dual	plural
1	أَسِفْتُ ʔasiftu	أَسِفْنَا ʔasifnā	
2m	أَسِفْتَ ʔasifta	أَسِفْتُمَا ʔasiftumā	أَسِفْتُمْ ʔasiftum
2f	أَسِفْتِ ʔasifti		أَسِفْتُنَّ ʔasiftunna
3m	أَسِفَ ʔasifa	أَسِفَا ʔasifā	أَسِفُوا ʔasifū
3f	أَسِفَتْ ʔasifat	أَسِفَتَا ʔasifatā	أَسِفْنَ ʔasifna

indicative

	singular	dual	plural
1	آسَفُ ʔāsafu	نَأْسَفُ naʔsafu	
2m	تَأْسَفُ taʔsafu	تَأْسَفَانِ taʔsafāni	تَأْسَفُونَ taʔsafūna
2f	تَأْسَفِينَ taʔsafīna		تَأْسَفْنَ taʔsafna
3m	يَأْسَفُ yaʔsafu	يَأْسَفَانِ yaʔsafāni	يَأْسَفُونَ yaʔsafūna
3f	تَأْسَفُ taʔsafu	تَأْسَفَانِ taʔsafāni	يَأْسَفْنَ yaʔsafna

subjunctive

	singular	dual	plural
1	آسَفَ ʔāsafa	نَأْسَفَ naʔsafa	
2m	تَأْسَفَ taʔsafa	تَأْسَفَا taʔsafā	تَأْسَفُوا taʔsafū
2f	تَأْسَفِي taʔsafī		تَأْسَفْنَ taʔsafna
3m	يَأْسَفَ yaʔsafa	يَأْسَفَا yaʔsafā	يَأْسَفُوا yaʔsafū
3f	تَأْسَفَ taʔsafa	تَأْسَفَا taʔsafā	يَأْسَفْنَ yaʔsafna

jussive

	singular	dual	plural
1	آسَفْ ʔāsaf	نَأْسَفْ naʔsaf	
2m	تَأْسَفْ taʔsaf	تَأْسَفَا taʔsafā	تَأْسَفُوا taʔsafū
2f	تَأْسَفِي taʔsafī		تَأْسَفْنَ taʔsafna
3m	يَأْسَفْ yaʔsaf	يَأْسَفَا yaʔsafā	يَأْسَفُوا yaʔsafū
3f	تَأْسَفْ taʔsaf	تَأْسَفَا taʔsafā	يَأْسَفْنَ yaʔsafna

imperative

	singular	dual	plural
2m	اِئْسَفْ iʔsaf	اِئْسَفَا iʔsafā	اِئْسَفُوا iʔsafū
2f	اِئْسَفِي iʔsafī		اِئْسَفْنَ iʔsafna

participles

active	passive
آسِف ʔāsif	مَأْسُوف maʔsūf

passive

perfect	imperfect
أُسِفَ ʔusifa	يُؤْسَفُ yaʔsafu

hamzated measure I		و	ي	ء	*other*	**1s4(b)**
perfect vowel: **i**	*R¹*		✓		✓	to give up hope
imperfect vowel: **a**	*R²*			✓		
	R³				✓	

perfect

	singular	dual	plural
1	يَئِسْتُ yaʔistu	يَئِسْنَا yaʔisnā	
2m	يَئِسْتَ yaʔista	يَئِسْتُمَا yaʔistumā	يَئِسْتُمْ yaʔistum
2f	يَئِسْتِ yaʔisti		يَئِسْتُنَّ yaʔistunna
3m	يَئِسَ yaʔisa	يَئِسَا yaʔisā	يَئِسُوا yaʔisū
3f	يَئِسَتْ yaʔisat	يَئِسَتَا yaʔisatā	يَئِسْنَ yaʔisna

indicative

	singular	dual	plural
1	أَيْأَسُ ʔayʔasu	نَيْأَسُ nayʔasu	
2m	تَيْأَسُ tayʔasu	تَيْأَسَانِ tayʔasāni	تَيْأَسُونَ tayʔasūna
2f	تَيْأَسِينَ tayʔasīna		تَيْأَسْنَ tayʔasna
3m	يَيْأَسُ yayʔasu	يَيْأَسَانِ yayʔasāni	يَيْأَسُونَ yayʔasūna
3f	تَيْأَسُ tayʔasu	تَيْأَسَانِ tayʔasāni	يَيْأَسْنَ yayʔasna

subjunctive

	singular	dual	plural
1	أَيْأَسَ ʔayʔasa	نَيْأَسَ nayʔasa	
2m	تَيْأَسَ tayʔasa	تَيْأَسَا tayʔasā	تَيْأَسُوا tayʔasū
2f	تَيْأَسِي tayʔasī		تَيْأَسْنَ tayʔasna
3m	يَيْأَسَ yayʔasa	يَيْأَسَا yayʔasā	يَيْأَسُوا yayʔasū
3f	تَيْأَسَ tayʔasa	تَيْأَسَا tayʔasā	يَيْأَسْنَ yayʔasna

jussive

	singular	dual	plural
1	أَيْأَسْ ʔayʔas	نَيْأَسْ nayʔas	
2m	تَيْأَسْ tayʔas	تَيْأَسَا tayʔasā	تَيْأَسُوا tayʔasū
2f	تَيْأَسِي tayʔasī		تَيْأَسْنَ tayʔasna
3m	يَيْأَسْ yayʔas	يَيْأَسَا yayʔasā	يَيْأَسُوا yayʔasū
3f	تَيْأَسْ tayʔas	تَيْأَسَا tayʔasā	يَيْأَسْنَ yayʔasna

imperative

	singular	dual	plural
2m	اِيْأَسْ iyʔas	اِيْأَسَا iyʔasā	اِيْأَسُوا iyʔasū
2f	اِيْأَسِي iyʔasī		اِيْأَسْنَ iyʔasna

participles

active	passive
يَائِس yāʔis	مَيْؤُوس mayʔūs

passive

perfect	imperfect
يُئِسَ yuʔisa	يُيْأَسُ yuyʔasu

hamzated measure I

perfect vowel: **i**
imperfect vowel: **a**

	و	ي	ء	*other*
*R*¹				✓
*R*²				✓
*R*³			✓	

1s4(c)

to be mistaken

perfect

	singular	dual	plural
1	خَطِئْتُ xaṭiʔtu	خَطِئْنَا xaṭiʔnā	
2m	خَطِئْتَ xaṭiʔta	خَطِئْتُمَا xaṭiʔtumā	خَطِئْتُمْ xaṭiʔtum
2f	خَطِئْتِ xaṭiʔti		خَطِئْتُنَّ xaṭiʔtunna
3m	خَطِئَ xaṭiʔa	خَطِئَا xaṭiʔā	خَطِئُوا xaṭiʔū
3f	خَطِئَتْ xaṭiʔat	خَطِئَتَا xaṭiʔatā	خَطِئْنَ xaṭiʔna

indicative

	singular	dual	plural
1	أَخْطَأُ ʔaxṭaʔu	نَخْطَأُ naxṭaʔu	
2m	تَخْطَأُ taxṭaʔu	تَخْطَآنِ taxṭaʔāni	تَخْطَؤُونَ taxṭaʔūna
2f	تَخْطَئِينَ taxṭaʔīna		تَخْطَأْنَ taxṭaʔna
3m	يَخْطَأُ yaxṭaʔu	يَخْطَآنِ yaxṭaʔāni	يَخْطَؤُونَ yaxṭaʔūna
3f	تَخْطَأُ taxṭaʔu	تَخْطَآنِ taxṭaʔāni	يَخْطَأْنَ yaxṭaʔna

subjunctive

	singular	dual	plural
1	أَخْطَأَ ʔaxṭaʔa	نَخْطَأَ naxṭaʔa	
2m	تَخْطَأَ taxṭaʔa	تَخْطَآ taxṭaʔā	تَخْطَؤُوا taxṭaʔū
2f	تَخْطَئِي taxṭaʔī		تَخْطَأْنَ taxṭaʔna
3m	يَخْطَأَ yaxṭaʔa	يَخْطَآ yaxṭaʔā	يَخْطَؤُوا yaxṭaʔū
3f	تَخْطَأَ taxṭaʔa	تَخْطَآ taxṭaʔā	يَخْطَأْنَ yaxṭaʔna

jussive

	singular	dual	plural
1	أَخْطَأْ ʔaxṭaʔ	نَخْطَأْ naxṭaʔ	
2m	تَخْطَأْ taxṭaʔ	تَخْطَآ taxṭaʔā	تَخْطَؤُوا taxṭaʔū
2f	تَخْطَئِي taxṭaʔī		تَخْطَأْنَ taxṭaʔna
3m	يَخْطَأْ yaxṭaʔ	يَخْطَآ yaxṭaʔā	يَخْطَؤُوا yaxṭaʔū
3f	تَخْطَأْ taxṭaʔ	تَخْطَآ taxṭaʔā	يَخْطَأْنَ yaxṭaʔna

imperative

	singular	dual	plural
2m	اِخْطَأْ ixṭaʔ	اِخْطَآ ixṭaʔā	اِخْطَؤُوا ixṭaʔū
2f	اِخْطَئِي ixṭaʔī		اِخْطَأْنَ ixṭaʔna

participles

active	passive
خَاطِئ xāṭiʔ	مَخْطُوء maxṭūʔ

passive

perfect	imperfect
خُطِئَ xuṭiʔa	يُخْطَأُ yuxṭaʔu

sound measure I *perfect vowel:* **i** *imperfect vowel:* **i**		و	ي	ء	*other*	**1s5** **to gain**
	R¹				✓	
	R²				✓	
	R³				✓	

perfect

	singular	dual	plural
1	رَبِحْتُ rabiɧtu	رَبِحْنَا rabiɧnā	
2m	رَبِحْتَ rabiɧta	رَبِحْتُمَا rabiɧtumā	رَبِحْتُمْ rabiɧtum
2f	رَبِحْتِ rabiɧti		رَبِحْتُنَّ rabiɧtunna
3m	رَبِحَ rabiɧa	رَبِحَا rabiɧā	رَبِحُوا rabiɧū
3f	رَبِحَتْ rabiɧat	رَبِحَتَا rabiɧatā	رَبِحْنَ rabiɧna

indicative

	singular	dual	plural
1	أَرْبِحُ ʔarbiɧu	نَرْبِحُ narbiɧu	
2m	تَرْبِحُ tarbiɧu	تَرْبِحَانِ tarbiɧāni	تَرْبِحُونَ tarbiɧūna
2f	تَرْبِحِينَ tarbiɧīna		تَرْبِحْنَ tarbiɧna
3m	يَرْبِحُ yarbiɧu	يَرْبِحَانِ yarbiɧāni	يَرْبِحُونَ yarbiɧūna
3f	تَرْبِحُ tarbiɧu	تَرْبِحَانِ tarbiɧāni	يَرْبِحْنَ yarbiɧna

subjunctive

	singular	dual	plural
1	أَرْبِحَ ʔarbiɧa	نَرْبِحَ narbiɧa	
2m	تَرْبِحَ tarbiɧa	تَرْبِحَا tarbiɧā	تَرْبِحُوا tarbiɧū
2f	تَرْبِحِي tarbiɧī		تَرْبِحْنَ tarbiɧna
3m	يَرْبِحَ yarbiɧa	يَرْبِحَا yarbiɧā	يَرْبِحُوا yarbiɧū
3f	تَرْبِحَ tarbiɧa	تَرْبِحَا tarbiɧā	يَرْبِحْنَ yarbiɧna

jussive

	singular	dual	plural
1	أَرْبِحْ ʔarbiɧ	نَرْبِحْ narbiɧ	
2m	تَرْبِحْ tarbiɧ	تَرْبِحَا tarbiɧā	تَرْبِحُوا tarbiɧū
2f	تَرْبِحِي tarbiɧī		تَرْبِحْنَ tarbiɧna
3m	يَرْبِحْ yarbiɧ	يَرْبِحَا yarbiɧā	يَرْبِحُوا yarbiɧū
3f	تَرْبِحْ tarbiɧ	تَرْبِحَا tarbiɧā	يَرْبِحْنَ yarbiɧna

imperative

	singular	dual	plural
2m	اِرْبِحْ irbiɧ	اِرْبِحَا irbiɧā	اِرْبِحُوا irbiɧū
2f	اِرْبِحِي irbiɧī		اِرْبِحْنَ irbiɧna

participles

active	passive
رَابِح rābiɧ	مَرْبُوح marbūɧ

passive

perfect	imperfect
رُبِحَ rubiɧa	يُرْبَحُ yurbaɧu

sound measure I *perfect vowel:* **u** *imperfect vowel:* **u**		و	ي	ء	*other*	**1s6** **to grow**
	R¹	(✓)			✓	
	R²				✓	
	R³				✓	

perfect

	singular	dual	plural
1	كَبُرْتُ kaburtu	كَبُرْنَا kaburnā	
2m	كَبُرْتَ kaburta	كَبُرْتُمَا kaburtumā	كَبُرْتُمْ kaburtum
2f	كَبُرْتِ kaburti		كَبُرْتُنَّ kaburtunna
3m	كَبُرَ kabura	كَبُرَا kaburā	كَبُرُوا kaburū
3f	كَبُرَتْ kaburat	كَبُرَتَا kaburatā	كَبُرْنَ kaburna

indicative

	singular	dual	plural
1	أَكْبُرُ ʔakburu	نَكْبُرُ nakburu	
2m	تَكْبُرُ takburu	تَكْبُرَانِ takburāni	تَكْبُرُونَ takburūna
2f	تَكْبُرِينَ takburīna		تَكْبُرْنَ takburna
3m	يَكْبُرُ yakburu	يَكْبُرَانِ yakburāni	يَكْبُرُونَ yakburūna
3f	تَكْبُرُ takburu	تَكْبُرَانِ takburāni	يَكْبُرْنَ yakburna

subjunctive

	singular	dual	plural
1	أَكْبُرَ ʔakbura	نَكْبُرَ nakbura	
2m	تَكْبُرَ takbura	تَكْبُرَا takburā	تَكْبُرُوا takburū
2f	تَكْبُرِي takburī		تَكْبُرْنَ takburna
3m	يَكْبُرَ yakbura	يَكْبُرَا yakburā	يَكْبُرُوا yakburū
3f	تَكْبُرَ takbura	تَكْبُرَا takburā	يَكْبُرْنَ yakburna

jussive

	singular	dual	plural
1	أَكْبُرْ ʔakbur	نَكْبُرْ nakbur	
2m	تَكْبُرْ takbur	تَكْبُرَا takburā	تَكْبُرُوا takburū
2f	تَكْبُرِي takburī		تَكْبُرْنَ takburna
3m	يَكْبُرْ yakbur	يَكْبُرَا yakburā	يَكْبُرُوا yakburū
3f	تَكْبُرْ takbur	تَكْبُرَا takburā	يَكْبُرْنَ yakburna

imperative

	singular	dual	plural
2m	أُكْبُرْ ukbur	أُكْبُرَا ukburā	أُكْبُرُوا ukburū
2f	أُكْبُرِي ukburī		أُكْبُرْنَ ukburna

participle

active
كَبِير kabīr

hamzated measure I *perfect vowel:* **u** *imperfect vowel:* **u**		و	ي	ء	*other*
	R^1			✓	
	R^2				✓
	R^3				✓

1s6(a)

to be faithful

perfect

	singular	dual	plural
1	أَمُنْتُ ʔamuntu	أَمُنَّا ʔamunnā	
2m	أَمُنْتَ ʔamunta	أَمُنْتُمَا ʔamuntumā	أَمُنْتُمْ ʔamuntum
2f	أَمُنْتِ ʔamunti		أَمُنْتُنَّ ʔamuntunna
3m	أَمُنَ ʔamuna	أَمُنَا ʔamunā	أَمُنُوا ʔamunū
3f	أَمُنَتْ ʔamunat	أَمُنَتَا ʔamunatā	أَمُنَّ ʔamunna

indicative

	singular	dual	plural
1	آمُنُ ʔāmunu	نَأْمُنُ naʔmunu	
2m	تَأْمُنُ taʔmunu	تَأْمُنَانِ taʔmunāni	تَأْمُنُونَ taʔmunūna
2f	تَأْمُنِينَ taʔmunīna		تَأْمُنَّ taʔmunna
3m	يَأْمُنُ yaʔmunu	يَأْمُنَانِ yaʔmunāni	يَأْمُنُونَ yaʔmunūna
3f	تَأْمُنُ taʔmunu	تَأْمُنَانِ taʔmunāni	يَأْمُنَّ yaʔmunna

subjunctive

	singular	dual	plural
1	آمُنَ ʔāmuna	نَأْمُنَ naʔmuna	
2m	تَأْمُنَ taʔmuna	تَأْمُنَا taʔmunā	تَأْمُنُوا taʔmunū
2f	تَأْمُنِي taʔmunī		تَأْمُنَّ taʔmunna
3m	يَأْمُنَ yaʔmuna	يَأْمُنَا yaʔmunā	يَأْمُنُوا yaʔmunū
3f	تَأْمُنَ taʔmuna	تَأْمُنَا taʔmunā	يَأْمُنَّ yaʔmunna

jussive

	singular	dual	plural
1	آمُنْ ʔāmun	نَأْمُنْ naʔmun	
2m	تَأْمُنْ taʔmun	تَأْمُنَا taʔmunā	تَأْمُنُوا taʔmunū
2f	تَأْمُنِي taʔmunī		تَأْمُنَّ taʔmunna
3m	يَأْمُنْ yaʔmun	يَأْمُنَا yaʔmunā	يَأْمُنُوا yaʔmunū
3f	تَأْمُنْ taʔmun	تَأْمُنَا taʔmunā	يَأْمُنَّ yaʔmunna

imperative

	singular	dual	plural
2m	أُؤْمُنْ uʔmun	أُؤْمُنَا uʔmunā	أُؤْمُنُوا uʔmunū
2f	أُؤْمُنِي uʔmunī		أُؤْمُنَّ uʔmunna

participle

active
أَمِين ʔamīn

hamzated measure I *perfect vowel:* **u** *imperfect vowel:* **u**		و	ي	ء	*other*	**1s6(b)** **to be brave**
	R^1				✓	
	R^2			✓		
	R^3				✓	

perfect

	singular	dual	plural
1	بَؤُسْتُ baʔustu	بَؤُسْنَا baʔusnā	
2m	بَؤُسْتَ baʔusta	بَؤُسْتُمَا baʔustumā	بَؤُسْتُمْ baʔustum
2f	بَؤُسْتِ baʔusti		بَؤُسْتُنَّ baʔustunna
3m	بَؤُسَ baʔusa	بَؤُسَا baʔusā	بَؤُسُوا baʔusū
3f	بَؤُسَتْ baʔusat	بَؤُسَتَا baʔusatā	بَؤُسْنَ baʔusna

indicative

	singular	dual	plural
1	أَبْؤُسُ ʔabʔusu	نَبْؤُسُ nabʔusu	
2m	تَبْؤُسُ tabʔusu	تَبْؤُسَانِ tabʔusāni	تَبْؤُسُونَ tabʔusūna
2f	تَبْؤُسِينَ tabʔusīna		تَبْؤُسْنَ tabʔusna
3m	يَبْؤُسُ yabʔusu	يَبْؤُسَانِ yabʔusāni	يَبْؤُسُونَ yabʔusūna
3f	تَبْؤُسُ tabʔusu	تَبْؤُسَانِ tabʔusāni	يَبْؤُسْنَ yabʔusna

subjunctive

	singular	dual	plural
1	أَبْؤُسَ ʔabʔusa	نَبْؤُسَ nabʔusa	
2m	تَبْؤُسَ tabʔusa	تَبْؤُسَا tabʔusā	تَبْؤُسُوا tabʔusū
2f	تَبْؤُسِي tabʔusī		تَبْؤُسْنَ tabʔusna
3m	يَبْؤُسَ yabʔusa	يَبْؤُسَا yabʔusā	يَبْؤُسُوا yabʔusū
3f	تَبْؤُسَ tabʔusa	تَبْؤُسَا tabʔusā	يَبْؤُسْنَ yabʔusna

jussive

	singular	dual	plural
1	أَبْؤُسْ ʔabʔus	نَبْؤُسْ nabʔus	
2m	تَبْؤُسْ tabʔus	تَبْؤُسَا tabʔusā	تَبْؤُسُوا tabʔusū
2f	تَبْؤُسِي tabʔusī		تَبْؤُسْنَ tabʔusna
3m	يَبْؤُسْ yabʔus	يَبْؤُسَا yabʔusā	يَبْؤُسُوا yabʔusū
3f	تَبْؤُسْ tabʔus	تَبْؤُسَا tabʔusā	يَبْؤُسْنَ yabʔusna

imperative

	singular	dual	plural
2m	أُبْؤُسْ ubʔus	أُبْؤُسَا ubʔusā	أُبْؤُسُوا ubʔusū
2f	أُبْؤُسِي ubʔusī		أُبْؤُسْنَ ubʔusna

participle

active
بَائِس bāʔis

hamzated measure I

perfect vowel: **u**
imperfect vowel: **u**

	و	ي	ء	*other*
R¹				✓
R²				✓
R³			✓	

1s6(c)
to be slow

perfect

	singular	dual	plural
1	بَطُؤْتُ baṭuʔtu	بَطُؤْنَا baṭuʔnā	
2m	بَطُؤْتَ baṭuʔta	بَطُؤْتُمَا baṭuʔtumā	بَطُؤْتُمْ baṭuʔtum
2f	بَطُؤْتِ baṭuʔti		بَطُؤْتُنَّ baṭuʔtunna
3m	بَطُؤَ baṭuʔa	بَطُؤَا baṭuʔā	بَطُؤُوا baṭuʔū
3f	بَطُؤَتْ baṭuʔat	بَطُؤَتَا baṭuʔatā	بَطُؤْنَ baṭuʔna

indicative

	singular	dual	plural
1	أَبْطُؤُ ʔabṭuʔu	نَبْطُؤُ nabṭuʔu	
2m	تَبْطُؤُ tabṭuʔu	تَبْطُؤَانِ tabṭuʔāni	تَبْطُؤُونَ tabṭuʔūna
2f	تَبْطُئِينَ tabṭuʔīna		تَبْطُؤْنَ tabṭuʔna
3m	يَبْطُؤُ yabṭuʔu	يَبْطُؤَانِ yabṭuʔāni	يَبْطُؤُونَ yabṭuʔūna
3f	تَبْطُؤُ tabṭuʔu	تَبْطُؤَانِ tabṭuʔāni	يَبْطُؤْنَ yabṭuʔna

subjunctive

	singular	dual	plural
1	أَبْطُؤَ ʔabṭuʔa	نَبْطُؤَ nabṭuʔa	
2m	تَبْطُؤَ tabṭuʔa	تَبْطُؤَا tabṭuʔā	تَبْطُؤُوا tabṭuʔū
2f	تَبْطُئِي tabṭuʔī		تَبْطُؤْنَ tabṭuʔna
3m	يَبْطُؤَ yabṭuʔa	يَبْطُؤَا yabṭuʔā	يَبْطُؤُوا yabṭuʔū
3f	تَبْطُؤَ tabṭuʔa	تَبْطُؤَا tabṭuʔā	يَبْطُؤْنَ yabṭuʔna

jussive

	singular	dual	plural
1	أَبْطُؤْ ʔabṭuʔ	نَبْطُؤْ nabṭuʔ	
2m	تَبْطُؤْ tabṭuʔ	تَبْطُؤَا tabṭuʔā	تَبْطُؤُوا tabṭuʔū
2f	تَبْطُئِي tabṭuʔī		تَبْطُؤْنَ tabṭuʔna
3m	يَبْطُؤْ yabṭuʔ	يَبْطُؤَا yabṭuʔā	يَبْطُؤُوا yabṭuʔū
3f	تَبْطُؤْ tabṭuʔ	تَبْطُؤَا tabṭuʔā	يَبْطُؤْنَ yabṭuʔna

imperative

	singular	dual	plural
2m	أُبْطُؤْ ubṭuʔ	أُبْطُؤَا ubṭuʔā	أُبْطُؤُوا ubṭuʔū
2f	أُبْطُئِي ubṭuʔī		أُبْطُؤْنَ ubṭuʔna

participle

active
بَطِيء baṭīʔ

geminate measure I

perfect vowel: **a**
imperfect vowel: **a**

	و	ي	ء	other
R^1	✓			✓
R^2				✓
R^3				✓

1g1
to continue

perfect

	singular	dual	plural
1	ظَلَلْتُ ẓalaltu	ظَلَلْنَا ẓalalnā	
2m	ظَلَلْتَ ẓalalta	ظَلَلْتُمَا ẓalaltumā	ظَلَلْتُمْ ẓalaltum
2f	ظَلَلْتِ ẓalalti		ظَلَلْتُنَّ ẓalaltunna
3m	ظَلَّ ẓalla	ظَلَّا ẓallā	ظَلُّوا ẓallū
3f	ظَلَّتْ ẓallat	ظَلَّتَا ẓallatā	ظَلَلْنَ ẓalalna

indicative

	singular	dual	plural
1	أَظَلُّ ʔaẓallu	نَظَلُّ naẓallu	
2m	تَظَلُّ taẓallu	تَظَلَّانِ taẓallāni	تَظَلُّونَ taẓallūna
2f	تَظَلِّينَ taẓallīna		تَظْلَلْنَ taẓlalna
3m	يَظَلُّ yaẓallu	يَظَلَّانِ yaẓallāni	يَظَلُّونَ yaẓallūna
3f	تَظَلُّ taẓallu	تَظَلَّانِ taẓallāni	يَظْلَلْنَ yaẓlalna

subjunctive

	singular	dual	plural
1	أَظَلَّ ʔaẓalla	نَظَلَّ naẓalla	
2m	تَظَلَّ taẓalla	تَظَلَّا taẓallā	تَظَلُّوا taẓallū
2f	تَظَلِّي taẓallī		تَظْلَلْنَ taẓlalna
3m	يَظَلَّ yaẓalla	يَظَلَّا yaẓallā	يَظَلُّوا yaẓallū
3f	تَظَلَّ taẓalla	تَظَلَّا taẓallā	يَظْلَلْنَ yaẓlalna

jussive

	singular	dual	plural
1	أَظَلَّ ʔaẓalla	نَظَلَّ naẓalla	
2m	تَظَلَّ taẓalla	تَظَلَّا taẓallā	تَظَلُّوا taẓallū
2f	تَظَلِّي taẓallī		تَظْلَلْنَ taẓlalna
3m	يَظَلَّ yaẓalla	يَظَلَّا yaẓallā	يَظَلُّوا yaẓallū
3f	تَظَلَّ taẓalla	تَظَلَّا taẓallā	يَظْلَلْنَ yaẓlalna

imperative

	singular	dual	plural
2m	ظَلَّ ẓalla	ظَلَّا ẓallā	ظَلُّوا ẓallū
2f	ظَلِّي ẓallī		اِظْلَلْنَ iẓlalna

participles

active	passive
ظَالّ ẓāll	مَظْلُول maẓlūl

passive

perfect	imperfect
ظُلَّ ẓulla	يُظَلُّ yuẓallu

geminate measure I		و	ي	ء	other	**1g2**
perfect vowel: **a**	R[1]				✓	to be less
imperfect vowel: **i**	R[2]				✓	
	R[3]				✓	

perfect

	singular	dual	plural
1	قَلَلْتُ qalaltu	قَلَلْنَا qalalnā	
2m	قَلَلْتَ qalalta	قَلَلْتُمَا qalaltumā	قَلَلْتُمْ qalaltum
2f	قَلَلْتِ qalalti		قَلَلْتُنَّ qalaltunna
3m	قَلَّ qalla	قَلَّا qallā	قَلُّوا qallū
3f	قَلَّتْ qallat	قَلَّتَا qallatā	قَلَلْنَ qalalna

indicative

	singular	dual	plural
1	أَقِلُّ ʔaqillu	نَقِلُّ naqillu	
2m	تَقِلُّ taqillu	تَقِلَّانِ taqillāni	تَقِلُّونَ taqillūna
2f	تَقِلِّينَ taqillīna		تَقْلِلْنَ taqlilna
3m	يَقِلُّ yaqillu	يَقِلَّانِ yaqillāni	يَقِلُّونَ yaqillūna
3f	تَقِلُّ taqillu	تَقِلَّانِ taqillāni	يَقْلِلْنَ yaqlilna

subjunctive

	singular	dual	plural
1	أَقِلَّ ʔaqilla	نَقِلَّ naqilla	
2m	تَقِلَّ taqilla	تَقِلَّا taqillā	تَقِلُّوا taqillū
2f	تَقِلِّي taqillī		تَقْلِلْنَ taqlilna
3m	يَقِلَّ yaqilla	يَقِلَّا yaqillā	يَقِلُّوا yaqillū
3f	تَقِلَّ taqilla	تَقِلَّا taqillā	يَقْلِلْنَ yaqlilna

jussive

	singular	dual	plural
1	أَقِلَّ ʔaqilla	نَقِلَّ naqilla	
2m	تَقِلَّ taqilla	تَقِلَّا taqillā	تَقِلُّوا taqillū
2f	تَقِلِّي taqillī		تَقْلِلْنَ taqlilna
3m	يَقِلَّ yaqilla	يَقِلَّا yaqillā	يَقِلُّوا yaqillū
3f	تَقِلَّ taqilla	تَقِلَّا taqillā	يَقْلِلْنَ yaqlilna

imperative

	singular	dual	plural
2m	قِلَّ qilla	قِلَّا qillā	قِلُّوا qillū
2f	قِلِّي qillī		اِقْلِلْنَ iqlilna

participles

active	passive
قَالّ qāll	مَقْلُول maqlūl

passive

perfect	imperfect
قُلَّ qulla	يُقَلُّ yuqallu

hamzated geminate measure I *perfect vowel:* **a** *imperfect vowel:* **i**		و	ي	ء	*other*	**1g2(a)** **to moan**
	R¹			✓		
	R²				✓	
	R³				✓	

perfect

	singular	dual	plural
1	أَنَنْتُ ʔanantu	أَنَنَّا ʔanannā	
2m	أَنَنْتَ ʔananta	أَنَنْتُمَا ʔanantumā	أَنَنْتُمْ ʔanantum
2f	أَنَنْتِ ʔananti		أَنَنْتُنَّ ʔanantunna
3m	أَنَّ ʔanna	أَنَّا ʔannā	أَنُّوا ʔannū
3f	أَنَّتْ ʔannat	أَنَّتَا ʔannatā	أَنَنَّ ʔananna

indicative

	singular	dual	plural
1	أَئِنُّ ʔaʔinnu	نَئِنُّ naʔinnu	
2m	تَئِنُّ taʔinnu	تَئِنَّانِ taʔinnāni	تَئِنُّونَ taʔinnūna
2f	تَئِنِّينَ taʔinnīna		تَأْنِنَّ taʔninna
3m	يَئِنُّ yaʔinnu	يَئِنَّانِ yaʔinnāni	يَئِنُّونَ yaʔinnūna
3f	تَئِنُّ taʔinnu	تَئِنَّانِ taʔinnāni	يَأْنِنَّ yaʔninna

subjunctive

	singular	dual	plural
1	أَئِنَّ ʔaʔinna	نَئِنَّ naʔinna	
2m	تَئِنَّ taʔinna	تَئِنَّا taʔinnā	تَئِنُّوا taʔinnū
2f	تَئِنِّي taʔinnī		تَأْنِنَّ taʔninna
3m	يَئِنَّ yaʔinna	يَئِنَّا yaʔinnā	يَئِنُّوا yaʔinnū
3f	تَئِنَّ taʔinna	تَئِنَّا taʔinnā	يَأْنِنَّ yaʔninna

jussive

	singular	dual	plural
1	أَئِنَّ ʔaʔinna	نَئِنَّ naʔinna	
2m	تَئِنَّ taʔinna	تَئِنَّا taʔinnā	تَئِنُّوا taʔinnū
2f	تَئِنِّي taʔinnī		تَأْنِنَّ taʔninna
3m	يَئِنَّ yaʔinna	يَئِنَّا yaʔinnā	يَئِنُّوا yaʔinnū
3f	تَئِنَّ taʔinna	تَئِنَّا taʔinnā	يَأْنِنَّ yaʔninna

imperative

	singular	dual	plural
2m	إِنَّ ʔinna	إِنَّا ʔinnā	إِنُّوا ʔinnū
2f	إِنِّي ʔinnī		اِئْنِنَّ iʔninna

participles

active	passive
آنّ ʔānn	مَأْنُون maʔnūn

passive

perfect	imperfect
أُنَّ ʔunna	يُؤَنُّ yuʔannu

geminate measure I		و	ي	ء	other	**1g3**
perfect vowel: **a**	*R¹*				✓	**to reply**
imperfect vowel: **u**	*R²*				✓	
	R³				✓	

perfect

	singular	dual	plural
1	رَدَدْتُ radadtu	رَدَدْنَا radadnā	
2m	رَدَدْتَ radadta	رَدَدْتُمَا radadtumā	رَدَدْتُمْ radadtum
2f	رَدَدْتِ radadti		رَدَدْتُنَّ radadtunna
3m	رَدَّ radda	رَدَّا raddā	رَدُّوا raddū
3f	رَدَّتْ raddat	رَدَّتَا raddatā	رَدَدْنَ radadna

indicative

	singular	dual	plural
1	أَرُدُّ ʔaruddu	نَرُدُّ naruddu	
2m	تَرُدُّ taruddu	تَرُدَّانِ taruddāni	تَرُدُّونَ taruddūna
2f	تَرُدِّينَ taruddīna		تَرْدُدْنَ tardudna
3m	يَرُدُّ yaruddu	يَرُدَّانِ yaruddāni	يَرُدُّونَ yaruddūna
3f	تَرُدُّ taruddu	تَرُدَّانِ taruddāni	يَرْدُدْنَ yardudna

subjunctive

	singular	dual	plural
1	أَرُدَّ ʔarudda	نَرُدَّ narudda	
2m	تَرُدَّ tarudda	تَرُدَّا taruddā	تَرُدُّوا taruddū
2f	تَرُدِّي taruddī		تَرْدُدْنَ tardudna
3m	يَرُدَّ yarudda	يَرُدَّا yaruddā	يَرُدُّوا yaruddū
3f	تَرُدَّ tarudda	تَرُدَّا taruddā	يَرْدُدْنَ yardudna

jussive

	singular	dual	plural
1	أَرُدَّ ʔarudda	نَرُدَّ narudda	
2m	تَرُدَّ tarudda	تَرُدَّا taruddā	تَرُدُّوا taruddū
2f	تَرُدِّي taruddī		تَرْدُدْنَ tardudna
3m	يَرُدَّ yarudda	يَرُدَّا yaruddā	يَرُدُّوا yaruddū
3f	تَرُدَّ tarudda	تَرُدَّا taruddā	يَرْدُدْنَ yardudna

imperative

	singular	dual	plural
2m	رُدَّ rudda	رُدَّا ruddā	رُدُّوا ruddū
2f	رُدِّي ruddī		أُرْدُدْنَ urdudna

participles

active	passive
رَادّ rādd	مَرْدُود mardūd

passive

perfect	imperfect
رُدَّ rudda	يُرَدُّ yuraddu

hamzated geminate measure I

perfect vowel: **a**
imperfect vowel: **u**

	و	ي	ء	*other*
R¹			✓	
R²				✓
R³				✓

1g3(a)
to buzz

perfect

	singular	dual	plural
1	أَزَزْتُ ʔazaztu	أَزَزْنَا ʔazaznā	
2m	أَزَزْتَ ʔazazta	أَزَزْتُمَا ʔazaztumā	أَزَزْتُمْ ʔazaztum
2f	أَزَزْتِ ʔazazti		أَزَزْتُنَّ ʔazaztunna
3m	أَزَّ ʔazza	أَزَّا ʔazzā	أَزُّوا ʔazzū
3f	أَزَّتْ ʔazzat	أَزَّتَا ʔazzatā	أَزَزْنَ ʔazazna

indicative

	singular	dual	plural
1	أَؤُزُّ ʔaʔuzzu	نَؤُزُّ naʔuzzu	
2m	تَؤُزُّ taʔuzzu	تَؤُزَّانِ taʔuzzāni	تَؤُزُّونَ taʔuzzūna
2f	تَؤُزِّينَ taʔuzzīna		تَأْزُزْنَ taʔzuzna
3m	يَؤُزُّ yaʔuzzu	يَؤُزَّانِ yaʔuzzāni	يَؤُزُّونَ yaʔuzzūna
3f	تَؤُزُّ taʔuzzu	تَؤُزَّانِ taʔuzzāni	يَأْزُزْنَ yaʔzuzna

subjunctive

	singular	dual	plural
1	أَؤُزَّ ʔaʔuzza	نَؤُزَّ naʔuzza	
2m	تَؤُزَّ taʔuzza	تَؤُزَّا taʔuzzā	تَؤُزُّوا taʔuzzū
2f	تَؤُزِّي taʔuzzī		تَأْزُزْنَ taʔzuzna
3m	يَؤُزَّ yaʔuzza	يَؤُزَّا yaʔuzzā	يَؤُزُّوا yaʔuzzū
3f	تَؤُزَّ taʔuzza	تَؤُزَّا taʔuzzā	يَأْزُزْنَ yaʔzuzna

jussive

	singular	dual	plural
1	أَؤُزَّ ʔaʔuzza	نَؤُزَّ naʔuzza	
2m	تَؤُزَّ taʔuzza	تَؤُزَّا taʔuzzā	تَؤُزُّوا taʔuzzū
2f	تَؤُزِّي taʔuzzī		تَأْزُزْنَ taʔzuzna
3m	يَؤُزَّ yaʔuzza	يَؤُزَّا yaʔuzzā	يَؤُزُّوا yaʔuzzū
3f	تَؤُزَّ taʔuzza	تَؤُزَّا taʔuzzā	يَأْزُزْنَ yaʔzuzna

imperative

	singular	dual	plural
2m	ؤُزَّ ʔuzza	ؤُزَّا ʔuzzā	ؤُزُّوا ʔuzzū
2f	ؤُزِّي ʔuzzī		أُؤْزُزْنَ uʔzuzna

participles

active	passive
آزّ ʔāzz	مَأْزُوز maʔzūz

passive

perfect	imperfect
ؤُزَّ ʔuzza	يُؤَزُّ yuʔazzu

assimilated measure I

perfect vowel: **a**
imperfect vowel: **a**

	و	ي	ء	other
R¹	✓			
R²				✓
R³				✓

1a1

to fall

perfect

	singular	dual	plural
1	وَقَعْتُ waqa3tu	وَقَعْنَا waqa3nā	
2m	وَقَعْتَ waqa3ta	وَقَعْتُمَا waqa3tumā	وَقَعْتُمْ waqa3tum
2f	وَقَعْتِ waqa3ti		وَقَعْتُنَّ waqa3tunna
3m	وَقَعَ waqa3a	وَقَعَا waqa3ā	وَقَعُوا waqa3ū
3f	وَقَعَتْ waqa3at	وَقَعَتَا waqa3atā	وَقَعْنَ waqa3na

indicative

	singular	dual	plural
1	أَقَعُ ʔaqa3u	نَقَعُ naqa3u	
2m	تَقَعُ taqa3u	تَقَعَانِ taqa3āni	تَقَعُونَ taqa3ūna
2f	تَقَعِينَ taqa3īna		تَقَعْنَ taqa3na
3m	يَقَعُ yaqa3u	يَقَعَانِ yaqa3āni	يَقَعُونَ yaqa3ūna
3f	تَقَعُ taqa3u	تَقَعَانِ taqa3āni	يَقَعْنَ yaqa3na

subjunctive

	singular	dual	plural
1	أَقَعَ ʔaqa3a	نَقَعَ naqa3a	
2m	تَقَعَ taqa3a	تَقَعَا taqa3ā	تَقَعُوا taqa3ū
2f	تَقَعِي taqa3ī		تَقَعْنَ taqa3na
3m	يَقَعَ yaqa3a	يَقَعَا yaqa3ā	يَقَعُوا yaqa3ū
3f	تَقَعَ taqa3a	تَقَعَا taqa3ā	يَقَعْنَ yaqa3na

jussive

	singular	dual	plural
1	أَقَعْ ʔaqa3	نَقَعْ naqa3	
2m	تَقَعْ taqa3	تَقَعَا taqa3ā	تَقَعُوا taqa3ū
2f	تَقَعِي taqa3ī		تَقَعْنَ taqa3na
3m	يَقَعْ yaqa3	يَقَعَا yaqa3ā	يَقَعُوا yaqa3ū
3f	تَقَعْ taqa3	تَقَعَا taqa3ā	يَقَعْنَ yaqa3na

imperative

	singular	dual	plural
2m	قَعْ qa3	قَعَا qa3ā	قَعُوا qa3ū
2f	قَعِي qa3ī		قَعْنَ qa3na

participles

active	passive
وَاقِع wāqi3	مَوْقُوع mawqū3

passive

perfect	imperfect
وُقِعَ wuqi3a	يُوقَعُ yūqa3u

hamzated assimilated meas. I *perfect vowel:* **a** *imperfect vowel:* **a**		و	ي	ء	*other*	**1a1(a)** **to sprain**
	R[1]	✓				
	R[2]				✓	
	R[3]			✓		

perfect

	singular	dual	plural
1	وَثَأْتُ waṯaʔtu	وَثَأْنَا waṯaʔnā	
2m	وَثَأْتَ waṯaʔta	وَثَأْتُمَا waṯaʔtumā	وَثَأْتُمْ waṯaʔtum
2f	وَثَأْتِ waṯaʔti		وَثَأْتُنَّ waṯaʔtunna
3m	وَثَأَ waṯaʔa	وَثَآ waṯaʔā	وَثَؤُوا waṯaʔū
3f	وَثَأَتْ waṯaʔat	وَثَأَتَا waṯaʔatā	وَثَأْنَ waṯaʔna

indicative

	singular	dual	plural
1	أَثَأُ ʔaṯaʔu	نَثَأُ naṯaʔu	
2m	تَثَأُ taṯaʔu	تَثَآنِ taṯaʔāni	تَثَؤُونَ taṯaʔūna
2f	تَثَئِينَ taṯaʔīna		تَثَأْنَ taṯaʔna
3m	يَثَأُ yaṯaʔu	يَثَآنِ yaṯaʔāni	يَثَؤُونَ yaṯaʔūna
3f	تَثَأُ taṯaʔu	تَثَآنِ taṯaʔāni	يَثَأْنَ yaṯaʔna

subjunctive

	singular	dual	plural
1	أَثَأَ ʔaṯaʔa	نَثَأَ naṯaʔa	
2m	تَثَأَ taṯaʔa	تَثَآ taṯaʔā	تَثَؤُوا taṯaʔū
2f	تَثَئِي taṯaʔī		تَثَأْنَ taṯaʔna
3m	يَثَأَ yaṯaʔa	يَثَآ yaṯaʔā	يَثَؤُوا yaṯaʔū
3f	تَثَأَ taṯaʔa	تَثَآ taṯaʔā	يَثَأْنَ yaṯaʔna

jussive

	singular	dual	plural
1	أَثَأْ ʔaṯaʔ	نَثَأْ naṯaʔ	
2m	تَثَأْ taṯaʔ	تَثَآ taṯaʔā	تَثَؤُوا taṯaʔū
2f	تَثَئِي taṯaʔī		تَثَأْنَ taṯaʔna
3m	يَثَأْ yaṯaʔ	يَثَآ yaṯaʔā	يَثَؤُوا yaṯaʔū
3f	تَثَأْ taṯaʔ	تَثَآ taṯaʔā	يَثَأْنَ yaṯaʔna

imperative

	singular	dual	plural
2m	ثَأْ ṯaʔ	ثَآ ṯaʔā	ثَؤُوا ṯaʔū
2f	ثَئِي ṯaʔī		ثَأْنَ ṯaʔna

participles

active	passive
وَاثِئ wāṯiʔ	مَوْثُوء mawṯūʔ

passive

perfect	imperfect
وُثِئَ wuṯiʔa	يُوثَأُ yūṯaʔu

assimilated measure I

perfect vowel: **a**
imperfect vowel: **i**

	و	ي	ء	other
R1	✓			
R2				✓
R3				✓

1a2
to find

perfect

	singular	dual	plural
1	وَجَدْتُ wajadtu	وَجَدْنَا wajadnā	
2m	وَجَدْتَ wajadta	وَجَدْتُمَا wajadtumā	وَجَدْتُمْ wajadtum
2f	وَجَدْتِ wajadti		وَجَدْتُنَّ wajadtunna
3m	وَجَدَ wajada	وَجَدَا wajadā	وَجَدُوا wajadū
3f	وَجَدَتْ wajadat	وَجَدَتَا wajadatā	وَجَدْنَ wajadna

indicative

	singular	dual	plural
1	أَجِدُ ʔajidu	نَجِدُ najidu	
2m	تَجِدُ tajidu	تَجِدَانِ tajidāni	تَجِدُونَ tajidūna
2f	تَجِدِينَ tajidīna		تَجِدْنَ tajidna
3m	يَجِدُ yajidu	يَجِدَانِ yajidāni	يَجِدُونَ yajidūna
3f	تَجِدُ tajidu	تَجِدَانِ tajidāni	يَجِدْنَ yajidna

subjunctive

	singular	dual	plural
1	أَجِدَ ʔajida	نَجِدَ najida	
2m	تَجِدَ tajida	تَجِدَا tajidā	تَجِدُوا tajidū
2f	تَجِدِي tajidī		تَجِدْنَ tajidna
3m	يَجِدَ yajida	يَجِدَا yajidā	يَجِدُوا yajidū
3f	تَجِدَ tajida	تَجِدَا tajidā	يَجِدْنَ yajidna

jussive

	singular	dual	plural
1	أَجِدْ ʔajid	نَجِدْ najid	
2m	تَجِدْ tajid	تَجِدَا tajidā	تَجِدُوا tajidū
2f	تَجِدِي tajidī		تَجِدْنَ tajidna
3m	يَجِدْ yajid	يَجِدَا yajidā	يَجِدُوا yajidū
3f	تَجِدْ tajid	تَجِدَا tajidā	يَجِدْنَ yajidna

imperative

	singular	dual	plural
2m	جِدْ jid	جِدَا jidā	جِدُوا jidū
2f	جِدِي jidī		جِدْنَ jidna

participles

active	passive
وَاجِد wājid	مَوْجُود mawjūd

passive

perfect	imperfect
وُجِدَ wujida	يُوجَدُ yūjadu

assimilated measure I *perfect vowel:* **i** *imperfect vowel:* **a**		و	ي	ء	*other*	**1a3** **to be wide**
	R^1	✓				
	R^2				✓	
	R^3				✓	

perfect

	singular	dual	plural
1	وَسِعْتُ wasi3tu	وَسِعْنَا wasi3nā	
2m	وَسِعْتَ wasi3ta	وَسِعْتُمَا wasi3tumā	وَسِعْتُمْ wasi3tum
2f	وَسِعْتِ wasi3ti		وَسِعْتُنَّ wasi3tunna
3m	وَسِعَ wasi3a	وَسِعَا wasi3ā	وَسِعُوا wasi3ū
3f	وَسِعَتْ wasi3at	وَسِعَتَا wasi3atā	وَسِعْنَ wasi3na

indicative

	singular	dual	plural
1	أَسَعُ ʔasa3u	نَسَعُ nasa3u	
2m	تَسَعُ tasa3u	تَسَعَانِ tasa3āni	تَسَعُونَ tasa3ūna
2f	تَسَعِينَ tasa3īna		تَسَعْنَ tasa3na
3m	يَسَعُ yasa3u	يَسَعَانِ yasa3āni	يَسَعُونَ yasa3ūna
3f	تَسَعُ tasa3u	تَسَعَانِ tasa3āni	يَسَعْنَ yasa3na

subjunctive

	singular	dual	plural
1	أَسَعَ ʔasa3a	نَسَعَ nasa3a	
2m	تَسَعَ tasa3a	تَسَعَا tasa3ā	تَسَعُوا tasa3ū
2f	تَسَعِي tasa3ī		تَسَعْنَ tasa3na
3m	يَسَعَ yasa3a	يَسَعَا yasa3ā	يَسَعُوا yasa3ū
3f	تَسَعَ tasa3a	تَسَعَا tasa3ā	يَسَعْنَ yasa3na

jussive

	singular	dual	plural
1	أَسَعْ ʔasa3	نَسَعْ nasa3	
2m	تَسَعْ tasa3	تَسَعَا tasa3ā	تَسَعُوا tasa3ū
2f	تَسَعِي tasa3ī		تَسَعْنَ tasa3na
3m	يَسَعْ yasa3	يَسَعَا yasa3ā	يَسَعُوا yasa3ū
3f	تَسَعْ tasa3	تَسَعَا tasa3ā	يَسَعْنَ yasa3na

imperative

	singular	dual	plural
2m	سَعْ sa3	سَعَا sa3ā	سَعُوا sa3ū
2f	سَعِي sa3ī		سَعْنَ sa3na

participles

active	passive
وَاسِع wāsi3	مَوْسُوع mawsū3

passive

perfect	imperfect
وُسِعَ wusi3a	يُوسَعُ yūsa3u

hamzated assimilated meas. I *perfect vowel:* **i** *imperfect vowel:* **a**		و	ي	ء	*other*	**1a3(a)** to tread
	***R*[1]**	✓				
	***R*[2]**				✓	
	***R*[3]**			✓		

perfect

	singular	dual	plural
1	وَطِئْتُ waṭiʔtu	وَطِئْنَا waṭiʔnā	
2m	وَطِئْتَ waṭiʔta	وَطِئْتُمَا waṭiʔtumā	وَطِئْتُمْ waṭiʔtum
2f	وَطِئْتِ waṭiʔti		وَطِئْتُنَّ waṭiʔtunna
3m	وَطِئَ waṭiʔa	وَطِئَا waṭiʔā	وَطِئُوا waṭiʔū
3f	وَطِئَتْ waṭiʔat	وَطِئَتَا waṭiʔatā	وَطِئْنَ waṭiʔna

indicative

	singular	dual	plural
1	أَطَأُ ʔaṭaʔu	نَطَأُ naṭaʔu	
2m	تَطَأُ taṭaʔu	تَطَآنِ taṭaʔāni	تَطَؤُونَ taṭaʔūna
2f	تَطَئِينَ taṭaʔīna		تَطَأْنَ taṭaʔna
3m	يَطَأُ yaṭaʔu	يَطَآنِ yaṭaʔāni	يَطَؤُونَ yaṭaʔūna
3f	تَطَأُس taṭaʔu	تَطَآنِ taṭaʔāni	يَطَأْنَ yaṭaʔna

subjunctive

	singular	dual	plural
1	أَطَأَ ʔaṭaʔa	نَطَأَ naṭaʔa	
2m	تَطَأَ taṭaʔa	تَطَآ taṭaʔā	تَطَؤُوا taṭaʔū
2f	تَطَئِي taṭaʔī		تَطَأْنَ taṭaʔna
3m	يَطَأَ yaṭaʔa	يَطَآ yaṭaʔā	يَطَؤُوا yaṭaʔū
3f	تَطَأَ taṭaʔa	تَطَآ taṭaʔā	يَطَأْنَ yaṭaʔna

jussive

	singular	dual	plural
1	أَطَأْ ʔaṭaʔ	نَطَأْ naṭaʔ	
2m	تَطَأْ taṭaʔ	تَطَآ taṭaʔā	تَطَؤُوا taṭaʔū
2f	تَطَئِي taṭaʔī		تَطَأْنَ taṭaʔna
3m	يَطَأْ yaṭaʔ	يَطَآ yaṭaʔā	يَطَؤُوا yaṭaʔū
3f	تَطَأْ taṭaʔ	تَطَآ taṭaʔā	يَطَأْنَ yaṭaʔna

imperative

	singular	dual	plural
2m	طَأْ ṭaʔ	طَآ ṭaʔā	طَؤُوا ṭaʔū
2f	طَئِي ṭaʔī		طَأْنَ ṭaʔna

participles

active	passive
وَاطِئ wāṭiʔ	مَوْطُوؤ mawṭūʔ

passive

perfect	imperfect
وُطِئَ wuṭiʔa	يُوطَأُ yūṭaʔu

assimilated measure I

perfect vowel: **i**
imperfect vowel: **i**

	و	ي	ء	*other*
R^1	✓			
R^2				✓
R^3				✓

1a4
to inherit

perfect

	singular	dual	plural
1	وَرِثْتُ wariŧtu	وَرِثْنَا wariŧnā	
2m	وَرِثْتَ wariŧta	وَرِثْتُمَا wariŧtumā	وَرِثْتُمْ wariŧtum
2f	وَرِثْتِ wariŧti		وَرِثْتُنَّ wariŧtunna
3m	وَرِثَ wariŧa	وَرِثَا wariŧā	وَرِثُوا wariŧū
3f	وَرِثَتْ wariŧat	وَرِثَتَا wariŧatā	وَرِثْنَ wariŧna

indicative

	singular	dual	plural
1	أَرِثُ ʔariŧu	نَرِثُ nariŧu	
2m	تَرِثُ tariŧu	تَرِثَانِ tariŧāni	تَرِثُونَ tariŧūna
2f	تَرِثِينَ tariŧīna		تَرِثْنَ tariŧna
3m	يَرِثُ yariŧu	يَرِثَانِ yariŧāni	يَرِثُونَ yariŧūna
3f	تَرِثُ tariŧu	تَرِثَانِ tariŧāni	يَرِثْنَ yariŧna

subjunctive

	singular	dual	plural
1	أَرِثَ ʔariŧa	نَرِثَ nariŧa	
2m	تَرِثَ tariŧa	تَرِثَا tariŧā	تَرِثُوا tariŧū
2f	تَرِثِي tariŧī		تَرِثْنَ tariŧna
3m	يَرِثَ yariŧa	يَرِثَا yariŧā	يَرِثُوا yariŧū
3f	تَرِثَ tariŧa	تَرِثَا tariŧā	يَرِثْنَ yariŧna

jussive

	singular	dual	plural
1	أَرِثْ ʔariŧ	نَرِثْ nariŧ	
2m	تَرِثْ tariŧ	تَرِثَا tariŧā	تَرِثُوا tariŧū
2f	تَرِثِي tariŧī		تَرِثْنَ tariŧna
3m	يَرِثْ yariŧ	يَرِثَا yariŧā	يَرِثُوا yariŧū
3f	تَرِثْ tariŧ	تَرِثَا tariŧā	يَرِثْنَ yariŧna

imperative

	singular	dual	plural
2m	رِثْ riŧ	رِثَا riŧā	رِثُوا riŧū
2f	رِثِي riŧī		رِثْنَ riŧna

participles

active	passive
وَارِث wāriŧ	مَوْرُوث mawrūŧ

passive

perfect	imperfect
وُرِثَ wuriŧa	يُورَثُ yūraŧu

hollow measure I
perfect vowel: **ā(i)**
imperfect vowel: **a**

	و	ي	ء	other
R[1]				✓
R[2]	✓	✓		
R[3]				✓

1h1
to sleep

perfect

	singular	dual	plural
1	نِمْتُ nimtu	نِمْنَا nimnā	
2m	نِمْتَ nimta	نِمْتُمَا nimtumā	نِمْتُمْ nimtum
2f	نِمْتِ nimti		نِمْتُنَّ nimtunna
3m	نَامَ nāma	نَامَا nāmā	نَامُوا nāmū
3f	نَامَتْ nāmat	نَامَتَا nāmatā	نِمْنَ nimna

indicative

	singular	dual	plural
1	أَنَامُ ʔanāmu	نَنَامُ nanāmu	
2m	تَنَامُ tanāmu	تَنَامَانِ tanāmāni	تَنَامُونَ tanāmūna
2f	تَنَامِينَ tanāmīna		تَنَمْنَ tanamna
3m	يَنَامُ yanāmu	يَنَامَانِ yanāmāni	يَنَامُونَ yanāmūna
3f	تَنَامُ tanāmu	تَنَامَانِ tanāmāni	يَنَمْنَ yanamna

subjunctive

	singular	dual	plural
1	أَنَامَ ʔanāma	نَنَامَ nanāma	
2m	تَنَامَ tanāma	تَنَامَا tanāmā	تَنَامُوا tanāmū
2f	تَنَامِي tanāmi		تَنَمْنَ tanamna
3m	يَنَامَ yanāma	يَنَامَا yanāmā	يَنَامُوا yanāmū
3f	تَنَامَ tanāma	تَنَامَا tanāmā	يَنَمْنَ yanamna

jussive

	singular	dual	plural
1	أَنَمْ ʔanam	نَنَمْ nanam	
2m	تَنَمْ tanam	تَنَامَا tanāmā	تَنَامُوا tanāmū
2f	تَنَامِي tanāmī		تَنَمْنَ tanamna
3m	يَنَمْ yanam	يَنَامَا yanāmā	يَنَامُوا yanāmū
3f	تَنَمْ tanam	تَنَامَا tanāmā	يَنَمْنَ yanamna

imperative

	singular	dual	plural
2m	نَمْ nam	نَامَا nāmā	نَامُوا nāmū
2f	نَامِي nāmī		نَمْنَ namna

participles

active	passive*
نَائِم nāʔim	مَنُوم manūm

passive

perfect	imperfect
نِيمَ nīma	يُنَامُ yanāmu

* Roots having the radical ي follow the pattern مفيل mafūl.

hamzated hollow measure I *perfect vowel:* **ā(i)** *imperfect vowel:* **a**		و	ي	ء	*other*	**1h1(a)** to want
	R[1]				✓	
	R[2]		✓			
	R[3]			✓		

perfect

	singular	dual	plural
1	شِئْتُ šiʔtu	شِئْنَا šiʔnā	
2m	شِئْتَ šiʔta	شِئْتُمَا šiʔtumā	شِئْتُمْ šiʔtum
2f	شِئْتِ šiʔti		شِئْتُنَّ šiʔtunna
3m	شَاءَ šāʔa	شَاءَا šāʔā	شَاءُوا (شَاؤُوا) šāʔū
3f	شَاءَتْ šāʔat	شَاءَتَا šāʔatā	شِئْنَ šiʔna

indicative

	singular	dual	plural
1	أَشَاءُ ʔašāʔu	نَشَاءُ našāʔu	
2m	تَشَاءُ tašāʔu	تَشَاءَانِ tašāʔāni	تَشَاءُونَ (تَشَاؤُونَ) tašāʔūna
2f	تَشَائِينَ tašāʔīna		تَشَأْنَ tašaʔna
3m	يَشَاءُ yašāʔu	يَشَاءَانِ yašāʔāni	يَشَاءُونَ (يَشَاؤُونَ) yašāʔūna
3f	تَشَاءُ tašāʔu	تَشَاءَانِ tašāʔāni	يَشَأْنَ yašaʔna

subjunctive

	singular	dual	plural
1	أَشَاءَ ʔašāʔa	نَشَاءَ našāʔa	
2m	تَشَاءَ tašāʔa	تَشَاءَا tašāʔā	تَشَاءُوا (تَشَاؤُوا) tašāʔū
2f	تَشَائِي tašāʔī		تَشَأْنَ tašaʔna
3m	يَشَاءَ yašāʔa	يَشَاءَا yašāʔā	يَشَاءُوا (يَشَاؤُوا) yašāʔū
3f	تَشَاءَ tašāʔa	تَشَاءَا tašāʔā	يَشَأْنَ yašaʔna

jussive

	singular	dual	plural
1	أَشَأْ ʔašāʔ	نَشَأْ našāʔ	
2m	تَشَأْ tašāʔ	تَشَاءَا tašāʔā	تَشَاءُوا (تَشَاؤُوا) tašāʔū
2f	تَشَائِي tašāʔī		تَشَأْنَ tašaʔna
3m	يَشَأْ yašāʔ	يَشَاءَا yašāʔā	يَشَاءُوا (يَشَاؤُوا) yašāʔū
3f	تَشَأْ tašāʔ	تَشَاءَا tašāʔā	يَشَأْنَ yašaʔna

imperative

	singular	dual	plural
2m	شَأْ šaʔ	شَاءَا šāʔā	شَاءُوا (شَاؤُوا) šāʔū
2f	شَائِي šāʔī		شَأْنَ šaʔna

participles

active	passive
شَاءٍ šāʔ(in)	مَشِيءٌ mašīʔ

passive

perfect	imperfect
شِيءَ šīʔa	يُشَاءُ yašāʔu

hollow measure I *perfect vowel:* **ā(i)** *imperfect vowel:* **i**		و	ي	ء	*other*	**1h2** **to sell**
	R[1]				✓	
	R[2]		✓			
	R[3]				✓	

perfect

	singular	dual	plural
1	بِعْتُ bi3tu	بِعْنَا bi3nā	
2m	بِعْتَ bi3ta	بِعْتُمَا bi3tumā	بِعْتُمْ bi3tum
2f	بِعْتِ bi3ti		بِعْتُنَّ bi3tunna
3m	بَاعَ bā3a	بَاعَا bā3ā	بَاعُوا bā3ū
3f	بَاعَتْ bā3at	بَاعَتَا bā3atā	بِعْنَ bi3na

indicative

	singular	dual	plural
1	أَبِيعُ ʔabī3u	نَبِيعُ nabī3u	
2m	تَبِيعُ tabī3u	تَبِيعَانِ tabī3āni	تَبِيعُونَ tabī3ūna
2f	تَبِيعِينَ tabī3īna		تَبِعْنَ tabi3na
3m	يَبِيعُ yabī3u	يَبِيعَانِ yabī3āni	يَبِيعُونَ yabī3ūna
3f	تَبِيعُ tabī3u	تَبِيعَانِ tabī3āni	يَبِعْنَ yabi3na

subjunctive

	singular	dual	plural
1	أَبِيعَ ʔabī3a	نَبِيعَ nabī3a	
2m	تَبِيعَ tabī3a	تَبِيعَا tabī3ā	تَبِيعُوا tabī3ū
2f	تَبِيعِي tabī3ī		تَبِعْنَ tabi3na
3m	يَبِيعَ yabī3a	يَبِيعَا yabī3ā	يَبِيعُوا yabī3ū
3f	تَبِيعَ tabī3a	تَبِيعَا tabī3ā	يَبِعْنَ yabi3na

jussive

	singular	dual	plural
1	أَبِعْ ʔabi3	نَبِعْ nabi3	
2m	تَبِعْ tabi3	تَبِيعَا tabī3ā	تَبِيعُوا tabī3ū
2f	تَبِيعِي tabī3ī		تَبِعْنَ tabi3na
3m	يَبِعْ yabi3	يَبِيعَا yabī3ā	يَبِيعُوا yabī3ū
3f	تَبِعْ tabi3	تَبِيعَا tabī3ā	يَبِعْنَ yabi3na

imperative

	singular	dual	plural
2m	بِعْ bi3	بِيعَا bī3ā	بِيعُوا bī3ū
2f	بِيعِي bī3ī		بِعْنَ bi3na

participles

active	passive
بَائِع bāʔi3	مَبِيع mabī3

passive

perfect	imperfect
بِيعَ bī3a	يُبَاعُ yabā3u

hamzated hollow measure I *perfect vowel:* **ā(i)** *imperfect vowel:* **i**		و	ي	ء	*other*	**1h2(a)** **to come**
	R[1]				✓	
	R[2]		✓			
	R[3]			✓		

perfect

	singular	dual	plural
1	جِئْتُ jiʔtu	جِئْنَا jiʔnā	
2m	جِئْتَ jiʔta	جِئْتُمَا jiʔtumā	جِئْتُمْ jiʔtum
2f	جِئْتِ jiʔti		جِئْتُنَّ jiʔtunna
3m	جَاءَ jāʔa	جَاءَا jāʔā	جَاءُوا (جَاؤُوا) jāʔū
3f	جَاءَتْ jāʔat	جَاءَتَا jāʔatā	جِئْنَ jiʔna

indicative

	singular	dual	plural
1	أَجِيءُ ʔajīʔu	نَجِيءُ najīʔu	
2m	تَجِيءُ tajīʔu	تَجِيئَانِ tajīʔāni	تَجِيئُونَ (تَجِيؤُونَ) tajīʔūna
2f	تَجِيئِينَ tajīʔīna		تَجِئْنَ tajiʔna
3m	يَجِيءُ yajīʔu	يَجِيئَانِ yajīʔāni	يَجِيئُونَ (يَجِيؤُونَ) yajīʔūna
3f	تَجِيءُ tajīʔu	تَجِيئَانِ tajīʔāni	يَجِئْنَ yajiʔna

subjunctive

	singular	dual	plural
1	أَجِيءَ ʔajīʔa	نَجِيءَ najīʔa	
2m	تَجِيءَ tajīʔa	تَجِيئَا tajīʔā	تَجِيئُوا (تَجِيؤُوا) tajīʔū
2f	تَجِيئِي tajīʔī		تَجِئْنَ tajiʔna
3m	يَجِيءَ yajīʔa	يَجِيئَا yajīʔā	يَجِيئُوا (يَجِيؤُوا) yajīʔū
3f	تَجِيءَ tajīʔa	تَجِيئَا tajīʔā	يَجِئْنَ yajiʔna

jussive

	singular	dual	plural
1	أَجِئْ ʔajiʔ	نَجِئْ najiʔ	
2m	تَجِئْ tajiʔ	تَجِيئَا tajīʔā	تَجِيئُوا (تَجِيؤُوا) tajīʔū
2f	تَجِيئِي tajīʔī		تَجِئْنَ tajiʔna
3m	يَجِئْ yajiʔ	يَجِيئَا yajīʔā	يَجِيئُوا (يَجِيؤُوا) yajīʔū
3f	تَجِئْ tajiʔ	تَجِيئَا tajīʔā	يَجِئْنَ yajiʔna

imperative

	singular	dual	plural
2m	جِئْ jiʔ	جِيئَا jīʔā	جِيئُوا (جِيؤُوا) jīʔū
2f	جِيئِي jīʔī		جِئْنَ jiʔna

participles

active	passive
جَاءٍ jāʔ(in)	مَجِيء majīʔ

passive

perfect	imperfect
جِيءَ jīʔa	يُجَاءُ yajāʔu

hollow measure I *perfect vowel:* **ā(u)** *imperfect vowel:* **u**		و	ي	ء	*other*
	R[1]				✓
	R[2]	✓			
	R[3]				✓

1h3
to say

perfect

	singular	dual	plural
1	قُلْتُ qultu	قُلْنَا qulnā	
2m	قُلْتَ qulta	قُلْتُمَا qultumā	قُلْتُمْ qultum
2f	قُلْتِ qulti		قُلْتُنَّ qultunna
3m	قَالَ qāla	قَالَا qālā	قَالُوا qālū
3f	قَالَتْ qālat	قَالَتَا qālatā	قُلْنَ qulna

indicative

	singular	dual	plural
1	أَقُولُ ʔaqūlu	نَقُولُ naqūlu	
2m	تَقُولُ taqūlu	تَقُولَانِ taqūlāni	تَقُولُونَ taqūlūna
2f	تَقُولِينَ taqūlīna		تَقُلْنَ taqulna
3m	يَقُولُ yaqūlu	يَقُولَانِ yaqūlāni	يَقُولُونَ yaqūlūna
3f	تَقُولُ taqūlu	تَقُولَانِ taqūlāni	يَقُلْنَ yaqulna

subjunctive

	singular	dual	plural
1	أَقُولَ ʔaqūla	نَقُولَ naqūla	
2m	تَقُولَ taqūla	تَقُولَا taqūlā	تَقُولُوا taqūlū
2f	تَقُولِي taqūli		تَقُلْنَ taqulna
3m	يَقُولَ yaqūla	يَقُولَا yaqūlā	يَقُولُوا yaqūlū
3f	تَقُولَ taqūla	تَقُولَا taqūlā	يَقُلْنَ yaqulna

jussive

	singular	dual	plural
1	أَقُلْ ʔaqul	نَقُلْ naqul	
2m	تَقُلْ taqul	تَقُولَا taqūlā	تَقُولُوا taqūlū
2f	تَقُولِي taqūlī		تَقُلْنَ taqulna
3m	يَقُلْ yaqul	يَقُولَا yaqūlā	يَقُولُوا yaqūlū
3f	تَقُلْ taqul	تَقُولَا taqūlā	يَقُلْنَ yaqulna

imperative

	singular	dual	plural
2m	قُلْ qul	قُولَا qūlā	قُولُوا qūlū
2f	قُولِي qūlī		قُلْنَ qulna

participles

active	passive
قَائِل qāʔil	مَقُول maqūl

passive

perfect	imperfect
قِيلَ qīla	يُقَالُ yaqālu

hamzated hollow measure I *perfect vowel:* **ā(u)** *imperfect vowel:* **u**		و	ي	ء	*other*	**1h3(a)** to return
	R[1]			✓		
	R[2]	✓				
	R[3]				✓	

perfect

	singular	dual	plural
1	أُبْتُ ʔubtu	أُبْنَا ʔubnā	
2m	أُبْتَ ʔubta	أُبْتُمَا ʔubtumā	أُبْتُمْ ʔubtum
2f	أُبْتِ ʔubti		أُبْتُنَّ ʔubtunna
3m	آبَ ʔāba	آبَا ʔābā	آبُوا ʔābū
3f	آبَتْ ʔābat	آبَتَا ʔābatā	أُبْنَ ʔubna

indicative

	singular	dual	plural
1	أَؤُوبُ ʔaʔūbu	نَؤُوبُ naʔūbu	
2m	تَؤُوبُ taʔūbu	تَؤُوبَانِ taʔūbāni	تَؤُوبُونَ taʔūbūna
2f	تَؤُوبِينَ taʔūbīna		تَؤُبْنَ taʔubna
3m	يَؤُوبُ yaʔūbu	يَؤُوبَانِ yaʔūbāni	يَؤُوبُونَ yaʔūbūna
3f	تَؤُوبُ taʔūbu	تَؤُوبَانِ taʔūbāni	يَؤُبْنَ yaʔubna

subjunctive

	singular	dual	plural
1	أَؤُوبَ ʔaʔūba	نَؤُوبَ naʔūba	
2m	تَؤُوبَ taʔūba	تَؤُوبَا taʔūbā	تَؤُوبُوا taʔūbū
2f	تَؤُوبِي taʔūbi		تَؤُبْنَ taʔubna
3m	يَؤُوبَ yaʔūba	يَؤُوبَا yaʔūbā	يَؤُوبُوا yaʔūbū
3f	تَؤُوبَ taʔūba	تَؤُوبَا taʔūbā	يَؤُبْنَ yaʔubna

jussive

	singular	dual	plural
1	أَؤُبْ ʔaʔub	نَؤُبْ naʔub	
2m	تَؤُبْ taʔub	تَؤُوبَا taʔūbā	تَؤُوبُوا taʔūbū
2f	تَؤُوبِي taʔūbī		تَؤُبْنَ taʔubna
3m	يَؤُبْ yaʔub	يَؤُوبَا yaʔūbā	يَؤُوبُوا yaʔūbū
3f	تَؤُبْ taʔub	تَؤُوبَا taʔūbā	يَؤُبْنَ yaʔubna

imperative

	singular	dual	plural
2m	أُبْ ʔub	أُوبَا ʔūbā	أُوبُوا ʔūbū
2f	أُوبِي ʔūbī		أُبْنَ ʔubna

participles

active	passive
آئِب ʔāʔib	مَؤُوب maʔūb

passive

perfect	imperfect
إِيبَ ʔība	يُؤَابُ yuʔābu

hamzated hollow measure I

perfect vowel: **ā(u)**
imperfect vowel: **u**

	و	ي	ء	*other*
R¹				✓
R²	✓			
R³			✓	

1h3(b)
to become bad

perfect

	singular	dual	plural
1	سُؤْتُ suʔtu	سُؤْنَا suʔnā	
2m	سُؤْتَ suʔta	سُؤْتُمَا suʔtumā	سُؤْتُمْ suʔtum
2f	سُؤْتِ suʔti		سُؤْتُنَّ suʔtunna
3m	سَاءَ sāʔa	سَاءَا sāʔā	سَاءُوا (سَاؤُوا) sāʔū
3f	سَاءَتْ sāʔat	سَاءَتَا sāʔatā	سُؤْنَ suʔna

indicative

	singular	dual	plural
1	أَسُوءُ ʔasūʔu	نَسُوءُ nasūʔu	
2m	تَسُوءُ tasūʔu	تَسُوءَانِ tasūʔāni	تَسُوؤُونَ (تَسُوءُونَ) tasūʔūna
2f	تَسُوئِينَ tasūʔīna		تَسُؤْنَ tasuʔna
3m	يَسُوءُ yasūʔu	يَسُوءَانِ yasūʔāni	يَسُوؤُونَ (يَسُوءُونَ) yasūʔūna
3f	تَسُوءُ tasūʔu	تَسُوءَانِ tasūʔāni	يَسُؤْنَ yasuʔna

subjunctive

	singular	dual	plural
1	أَسُوءَ ʔasūʔa	نَسُوءَ nasūʔa	
2m	تَسُوءَ tasūʔa	تَسُوءَا tasūʔā	تَسُوؤُوا (تَسُوءُوا) tasūʔū
2f	تَسُوئِي tasūʔī		تَسُؤْنَ tasuʔna
3m	يَسُوءَ yasūʔa	يَسُوءَا yasūʔā	يَسُوؤُوا (يَسُوءُوا) yasūʔū
3f	تَسُوءَ tasūʔa	تَسُوءَا tasūʔā	يَسُؤْنَ yasuʔna

jussive

	singular	dual	plural
1	أَسُؤْ ʔasuʔ	نَسُؤْ nasuʔ	
2m	تَسُؤْ tasuʔ	تَسُوءَا tasūʔā	تَسُوؤُوا (تَسُوءُوا) tasūʔū
2f	تَسُوئِي tasūʔī		تَسُؤْنَ tasuʔna
3m	يَسُؤْ yasuʔ	يَسُوءَا yasūʔā	يَسُوؤُوا (يَسُوءُوا) yasūʔū
3f	تَسُؤْ tasuʔ	تَسُوءَا tasūʔā	يَسُؤْنَ yasuʔna

imperative

	singular	dual	plural
2m	سُؤْ suʔ	سُوءَا sūʔā	سُوؤُوا(سُوءُوا) sūʔū
2f	سُوئِي sūʔī		سُؤْنَ suʔna

participles

active	passive
سَائِل sāʔil	مَسُول masūl

passive

perfect	imperfect
سِيءَ sīʔa	يُسَاءُ yusāʔu

defective measure I *perfect vowel:* **a** *imperfect vowel:* **a**		و	ي	ء	*other*	**1d1** **to strive**
	R¹				✓	
	R²				✓	
	R³		✓			

perfect

	singular	dual	plural
1	سَعَيْتُ sa3aytu	سَعَيْنَا sa3aynā	
2m	سَعَيْتَ sa3ayta	سَعَيْتُمَا sa3aytumā	سَعَيْتُمْ sa3aytum
2f	سَعَيْتِ sa3ayti		سَعَيْتُنَّ sa3aytunna
3m	سَعَى sa3ā	سَعَيَا sa3ayā	سَعَوْا sa3aw
3f	سَعَتْ sa3at	سَعَتَا sa3atā	سَعَيْنَ sa3ayna

indicative

	singular	dual	plural
1	أَسْعَى ʔas3ā	نَسْعَى nas3ā	
2m	تَسْعَى tas3ā	تَسْعَيَانِ tas3ayāni	تَسْعَوْنَ tas3awna
2f	تَسْعَيْنَ tas3ayna		تَسْعَيْنَ tas3ayna
3m	يَسْعَى yas3ā	يَسْعَيَانِ yas3ayāni	يَسْعَوْنَ yas3awna
3f	تَسْعَى tas3ā	تَسْعَيَانِ tas3ayāni	يَسْعَيْنَ yas3ayna

subjunctive

	singular	dual	plural
1	أَسْعَى ʔas3ā	نَسْعَى nas3ā	
2m	تَسْعَى tas3ā	تَسْعَيَا tas3ayā	تَسْعَوْا tas3aw
2f	تَسْعَيْ tas3ay		تَسْعَيْنَ tas3ayna
3m	يَسْعَى yas3ā	يَسْعَيَا yas3ayā	يَسْعَوْا yas3aw
3f	تَسْعَى tas3ā	تَسْعَيَا tas3ayā	يَسْعَيْنَ yas3ayna

jussive

	singular	dual	plural
1	أَسْعَ ʔas3a	نَسْعَ nas3a	
2m	تَسْعَ tas3a	تَسْعَيَا tas3ayā	تَسْعَوْا tas3aw
2f	تَسْعَيْ tas3ay		تَسْعَيْنَ tas3ayna
3m	يَسْعَ yas3a	يَسْعَيَا yas3ayā	يَسْعَوْا yas3aw
3f	تَسْعَ tas3a	تَسْعَيَا tas3ayā	يَسْعَيْنَ yas3ayna

imperative

	singular	dual	plural
2m	اِسْعَ is3a	اِسْعَيَا is3ayā	اِسْعَوْا is3aw
2f	اِسْعَيْ is3ay		اِسْعَيْنَ is3ayna

participles

active	passive
سَاعٍ sā3(in)	مَسْعِيّ mas3īy

passive

perfect	imperfect
سُعِيَ su3iya	يُسْعَى yus3ā

hamzated defective measure I *perfect vowel:* **a** *imperfect vowel:* **a**		و	ي	ء	other	**1d1(a)** **to refuse**
	R[1]			✓		
	R[2]				✓	
	R[3]		✓			

perfect

	singular	dual	plural
1	أَبَيْتُ ʔabaytu	أَبَيْنَا ʔabaynā	
2m	أَبَيْتَ ʔabayta	أَبَيْتُمَا ʔabaytumā	أَبَيْتُمْ ʔabaytum
2f	أَبَيْتِ ʔabayti		أَبَيْتُنَّ ʔabaytunna
3m	أَبَى ʔabā	أَبَيَا ʔabayā	أَبَوْا ʔabaw
3f	أَبَتْ ʔabat	أَبَتَا ʔabatā	أَبَيْنَ ʔabayna

indicative

	singular	dual	plural
1	آبَى ʔābā	نَأْبَى naʔbā	
2m	تَأْبَى taʔbā	تَأْبَيَانِ taʔbayāni	تَأْبَوْنَ taʔbawna
2f	تَأْبَيْنَ taʔbayna		تَأْبَيْنَ taʔbayna
3m	يَأْبَى yaʔbā	يَأْبَيَانِ yaʔbayāni	يَأْبَوْنَ yaʔbawna
3f	تَأْبَى taʔbā	تَأْبَيَانِ taʔbayāni	يَأْبَيْنَ yaʔbayna

subjunctive

	singular	dual	plural
1	آبَى ʔābā	نَأْبَى naʔbā	
2m	تَأْبَى taʔbā	تَأْبَيَا taʔbayā	تَأْبَوْا taʔbaw
2f	تَأْبَيْ taʔbay		تَأْبَيْنَ taʔbayna
3m	يَأْبَى yaʔbā	يَأْبَيَا yaʔbayā	يَأْبَوْا yaʔbaw
3f	تَأْبَى taʔbā	تَأْبَيَا taʔbayā	يَأْبَيْنَ yaʔbayna

jussive

	singular	dual	plural
1	آبَ ʔāba	نَأْبَ naʔba	
2m	تَأْبَ taʔba	تَأْبَيَا taʔbayā	تَأْبَوْا taʔbaw
2f	تَأْبَيْ taʔbay		تَأْبَيْنَ taʔbayna
3m	يَأْبَ yaʔba	يَأْبَيَا yaʔbayā	يَأْبَوْا yaʔbaw
3f	تَأْبَ taʔba	تَأْبَيَا taʔbayā	يَأْبَيْنَ yaʔbayna

imperative

	singular	dual	plural
2m	اِئْبَ iʔba	اِئْبَيَا iʔbayā	اِئْبَوْا iʔbaw
2f	اِئْبَيْ iʔbay		اِئْبَيْنَ iʔbayna

participles

active	passive
آبٍ ʔāb(in)	مَأْبِيّ maʔbīy

passive

perfect	imperfect
أُبِيَ ʔubiya	يُؤْبَى yuʔbā

irregular* defective measure I		و	ي	ء	other	
perfect vowel: **a**	R¹				✓	**1d1(b)**
imperfect vowel: **a**	R²			✓		
	R³		✓			to see

perfect / indicative

		perfect			**indicative**		
		singular	dual	plural	singular	dual	plural
1		رَأَيْتُ raʔaytu	رَأَيْنَا raʔaynā		أَرَى ʔarā	نَرَى narā	
2m		رَأَيْتَ raʔayta	رَأَيْتُمَا raʔaytumā	رَأَيْتُمْ raʔaytum	تَرَى tarā	تَرَيَانِ tarayāni	تَرَوْنَ tarawna
2f		رَأَيْتِ raʔayti		رَأَيْتُنَّ raʔaytunna	تَرَيْنَ tarayna		تَرَيْنَ tarayna
3m		رَأَى raʔā	رَأَيَا raʔayā	رَأَوْا raʔaw	يَرَى yarā	يَرَيَانِ yarayāni	يَرَوْنَ yarawna
3f		رَأَتْ raʔat	رَأَتَا raʔatā	رَأَيْنَ raʔayna	تَرَى tarā	تَرَيَانِ tarayāni	يَرَيْنَ yarayna

subjunctive / jussive

		subjunctive			**jussive**		
		singular	dual	plural	singular	dual	plural
1		أَرَى ʔarā	نَرَى narā		أَرَ ʔara	نَرَ nara	
2m		تَرَى tarā	تَرَيَا tarayā	تَرَوْ taraw	تَرَ tara	تَرَيَا tarayā	تَرَوْ taraw
2f		تَرَيْ taray		تَرَيْنَ tarayna	تَرَيْ taray		تَرَيْنَ tarayna
3m		يَرَى yarā	يَرَيَا yarayā	يَرَوْ yaraw	يَرَ yara	يَرَيَا yarayā	يَرَوْ yaraw
3f		تَرَى tarā	تَرَيَا tarayā	يَرَيْنَ yarayna	تَرَ tara	تَرَيَا tarayā	يَرَيْنَ yarayna

imperative / participles / passive

		imperative			**participles**		**passive**	
		singular	dual	plural	active	passive	perfect	imperfect
2m		رَ ra	رَيَا rayā	رَوْا raw	رَاءٍ rāʔ(in)	مَرْئِيّ marʔīy	رُئِيَ ruʔiya	يُرَى yurā
2f		رَيْ ray		رَيْنَ rayna				

* The verb رَأَى raʔā (*see*) is irregular in that the second radical (ء) is absent in all forms except the perfect forms.

defective measure I

perfect vowel: **a**
imperfect vowel: **i**

	و	ي	ء	other
R[1]				✓
R[2]	✓			✓
R[3]		✓		

1d2

to walk

perfect

	singular	dual	plural
1	مَشَيْتُ mašaytu	مَشَيْنَا mašaynā	
2m	مَشَيْتَ mašayta	مَشَيْتُمَا mašaytumā	مَشَيْتُمْ mašaytum
2f	مَشَيْتِ mašayti		مَشَيْتُنَّ mašaytunna
3m	مَشَى mašā	مَشَيَا mašayā	مَشَوْا mašaw
3f	مَشَتْ mašat	مَشَتَا mašatā	مَشَيْنَ mašayna

indicative

	singular	dual	plural
1	أَمْشِي ʔamšī	نَمْشِي namšī	
2m	تَمْشِي tamšī	تَمْشِيَانِ tamšiyāni	تَمْشُونَ tamšūna
2f	تَمْشِينَ tamšīna		تَمْشِينَ tamšīna
3m	يَمْشِي yamšī	يَمْشِيَانِ yamšiyāni	يَمْشُونَ yamšūna
3f	تَمْشِي tamšī	تَمْشِيَانِ tamšiyāni	يَمْشِينَ yamšīna

subjunctive

	singular	dual	plural
1	أَمْشِيَ ʔamšiya	نَمْشِيَ namšiya	
2m	تَمْشِيَ tamšiya	تَمْشِيَا tamšiyā	تَمْشُوا tamšū
2f	تَمْشِي tamšī		تَمْشِينَ tamšīna
3m	يَمْشِيَ yamšiya	يَمْشِيَا yamšiyā	يَمْشُوا yamšū
3f	تَمْشِيَ tamšiya	تَمْشِيَا tamšiyā	يَمْشِينَ yamšīna

jussive

	singular	dual	plural
1	أَمْشِ ʔamši	نَمْشِ namši	
2m	تَمْشِ tamši	تَمْشِيَا tamšiyā	تَمْشُوا tamšū
2f	تَمْشِي tamšī		تَمْشِينَ tamšīna
3m	يَمْشِ yamši	يَمْشِيَا yamšiyā	يَمْشُوا yamšū
3f	تَمْشِ tamši	تَمْشِيَا tamšiyā	يَمْشِينَ yamšīna

imperative

	singular	dual	plural
2m	اِمْشِ imši	اِمْشِيَا imšiyā	اِمْشُوا imšū
2f	اِمْشِي imšī		اِمْشِينَ imšīna

participles

active	passive
مَاشٍ māš(in)	مَمْشِيّ mamšīy

passive

perfect	imperfect
مُشِيَ mušiya	يُمْشَى yumšā

hamzated defective measure I

perfect vowel: **a**
imperfect vowel: **i**

	و	ي	ء	*other*
R[1]			✓	
R[2]	✓			✓
R[3]		✓		

1d2(a)
to come

perfect

	singular	dual	plural
1	أَتَيْتُ ʔataytu	أَتَيْنَا ʔataynā	
2m	أَتَيْتَ ʔatayta	أَتَيْتُمَا ʔataytumā	أَتَيْتُمْ ʔataytum
2f	أَتَيْتِ ʔatayti		أَتَيْتُنَّ ʔataytunna
3m	أَتَى ʔatā	أَتَيَا ʔatayā	أَتَوْا ʔataw
3f	أَتَتْ ʔatat	أَتَتَا ʔatatā	أَتَيْنَ ʔatayna

indicative

	singular	dual	plural
1	آتِي ʔaʔtī	نَأْتِي naʔtī	
2m	تَأْتِي taʔtī	تَأْتِيَانِ taʔtiyāni	تَأْتُونَ taʔtūna
2f	تَأْتِينَ taʔtīna		تَأْتِينَ taʔtīna
3m	يَأْتِي yaʔtī	يَأْتِيَانِ yaʔtiyāni	يَأْتُونَ yaʔtūna
3f	تَأْتِي taʔtī	تَأْتِيَانِ taʔtiyāni	يَأْتِينَ yaʔtīna

subjunctive

	singular	dual	plural
1	آتِيَ ʔaʔtiya	نَأْتِيَ naʔtiya	
2m	تَأْتِيَ taʔtiya	تَأْتِيَا taʔtiyā	تَأْتُوا taʔtū
2f	تَأْتِي taʔtī		تَأْتِينَ taʔtīna
3m	يَأْتِيَ yaʔtiya	يَأْتِيَا yaʔtiyā	يَأْتُوا yaʔtū
3f	تَأْتِيَ taʔtiya	تَأْتِيَا taʔtiyā	يَأْتِينَ yaʔtīna

jussive

	singular	dual	plural
1	آتِ ʔāti	نَأْتِ naʔti	
2m	تَأْتِ taʔti	تَأْتِيَا taʔtiyā	تَأْتُوا taʔtū
2f	تَفْتِي taʔtī		تَأْتِينَ taʔtīna
3m	يَفْتِ yaʔti	يَأْتِيَا yaʔtiyā	يَأْتُوا yaʔtū
3f	تَفْتِ taʔti	تَأْتِيَا taʔtiyā	يَأْتِينَ yaʔtīna

imperative

	singular	dual	plural
2m	اِفْتِ ifti	اِفْتِيَا iftiyā	اِفْتُوا iftū
2f	اِفْتِي iftī		اِفْتِينَ iftīna

participles

active	passive
فَاتٍ fāt(in)	مَفْتِيّ maftīy

passive

perfect	imperfect
فُتِيَ futiya	يُفْتَى yuftā

assimilated defective measure I

perfect vowel: **a**
imperfect vowel: **i**

	و	ي	ء	other
R1	✓			
R2				✓
R3		✓		

1d2(b) to perceive

perfect

	singular	dual	plural
1	وَعَيْتُ wa3aytu	وَعَيْنَا wa3aynā	
2m	وَعَيْتَ wa3ayta	وَعَيْتُمَا wa3aytumā	وَعَيْتُمْ wa3aytum
2f	وَعَيْتِ wa3ayti		وَعَيْتُنَّ wa3aytunna
3m	وَعَى wa3ā	وَعَيَا wa3ayā	وَعَوْا wa3aw
3f	وَعَتْ wa3at	وَعَتَا wa3atā	وَعَيْنَ wa3ayna

indicative

	singular	dual	plural
1	أَعِي ʔa3ī	نَعِي na3ī	
2m	تَعِي ta3ī	تَعِيَانِ ta3iyāni	تَعُونَ ta3ūna
2f	تَعِينَ ta3īna		تَعِينَ ta3īna
3m	يَعِي ya3ī	يَعِيَانِ ya3iyāni	يَعُونَ ya3ūna
3f	تَعِي ta3ī	تَعِيَانِ ta3iyāni	يَعِينَ ya3īna

subjunctive

	singular	dual	plural
1	أَعِيَ ʔa3iya	نَعِيَ na3iya	
2m	تَعِيَ ta3iya	تَعِيَا ta3iyā	تَعُوا ta3ū
2f	تَعِي ta3ī		تَعِينَ ta3īna
3m	يَعِيَ ya3iya	يَعِيَا ya3iyā	يَعُوا ya3ū
3f	تَعِيَ ta3iya	تَعِيَا ta3iyā	يَعِينَ ya3īna

jussive

	singular	dual	plural
1	أَعِ ʔa3i	نَعِ na3i	
2m	تَعِ ta3i	تَعِيَا ta3iyā	تَعُوا ta3ū
2f	تَعِي ta3ī		تَعِينَ ta3īna
3m	يَعِ ya3i	يَعِيَا ya3iyā	يَعُوا ya3ū
3f	تَعِ ta3i	تَعِيَا ta3iyā	يَعِينَ ya3īna

imperative

	singular	dual	plural
2m	عِ 3i	عِيَا 3iyā	عُوا 3ū
2f	عِي 3ī		عِينَ 3īna

participles

active	passive
وَاعٍ wā3(in)	مَوْعِيّ maw3īy

passive

perfect	imperfect
وُعِيَ wu3iya	يُوعَى yū3ā

defective measure I *perfect vowel:* **a** *imperfect vowel:* **u**		و	ي	ء	*other*	**1d3** **to seem**
	R¹				✓	
	R²				✓	
	R³	✓				

perfect

	singular	dual	plural
1	بَدَوْتُ badawtu	بَدَوْنَا badawnā	
2m	بَدَوْتَ badawta	بَدَوْتُمَا badawtumā	بَدَوْتُمْ badawtum
2f	بَدَوْتِ badawti		بَدَوْتُنَّ badawtunna
3m	بَدَا badā	بَدَيَا badawā	بَدَوْا badaw
3f	بَدَتْ badat	بَدَتَا badatā	بَدَوْنَ badawna

indicative

	singular	dual	plural
1	أَبْدُو ʔabdū	نَبْدُو nabdū	
2m	تَبْدُو tabdū	تَبْدُوَانِ tabduwāni	تَبْدُونَ tabdūna
2f	تَبْدِينَ tabdīna		تَبْدُونَ tabdūna
3m	يَبْدُو yabdū	يَبْدُوَانِ yabduwāni	يَبْدُونَ yabdūna
3f	تَبْدُو tabdū	تَبْدُوَانِ tabduwāni	يَبْدُونَ yabdūna

subjunctive

	singular	dual	plural
1	أَبْدُوَ ʔabduwa	نَبْدُوَ nabduwa	
2m	تَبْدُوَ tabduwa	تَبْدُوَا tabduwā	تَبْدُوا tabdū
2f	تَبْدِي tabdī		تَبْدُونَ tabdūna
3m	يَبْدُوَ yabduwa	يَبْدُوَا yabduwā	يَبْدُوا yabdū
3f	تَبْدُوَ tabduwa	تَبْدُوَا tabduwā	يَبْدُونَ yabdūna

jussive

	singular	dual	plural
1	أَبْدُ ʔabdu	نَبْدُ nabdu	
2m	تَبْدُ tabdu	تَبْدُوَا tabduwā	تَبْدُوا tabdū
2f	تَبْدِي tabdī		تَبْدُونَ tabdūna
3m	يَبْدُ yabdu	يَبْدُوَا yabduwā	يَبْدُوا yabdū
3f	تَبْدُ tabdu	تَبْدُوَا tabduwā	يَبْدُونَ yabdūna

imperative

	singular	dual	plural
2m	أُبْدُ ubdu	أُبْدُوَا ubduwa	أُبْدُوا ubdū
2f	أُبْدِي ubdī		أُبْدُونَ ubdūna

participles

active	passive
بَادٍ bād(in)	مَبْدُوّ mabdūw

passive

perfect	imperfect
بُدِيَ budiya	يُبْدَى yubdā

defective measure I

perfect vowel: **i**
imperfect vowel: **a**

	و	ي	ء	other
R^1				✓
R^2				✓
R^3		✓		

1d4
to stay

perfect

	singular	dual	plural
1	بَقِيتُ baqītu	بَقِينَا baqīnā	
2m	بَقِيتَ baqīta	بَقِيتُمَا baqītumā	بَقِيتُمْ baqītum
2f	بَقِيتِ baqīti		بَقِيتُنَّ baqītunna
3m	بَقِيَ baqiya	بَقِيَا baqiyā	بَقُوا baqū
3f	بَقِيَتْ baqiyat	بَقِيَتَا baqiyatā	بَقِينَ baqīna

indicative

	singular	dual	plural
1	أَبْقَى ʔabqā	نَبْقَى nabqā	
2m	تَبْقَى tabqā	تَبْقَيَانِ tabqayāni	تَبْقَوْنَ tabqawna
2f	تَبْقَيْنَ tabqayna		تَبْقَيْنَ tabqayna
3m	يَبْقَى yabqā	يَبْقَيَانِ yabqayāni	يَبْقَوْنَ yabqawna
3f	تَبْقَى tabqā	تَبْقَيَانِ tabqayāni	يَبْقَيْنَ yabqayna

subjunctive

	singular	dual	plural
1	أَبْقَى ʔabqā	نَبْقَى nabqā	
2m	تَبْقَى tabqā	تَبْقَيَا tabqayā	تَبْقَوْا tabqaw
2f	تَبْقَيْ tabqay		تَبْقَيْنَ tabqayna
3m	يَبْقَى yabqā	يَبْقَيَا yabqayā	يَبْقَوْا yabqaw
3f	تَبْقَى tabqā	تَبْقَيَا tabqayā	يَبْقَيْنَ yabqayna

jussive

	singular	dual	plural
1	أَبْقَ ʔabqa	نَبْقَ nabqa	
2m	تَبْقَ tabqa	تَبْقَيَا tabqayā	تَبْقَوْا tabqaw
2f	تَبْقَيْ tabqay		تَبْقَيْنَ tabqayna
3m	يَبْقَ yabqa	يَبْقَيَا yabqayā	يَبْقَوْا yabqaw
3f	تَبْقَ tabqa	تَبْقَيَا tabqayā	يَبْقَيْنَ yabqayna

imperative

	singular	dual	plural
2m	اِبْقَ ibqa	اِبْقَيَا ibqayā	اِبْقَوْا ibqaw
2f	اِبْقَيْ ibqay		اِبْقَيْنَ ibqayna

participles

active	passive
بَاقٍ bāq(in)	مَبْقِيّ mabqīy

passive

perfect	imperfect
بُقِيَ buqiya	يُبْقَى yubqā

hamzated defective measure I *perfect vowel:* **i** *imperfect vowel:* **a**		و	ي	ء	*other*	**1d4(a)** **to grieve**
	R^1			✓		
	R^2				✓	
	R^3		✓			

perfect

	singular	dual	plural
1	أَسِيتُ ʔasītu	أَسِينَا ʔasīnā	
2m	أَسِيتَ ʔasīta	أَسِيتُمَا ʔasītumā	أَسِيتُمْ ʔasītum
2f	أَسِيتِ ʔasīti		أَسِيتُنَّ ʔasītunna
3m	أَسِيَ ʔasiya	أَسِيَا ʔasiyā	أَسُوا ʔasū
3f	أَسِيَتْ ʔasiyat	أَسِيَتَا ʔasiyatā	أَسِينَ ʔasīna

indicative

	singular	dual	plural
1	آسَى ʔāsā	نَأْسَى naʔsā	
2m	تَأْسَى taʔsā	تَأْسَيَانِ taʔsayāni	تَأْسَوْنَ taʔsawna
2f	تَأْسَيْنَ taʔsayna		تَأْسَيْنَ taʔsayna
3m	يَأْسَى yaʔsā	يَأْسَيَانِ yaʔsayāni	يَأْسَوْنَ yaʔsawna
3f	تَأْسَى taʔsā	تَأْسَيَانِ taʔsayāni	يَأْسَيْنَ yaʔsayna

subjunctive

	singular	dual	plural
1	آسَى ʔāsā	نَأْسَى naʔsā	
2m	تَأْسَى taʔsā	تَأْسَيَا taʔsayā	تَأْسَوْا taʔsaw
2f	تَأْسَيْ taʔsay		تَأْسَيْنَ taʔsayna
3m	يَأْسَى yaʔsā	يَأْسَيَا yaʔsayā	يَأْسَوْا yaʔsaw
3f	تَأْسَى taʔsā	تَأْسَيَا taʔsayā	يَأْسَيْنَ yaʔsayna

jussive

	singular	dual	plural
1	آسَ ʔāsa	نَأْسَ naʔsa	
2m	تَأْسَ taʔsa	تَأْسَيَا taʔsayā	تَأْسَوْا taʔsaw
2f	تَأْسَيْ taʔsay		تَأْسَيْنَ taʔsayna
3m	يَأْسَ yaʔsa	يَأْسَيَا yaʔsayā	يَأْسَوْا yaʔsaw
3f	تَأْسَ taʔsa	تَأْسَيَا taʔsayā	يَأْسَيْنَ yaʔsayna

imperative

	singular	dual	plural
2m	اِئْسَ iʔsa	اِئْسَيَا iʔsayā	اِئْسَوْا iʔsaw
2f	اِئْسَيْ iʔsay		اِئْسَيْنَ iʔsayna

participles

active	passive
آسٍ ʔās(in)	مَأْسِيّ maʔsīy

passive

perfect	imperfect
أُسِيَ ʔusiya	يُؤْسَى yuʔsā

irregular defective measure I		و	ي	ء	*other*	**1d4(b)**
perfect vowel: **i**	*R¹*				✓	**to live**
imperfect vowel: **a**	*R²*		✓			
	R³		✓			

perfect

	singular	dual	plural
1	حَيِيتُ ɦayītu	حَيِينَا ɦayīna	
2m	حَيِيتَ ɦayīta	حَيِيتُمَا ɦayītumā	حَيِيتُمْ ɦayītum
2f	حَيِيتِ ɦayīti		حَيِيتُنَّ ɦayītunna
3m	حَيِيَ (حَيَّ) ɦayiya (ɦayya)	حَيِيَا (حَيَّا) ɦayiyā (ɦayyā)	حَيُّوا ɦayyū
3f	حَيِيَتْ (حَيَّتْ) ɦayiyat (ɦayyat)	حَيِيَتَا (حَيَّتَا) ɦayiyatā (ɦayyatā)	حَيِينَ ɦayīna

indicative

	singular	dual	plural
1	أَحْيَا ʔaɦyā	نَحْيَا naɦyā	
2m	تَحْيَا taɦyā	تَحْيَيَانِ taɦyayāni	تَحْيَوْنَ taɦyawna
2f	تَحْيَيْنَ taɦyayna		تَحْيَيْنَ taɦyayna
3m	يَحْيَا yaɦyā	يَحْيَيَانِ yaɦyayāni	يَحْيَوْنَ yaɦyawna
3f	تَحْيَا taɦyā	تَحْيَيَانِ taɦyayāni	يَحْيَيْنَ yaɦyayna

subjunctive

	singular	dual	plural
1	أَحْيَا ʔaɦyā	نَحْيَا naɦyā	
2m	تَحْيَا taɦyā	تَحْيَيَا taɦyayā	تَحْيَوْا taɦyaw
2f	تَحْيَيْ taɦyay		تَحْيَيْنَ taɦyayna
3m	يَحْيَا yaɦyā	يَحْيَيَا yaɦyayā	يَحْيَوْا yaɦyaw
3f	تَحْيَا taɦyā	تَحْيَيَا taɦyayā	يَحْيَيْنَ yaɦyayna

jussive

	singular	dual	plural
1	أَحْيَ ʔaɦya	نَحْيَ naɦya	
2m	تَحْيَ taɦya	تَحْيَيَا taɦyayā	تَحْيَوْا taɦyaw
2f	تَحْيَيْ taɦyay		تَحْيَيْنَ taɦyayna
3m	يَحْيَ yaɦya	يَحْيَيَا yaɦyayā	يَحْيَوْا yaɦyaw
3f	تَحْيَ taɦya	تَحْيَيَا taɦyayā	يَحْيَيْنَ yaɦyayna

imperative

	singular	dual	plural
2m	اِحْيَ iɦya	اِحْيَيَا iɦyayā	اِحْيَوْا iɦyaw
2f	اِحْيَيْ iɦyay		اِحْيَيْنَ iɦyayna

participles

active	passive
حَايٍ ɦāy(in)	مَحْيِيّ maɦyīy

passive

perfect	imperfect
حُيِيَ ɦuyiya	يُحْيَا yuɦyā

assimilated defective measure I

perfect vowel: **i**
imperfect vowel: **i**

	و	ي	ء	*other*
R¹	✓			
R²				✓
R³		✓		

1d5
to follow

perfect

	singular	dual	plural
1	وَلِيتُ walītu	وَلِينَا walīnā	
2m	وَلِيتَ walīta	وَلِيتُمَا walītumā	وَلِيتُمْ walītum
2f	وَلِيتِ walīti		وَلِيتُنَّ walītunna
3m	وَلِيَ waliya	وَلِيَا waliyā	وَلُوا walū
3f	وَلِيَتْ waliyat	وَلِيَتَا waliyatā	وَلِينَ walīna

indicative

	singular	dual	plural
1	أَلِي ʔalī	نَلِي nalī	
2m	تَلِي talī	تَلِيَانِ taliyāni	تَلُونَ talūna
2f	تَلِينَ talīna		تَلِينَ talīna
3m	يَلِي yalī	يَلِيَانِ yaliyāni	يَلُونَ yalūna
3f	تَلِي talī	تَلِيَانِ taliyāni	يَلِينَ yalīna

subjunctive

	singular	dual	plural
1	أَلِيَ ʔaliya	نَلِيَ naliya	
2m	تَلِيَ taliya	تَلِيَا taliyā	تَلُوا talū
2f	تَلِي talī		تَلِينَ talīna
3m	يَلِيَ yaliya	يَلِيَا yaliyā	يَلُوا yalū
3f	تَلِيَ taliya	تَلِيَا taliyā	يَلِينَ yalīna

jussive

	singular	dual	plural
1	أَلِ ʔali	نَلِ nali	
2m	تَلِ tali	تَلِيَا taliyā	تَلُوا talū
2f	تَلِي talī		تَلِينَ talīna
3m	يَلِ yali	يَلِيَا yaliyā	يَلُوا yalū
3f	تَلِ tali	تَلِيَا taliyā	يَلِينَ yalīna

imperative

	singular	dual	plural
2m	لِ li	لِيَا liyā	لُوا lū
2f	لِي lī		لِينَ līna

participles

active	passive
وَالٍ wāl(in)	مَوْلِيّ mawlīy

passive

perfect	imperfect
وُلِيَ wuliya	يُولَى yūlā

Measures II-X

Names	augmented verb, derived verb
	مزيد ثلاثي mazīd ŧulāŧī^{y}
Characteristics	• **triliteral**

	measure II
Names	مزيد ثلاثي وزن فعّل mazīd ŧulāŧī^{y} wazn fa33ala
Characteristics	• second radical doubled
Meanings	• transitive of intransitive measure I verbs • causative of transitive measure I verbs • do intensively and/or repeatedly ('__ to pieces')

	measure III
Names	مزيد ثلاثي وزن فاعل mazīd ŧulāŧī^{y} wazn fā3ala
Characteristics	• first radical followed by ā
Meanings	• attempt to do • do with someone else

	measure IV
Names	مزيد ثلاثي وزن أفعل mazīd ŧulāŧī^{y} wazn fa33ala
Characteristics	• first radical of the perfect verb is prefixed by ʔa-, which is omitted in the imperfect tense
Meanings	• transitive of intransitive measure I verbs • causative of transitive measure I verbs • often synonymous with measure II verbs

	measure V
Names	مزيد ثلاثي وزن تفعّل mazīd ŧulāŧī^{y} wazn tafa33ala
Characteristics	• first radical prefixed by ta- • second radical is doubled
Meaning	• reflexive or passive of measure II verbs

	measure VI
Names	مزيد ثلاثي وزن تفاعل mazīd ŧulāŧī^{y} wazn tafā3ala
Characteristics	• first radical prefixed by ta- • first radical followed by ā
Meaning	• reciprocal of measure III verbs ('__ each other')

	measure VII
Names	مزيد ثلاثي وزن انفعل mazīd ŧulāŧī^{y} wazn infa3ala
Characteristics	• first radical prefixed by in-
Meaning	• reflexive or passive of measure I verbs

	measure VIII
Names	مزيد ثلاثي وزن افتعل mazīd ŧulāŧī^{y} wazn ifta3ala
Characteristics	• first radical sandwiched by i_t-
Meanings	• reflexive or passive of measure I verbs • various other meanings

	measure IX
Names	مزيد ثلاثي وزن افعلّ mazīd ŧulāŧī^{y} wazn if3alla
Characteristics	• first radical prefixed by i- • third radical doubled
Meaning	• intransitive verbs referring to color or physical deficiencies

	measure X
Names	مزيد ثلاثي وزن استفعل mazīd ŧulāŧī^{y} wazn istaf3ala
Characteristics	• first radical prefixed by ista-
Meanings	• ask for __ • find, regard as __ • various other meanings

sound measure II

masdar: تَقْدِيم taqdīm

	و	ي	ء	other
R^1	✓	✓		✓
R^2	✓	✓		✓
R^3				✓

2s

to introduce

perfect

	singular	dual	plural
1	قَدَّمْتُ qaddamtu	قَدَّمْنَا qaddamnā	
2m	قَدَّمْتَ qaddamta	قَدَّمْتُمَا qaddamtumā	قَدَّمْتُمْ qaddamtum
2f	قَدَّمْتِ qaddamti		قَدَّمْتُنَّ qaddamtunna
3m	قَدَّمَ qaddama	قَدَّمَا qaddamā	قَدَّمُوا qaddamū
3f	قَدَّمَتْ qaddamat	قَدَّمَتَا qaddamatā	قَدَّمْنَ qaddamna

indicative

	singular	dual	plural
1	أُقَدِّمُ ʔuqaddimu	نُقَدِّمُ nuqaddimu	
2m	تُقَدِّمُ tuqaddimu	تُقَدِّمَانِ tuqaddimāni	تُقَدِّمُونَ tuqaddimūna
2f	تُقَدِّمِينَ tuqaddimīna		تُقَدِّمْنَ tuqaddimna
3m	يُقَدِّمُ yuqaddimu	يُقَدِّمَانِ yuqaddimāni	يُقَدِّمُونَ yuqaddimūna
3f	تُقَدِّمُ tuqaddimu	تُقَدِّمَانِ tuqaddimāni	يُقَدِّمْنَ yuqaddimna

subjunctive

	singular	dual	plural
1	أُقَدِّمَ ʔuqaddima	نُقَدِّمَ nuqaddima	
2m	تُقَدِّمَ tuqaddima	تُقَدِّمَا tuqaddimā	تُقَدِّمُوا tuqaddimū
2f	تُقَدِّمِي tuqaddimī		تُقَدِّمْنَ tuqaddimna
3m	يُقَدِّمَ yuqaddima	يُقَدِّمَا yuqaddimā	يُقَدِّمُوا yuqaddimū
3f	تُقَدِّمَ tuqaddima	تُقَدِّمَا tuqaddimā	يُقَدِّمْنَ yuqaddimna

jussive

	singular	dual	plural
1	أُقَدِّمْ ʔuqaddim	نُقَدِّمْ nuqaddim	
2m	تُقَدِّمْ tuqaddim	تُقَدِّمَا tuqaddimā	تُقَدِّمُوا tuqaddimū
2f	تُقَدِّمِي tuqaddimī		تُقَدِّمْنَ tuqaddimna
3m	يُقَدِّمْ yuqaddim	يُقَدِّمَا yuqaddimā	يُقَدِّمُوا yuqaddimū
3f	تُقَدِّمْ tuqaddim	تُقَدِّمَا tuqaddimā	يُقَدِّمْنَ yuqaddimna

imperative

	singular	dual	plural
2m	قَدِّمْ qaddim	قَدِّمَا qaddimā	قَدِّمُوا qaddimū
2f	قَدِّمِي qaddimī		قَدِّمْنَ qaddimna

participles

active	passive
مُقَدِّم muqaddim	مُقَدَّم muqaddam

passive

perfect	imperfect
قُدِّمَ quddima	يُقَدَّمُ yuqaddamu

hamzated measure II

masdar: تَأْكِيد taʔkīd

	و	ي	ء	*other*
R[1]			✓	
R[2]	✓	✓		✓
R[3]				✓

2s(a)
to confirm

perfect

	singular	dual	plural
1	أَكَّدْتُ ʔakkadtu	أَكَّدْنَا ʔakkadnā	
2m	أَكَّدْتَ ʔakkadta	أَكَّدْتُمَا ʔakkadtumā	أَكَّدْتُمْ ʔakkadtum
2f	أَكَّدْتِ ʔakkadti		أَكَّدْتُنَّ ʔakkadtunna
3m	أَكَّدَ ʔakkada	أَكَّدَا ʔakkadā	أَكَّدُوا ʔakkadū
3f	أَكَّدَتْ ʔakkadat	أَكَّدَتَا ʔakkadatā	أَكَّدْنَ ʔakkadna

indicative

	singular	dual	plural
1	أُؤَكِّدُ ʔuʔakkidu	نُؤَكِّدُ nuʔakkidu	
2m	تُؤَكِّدُ tuʔakkidu	تُؤَكِّدَانِ tuʔakkidāni	تُؤَكِّدُونَ tuʔakkidūna
2f	تُؤَكِّدِينَ tuʔakkidīna		تُؤَكِّدْنَ tuʔakkidna
3m	يُؤَكِّدُ yuʔakkidu	يُؤَكِّدَانِ yuʔakkidāni	يُؤَكِّدُونَ yuʔakkidūna
3f	تُؤَكِّدُ tuʔakkidu	تُؤَكِّدَانِ tuʔakkidāni	يُؤَكِّدْنَ yuʔakkidna

subjunctive

	singular	dual	plural
1	أُؤَكِّدَ ʔuʔakkida	نُؤَكِّدَ nuʔakkida	
2m	تُؤَكِّدَ tuʔakkida	تُؤَكِّدَا tuʔakkidā	تُؤَكِّدُوا tuʔakkidū
2f	تُؤَكِّدِي tuʔakkidī		تُؤَكِّدْنَ tuʔakkidna
3m	يُؤَكِّدَ yuʔakkida	يُؤَكِّدَا yuʔakkidā	يُؤَكِّدُوا yuʔakkidū
3f	تُؤَكِّدَ tuʔakkida	تُؤَكِّدَا tuʔakkidā	يُؤَكِّدْنَ yuʔakkidna

jussive

	singular	dual	plural
1	أُؤَكِّدْ ʔuʔakkid	نُؤَكِّدْ nuʔakkid	
2m	تُؤَكِّدْ tuʔakkid	تُؤَكِّدَا tuʔakkidā	تُؤَكِّدُوا tuʔakkidū
2f	تُؤَكِّدِي tuʔakkidī		تُؤَكِّدْنَ tuʔakkidna
3m	يُؤَكِّدْ yuʔakkid	يُؤَكِّدَا yuʔakkidā	يُؤَكِّدُوا yuʔakkidū
3f	تُؤَكِّدْ tuʔakkid	تُؤَكِّدَا tuʔakkidā	يُؤَكِّدْنَ yuʔakkidna

imperative

	singular	dual	plural
2m	أَكِّدْ ʔakkid	أَكِّدَا ʔakkidā	أَكِّدُوا ʔakkidū
2f	أَكِّدِي ʔakkidī		أَكِّدْنَ ʔakkidna

participles

active	passive
مُؤَكِّد muʔakkid	مُؤَكَّد muʔakkad

passive

perfect	imperfect
أُكِّدَ ʔukkida	يُؤَكَّدُ yuʔakkadu

hamzated measure II		و	ي	ء	other	**2s(b)**
masdar: تَرْئِيس tarʔīs	R^1	✓	✓		✓	to make president
	R^2			✓		
	R^3				✓	

perfect

	singular	dual	plural
1	رَأَّسْتُ raʔʔastu	رَأَّسْنَا raʔʔasnā	
2m	رَأَّسْتَ raʔʔasta	رَأَّسْتُمَا raʔʔastumā	رَأَّسْتُمْ raʔʔastum
2f	رَأَّسْتِ raʔʔasti		رَأَّسْتُنَّ raʔʔastunna
3m	رَأَّسَ raʔʔasa	رَأَّسَا raʔʔasā	رَأَّسُوا raʔʔasū
3f	رَأَّسَتْ raʔʔasat	رَأَّسَتَا raʔʔasatā	رَأَّسْنَ raʔʔasna

indicative

	singular	dual	plural
1	أُرَئِّسُ ʔuraʔʔisu	نُرَئِّسُ nuraʔʔisu	
2m	تُرَئِّسُ turaʔʔisu	تُرَئِّسَانِ turaʔʔisāni	تُرَئِّسُونَ turaʔʔisūna
2f	تُرَئِّسِينَ turaʔʔisīna		تُرَئِّسْنَ turaʔʔisna
3m	يُرَئِّسُ yuraʔʔisu	يُرَئِّسَانِ yuraʔʔisāni	يُرَئِّسُونَ yuraʔʔisūna
3f	تُرَئِّسُ turaʔʔisu	تُرَئِّسَانِ turaʔʔisāni	يُرَئِّسْنَ yuraʔʔisna

subjunctive

	singular	dual	plural
1	أُرَئِّسَ ʔuraʔʔisa	نُرَئِّسَ nuraʔʔisa	
2m	تُرَئِّسَ turaʔʔisa	تُرَئِّسَا turaʔʔisā	تُرَئِّسُوا turaʔʔisū
2f	تُرَئِّسِي turaʔʔisī		تُرَئِّسْنَ turaʔʔisna
3m	يُرَئِّسَ yuraʔʔisa	يُرَئِّسَا yuraʔʔisā	يُرَئِّسُوا yuraʔʔisū
3f	تُرَئِّسَ turaʔʔisa	تُرَئِّسَا turaʔʔisā	يُرَئِّسْنَ yuraʔʔisna

jussive

	singular	dual	plural
1	أُرَئِّسْ ʔuraʔʔis	نُرَئِّسْ nuraʔʔis	
2m	تُرَئِّسْ turaʔʔis	تُرَئِّسَا turaʔʔisā	تُرَئِّسُوا turaʔʔisū
2f	تُرَئِّسِي turaʔʔisī		تُرَئِّسْنَ turaʔʔisna
3m	يُرَئِّسْ yuraʔʔis	يُرَئِّسَا yuraʔʔisā	يُرَئِّسُوا yuraʔʔisū
3f	تُرَئِّسْ turaʔʔis	تُرَئِّسَا turaʔʔisā	يُرَئِّسْنَ yuraʔʔisna

imperative

	singular	dual	plural
2m	رَئِّسْ raʔʔis	رَئِّسَا raʔʔisā	رَئِّسُوا raʔʔisū
2f	رَئِّسِي raʔʔisī		رَئِّسْنَ raʔʔisna

participles

active	passive
مُرَئِّس muraʔʔis	مُرَأَّس muraʔʔas

passive

perfect	imperfect
رُئِّسَ ruʔʔisa	يُرَأَّسُ yuraʔʔasu

sound measure II

masdar: تَهْدِئَة tahdiʔa^t

	و	ي	ء	other
R¹	✓	✓		✓
R²	✓	✓		✓
R³			✓	

2s(c)
to calm

perfect

	singular	dual	plural
1	هَدَّأْتُ haddaʔtu	هَدَّأْنَا haddaʔnā	
2m	هَدَّأْتَ haddaʔta	هَدَّأْتُمَا haddaʔtumā	هَدَّأْتُمْ haddaʔtum
2f	هَدَّأْتِ haddaʔti		هَدَّأْتُنَّ haddaʔtunna
3m	هَدَّأَ haddaʔa	هَدَّآ haddaʔā	هَدَّؤُوا haddaʔū
3f	هَدَّأَتْ haddaʔat	هَدَّأَتَا haddaʔatā	هَدَّأْنَ haddaʔna

indicative

	singular	dual	plural
1	أُهَدِّئُ ʔuhaddiʔu	نُهَدِّئُ nuhaddiʔu	
2m	تُهَدِّئُ tuhaddiʔu	تُهَدِّئَانِ tuhaddiʔāni	تُهَدِّئُونَ tuhaddiʔūna
2f	تُهَدِّئِينَ tuhaddiʔīna		تُهَدِّئْنَ tuhaddiʔna
3m	يُهَدِّئُ yuhaddiʔu	يُهَدِّئَانِ yuhaddiʔāni	يُهَدِّئُونَ yuhaddiʔūna
3f	تُهَدِّئُ tuhaddiʔu	تُهَدِّئَانِ tuhaddiʔāni	يُهَدِّئْنَ yuhaddiʔna

subjunctive

	singular	dual	plural
1	أُهَدِّئَ ʔuhaddiʔa	نُهَدِّئَ nuhaddiʔa	
2m	تُهَدِّئَ tuhaddiʔa	تُهَدِّئَا tuhaddiʔā	تُهَدِّئُوا tuhaddiʔū
2f	تُهَدِّئِي tuhaddiʔī		تُهَدِّئْنَ tuhaddiʔna
3m	يُهَدِّئَ yuhaddiʔa	يُهَدِّئَا yuhaddiʔā	يُهَدِّئُوا yuhaddiʔū
3f	تُهَدِّئَ tuhaddiʔa	تُهَدِّئَا tuhaddiʔā	يُهَدِّئْنَ yuhaddiʔna

jussive

	singular	dual	plural
1	أُهَدِّئْ ʔuhaddiʔ	نُهَدِّئْ nuhaddiʔ	
2m	تُهَدِّئْ tuhaddiʔ	تُهَدِّئَا tuhaddiʔā	تُهَدِّئُوا tuhaddiʔū
2f	تُهَدِّئِي tuhaddiʔī		تُهَدِّئْنَ tuhaddiʔna
3m	يُهَدِّئْ yuhaddiʔ	يُهَدِّئَا yuhaddiʔā	يُهَدِّئُوا yuhaddiʔū
3f	تُهَدِّئْ tuhaddiʔ	تُهَدِّئَا tuhaddiʔā	يُهَدِّئْنَ yuhaddiʔna

imperative

	singular	dual	plural
2m	هَدِّئْ haddiʔ	هَدِّئَا haddiʔā	هَدِّئُوا haddiʔū
2f	هَدِّئِي haddiʔī		هَدِّئْنَ haddiʔna

participles

active	passive
مُهَدِّئ muhaddiʔ	مُهَدَّأ muhaddaʔ

passive

perfect	imperfect
هُدِّئَ huddiʔa	يُهَدَّأُ yuhaddaʔu

defective measure II

masdar: تَغْنِيَة taɣniyaᵗ

	و	ي	ء	*other*
R¹	✓	✓		✓
R²	✓	✓		✓
R³	✓	✓		

2d
to sing

perfect

	singular	dual	plural
1	غَنَّيْتُ ɣannaytu	غَنَّيْنَا ɣannaynā	
2m	غَنَّيْتَ ɣannayta	غَنَّيْتُمَا ɣannaytumā	غَنَّيْتُمْ ɣannaytum
2f	غَنَّيْتِ ɣannayti		غَنَّيْتُنَّ ɣannaytunna
3m	غَنَّى* ɣannā	غَنَّيَا ɣannayā	غَنَّوْا ɣannaw
3f	غَنَّتْ ɣannat	غَنَّتَا ɣannatā	غَنَّيْنَ ɣannayna

indicative

	singular	dual	plural
1	أُغَنِّي ʔuɣannī	نُغَنِّي nuɣannī	
2m	تُغَنِّي tuɣannī	تُغَنِّيَانِ tuɣanniyāni	تُغَنُّونَ tuɣannūna
2f	تُغَنِّينَ tuɣannīna		تُغَنِّينَ tuɣannīna
3m	يُغَنِّي yuɣannī	يُغَنِّيَانِ yuɣanniyāni	يُغَنُّونَ yuɣannūna
3f	تُغَنِّي tuɣannī	تُغَنِّيَانِ tuɣanniyāni	يُغَنِّينَ yuɣannīna

subjunctive

	singular	dual	plural
1	أُغَنِّيَ ʔuɣanniya	نُغَنِّيَ nuɣanniya	
2m	تُغَنِّيَ tuɣanniya	تُغَنِّيَا tuɣanniyā	تُغَنُّوا tuɣannū
2f	تُغَنِّي tuɣannī		تُغَنِّينَ tuɣannīna
3m	يُغَنِّيَ yuɣanniya	يُغَنِّيَا yuɣanniyā	يُغَنُّوا yuɣannū
3f	تُغَنِّيَ tuɣanniya	تُغَنِّيَا tuɣanniyā	يُغَنِّينَ yuɣannīna

jussive

	singular	dual	plural
1	أُغَنِّ ʔuɣanni	نُغَنِّ nuɣanni	
2m	تُغَنِّ tuɣanni	تُغَنِّيَا tuɣanniyā	تُغَنُّوا tuɣannū
2f	تُغَنِّي tuɣannī		تُغَنِّينَ tuɣannīna
3m	يُغَنِّ yuɣanni	يُغَنِّيَا yuɣanniyā	يُغَنُّوا yuɣannū
3f	تُغَنِّ tuɣanni	تُغَنِّيَا tuɣanniyā	يُغَنِّينَ yuɣannīna

imperative

	singular	dual	plural
2m	غَنِّ ɣanni	غَنِّيَا ɣanniyā	غَنُّوا ɣannū
2f	غَنِّي ɣannī		غَنِّينَ ɣannīna

participles

active	passive
مُغَنٍّ muɣann(in)	مُغَنًّى muɣann(an)

passive

perfect	imperfect
غُنِّيَ ɣunniya	يُغَنَّى yuɣannā

*The 3rd person masculine singular perfect form of حَيَّا is irregular in that it is spelled with ـا, not ى.

hamzated defective meas. II

masdar: تَأْدِيَة taʔdiyaᵗ

	و	ي	ء	*other*
R¹			✓	
R²	✓	✓		✓
R³	✓	✓		

2d(a)

to cause

perfect

	singular	dual	plural
1	أَدَّيْتُ ʔaddaytu	أَدَّيْنَا ʔaddaynā	
2m	أَدَّيْتَ ʔaddayta	أَدَّيْتُمَا ʔaddaytumā	أَدَّيْتُمْ ʔaddaytum
2f	أَدَّيْتِ ʔaddayti		أَدَّيْتُنَّ ʔaddaytunna
3m	أَدَّى ʔaddā	أَدَّيَا ʔaddayā	أَدَّوْا ʔaddaw
3f	أَدَّتْ ʔaddat	أَدَّتَا ʔaddatā	أَدَّيْنَ ʔaddayna

indicative

	singular	dual	plural
1	أُؤَدِّي ʔuʔaddī	نُؤَدِّي nuʔaddī	
2m	تُؤَدِّي tuʔaddī	تُؤَدِّيَانِ tuʔaddiyāni	تُؤَدُّونَ tuʔaddūna
2f	تُؤَدِّينَ tuʔaddīna		تُؤَدِّينَ tuʔaddīna
3m	يُؤَدِّي yuʔaddī	يُؤَدِّيَانِ yuʔaddiyāni	يُؤَدُّونَ yuʔaddūna
3f	تُؤَدِّي tuʔaddī	تُؤَدِّيَانِ tuʔaddiyāni	يُؤَدِّينَ yuʔaddīna

subjunctive

	singular	dual	plural
1	أُؤَدِّيَ ʔuʔaddiya	نُؤَدِّيَ nuʔaddiya	
2m	تُؤَدِّيَ tuʔaddiya	تُؤَدِّيَا tuʔaddiyā	تُؤَدُّوا tuʔaddū
2f	تُؤَدِّي tuʔaddī		تُؤَدِّينَ tuʔaddīna
3m	يُؤَدِّيَ yuʔaddiya	يُؤَدِّيَا yuʔaddiyā	يُؤَدُّوا yuʔaddū
3f	تُؤَدِّيَ tuʔaddiya	تُؤَدِّيَا tuʔaddiyā	يُؤَدِّينَ yuʔaddīna

jussive

	singular	dual	plural
1	أُؤَدِّ ʔuʔaddi	نُؤَدِّ nuʔaddi	
2m	تُؤَدِّ tuʔaddi	تُؤَدِّيَا tuʔaddiyā	تُؤَدُّوا tuʔaddū
2f	تُؤَدِّي tuʔaddī		تُؤَدِّينَ tuʔaddīna
3m	يُؤَدِّ yuʔaddi	يُؤَدِّيَا yuʔaddiyā	يُؤَدُّوا yuʔaddū
3f	تُؤَدِّ tuʔaddi	تُؤَدِّيَا tuʔaddiyā	يُؤَدِّينَ yuʔaddīna

imperative

	singular	dual	plural
2m	أَدِّ ʔaddi	أَدِّيَا ʔaddiyā	أَدُّوا ʔaddū
2f	أَدِّي ʔaddī		أَدِّينَ ʔaddīna

participles

active	passive
مُؤَدٍّ muʔadd(in)	مُؤَدًّى muʔadd(an)

passive

perfect	imperfect
أُدِّيَ ʔuddiya	يُؤَدَّى yuʔaddā

sound measure III **masdar:** مُحَاوَلَة muɧāwala^t		و	ي	ء	*other*	**3s** **to try**
	R^1	✓	✓		✓	
	R^2	✓	✓		✓	
	R^3				✓	

perfect

	singular	dual	plural
1	حَاوَلْتُ ɧāwaltu	حَاوَلْنَا ɧāwalnā	
2m	حَاوَلْتَ ɧāwalta	حَاوَلْتُمَا ɧāwaltumā	حَاوَلْتُمْ ɧāwaltum
2f	حَاوَلْتِ ɧāwalti		حَاوَلْتُنَّ ɧāwaltunna
3m	حَاوَلَ ɧāwala	حَاوَلَا ɧāwalā	حَاوَلُوا ɧāwalū
3f	حَاوَلَتْ ɧāwalat	حَاوَلَتَا ɧāwalatā	حَاوَلْنَ ɧāwalna

indicative

	singular	dual	plural
1	أُحَاوِلُ ʔuɧāwilu	نُحَاوِلُ nuɧāwilu	
2m	تُحَاوِلُ tuɧāwilu	تُحَاوِلَانِ tuɧāwilāni	تُحَاوِلُونَ tuɧāwilūna
2f	تُحَاوِلِينَ tuɧāwilīna		تُحَاوِلْنَ tuɧāwilna
3m	يُحَاوِلُ yuɧāwilu	يُحَاوِلَانِ yuɧāwilāni	يُحَاوِلُونَ yuɧāwilūna
3f	تُحَاوِلُ tuɧāwilu	تُحَاوِلَانِ tuɧāwilāni	يُحَاوِلْنَ yuɧāwilna

subjunctive

	singular	dual	plural
1	أُحَاوِلَ ʔuɧāwila	نُحَاوِلَ nuɧāwila	
2m	تُحَاوِلَ tuɧāwila	تُحَاوِلَا tuɧāwilā	تُحَاوِلُوا tuɧāwilū
2f	تُحَاوِلِي tuɧāwilī		تُحَاوِلْنَ tuɧāwilna
3m	يُحَاوِلَ yuɧāwila	يُحَاوِلَا yuɧāwilā	يُحَاوِلُوا yuɧāwilū
3f	تُحَاوِلَ tuɧāwila	تُحَاوِلَا tuɧāwilā	يُحَاوِلْنَ yuɧāwilna

jussive

	singular	dual	plural
1	أُحَاوِلْ ʔuɧāwil	نُحَاوِلْ nuɧāwil	
2m	تُحَاوِلْ tuɧāwil	تُحَاوِلَا tuɧāwilā	تُحَاوِلُوا tuɧāwilū
2f	تُحَاوِلِي tuɧāwilī		تُحَاوِلْنَ tuɧāwilna
3m	يُحَاوِلْ yuɧāwil	يُحَاوِلَا yuɧāwilā	يُحَاوِلُوا yuɧāwilū
3f	تُحَاوِلْ tuɧāwil	تُحَاوِلَا tuɧāwilā	يُحَاوِلْنَ yuɧāwilna

imperative

	singular	dual	plural
2m	حَاوِلْ ɧāwil	حَاوِلَا ɧāwilā	حَاوِلُوا ɧāwilū
2f	حَاوِلِي ɧāwilī		حَاوِلْنَ ɧāwilna

participles

active	passive
مُحَاوِل muɧāwil	مُحَاوَل muɧāwal

passive

perfect	imperfect
حُووِلَ ɧūwila	يُحَاوَلُ yuɧāwalu

hamzated measure III **masdar:** مُؤَاخَذَة muʔāxađa[t]		و	ي	ء	*other*	**3s(a)** **to blame**
	R¹			✓		
	R²	✓	✓		✓	
	R³				✓	

perfect

	singular	dual	plural
1	آخَذْتُ ʔāxađtu	آخَذْنَا ʔāxađnā	
2m	آخَذْتَ ʔāxađta	آخَذْتُمَا ʔāxađtumā	آخَذْتُمْ ʔāxađtum
2f	آخَذْتِ ʔāxađti		آخَذْتُنَّ ʔāxađtunna
3m	آخَذَ ʔāxađa	آخَذَا ʔāxađā	آخَذُوا ʔāxađū
3f	آخَذَتْ ʔāxađat	آخَذَتَا ʔāxađatā	آخَذْنَ ʔāxađna

indicative

	singular	dual	plural
1	أُؤَاخِذُ ʔuʔāxiđu	نُؤَاخِذُ nuʔāxiđu	
2m	تُؤَاخِذُ tuʔāxiđu	تُؤَاخِذَانِ tuʔāxiđāni	تُؤَاخِذُونَ tuʔāxiđūna
2f	تُؤَاخِذِينَ tuʔāxiđīna		تُؤَاخِذْنَ tuʔāxiđna
3m	يُؤَاخِذُ yuʔāxiđu	يُؤَاخِذَانِ yuʔāxiđāni	يُؤَاخِذُونَ yuʔāxiđūna
3f	تُؤَاخِذُ tuʔāxiđu	تُؤَاخِذَانِ tuʔāxiđāni	يُؤَاخِذْنَ yuʔāxiđna

subjunctive

	singular	dual	plural
1	أُؤَاخِذَ ʔuʔāxiđa	نُؤَاخِذَ nuʔāxiđa	
2m	تُؤَاخِذَ tuʔāxiđa	تُؤَاخِذَا tuʔāxiđā	تُؤَاخِذُوا tuʔāxiđū
2f	تُؤَاخِذِي tuʔāxiđī		تُؤَاخِذْنَ tuʔāxiđna
3m	يُؤَاخِذَ yuʔāxiđa	يُؤَاخِذَا yuʔāxiđā	يُؤَاخِذُوا yuʔāxiđū
3f	تُؤَاخِذَ tuʔāxiđa	تُؤَاخِذَا tuʔāxiđā	يُؤَاخِذْنَ yuʔāxiđna

jussive

	singular	dual	plural
1	أُؤَاخِذْ ʔuʔāxiđ	نُؤَاخِذْ nuʔāxiđ	
2m	تُؤَاخِذْ tuʔāxiđ	تُؤَاخِذَا tuʔāxiđā	تُؤَاخِذُوا tuʔāxiđū
2f	تُؤَاخِذِي tuʔāxiđī		تُؤَاخِذْنَ tuʔāxiđna
3m	يُؤَاخِذْ yuʔāxiđ	يُؤَاخِذَا yuʔāxiđā	يُؤَاخِذُوا yuʔāxiđū
3f	تُؤَاخِذْ tuʔāxiđ	تُؤَاخِذَا tuʔāxiđā	يُؤَاخِذْنَ yuʔāxiđna

imperative

	singular	dual	plural
2m	آخِذْ ʔāxiđ	آخِذَا ʔāxiđā	آخِذُوا ʔāxiđū
2f	آخِذِي ʔāxiđī		آخِذْنَ ʔāxiđna

participles

active	passive
مُؤَاخِذ muʔāxiđ	مُؤَاخَذ muʔāxađ

passive

perfect	imperfect
أُوخِذَ ʔūxiđa	يُؤَاخَذُ yuʔāxađu

hamzated measure III

masdar: مُسَاءَلَة musāʔalat

	و	ي	ء	other
R^1	✓	✓		✓
R^2			✓	
R^3				✓

3s(b)

to call to account

perfect

	singular	dual	plural
1	سَاءَلْتُ sāʔaltu	سَاءَلْنَا sāʔalnā	
2m	سَاءَلْتَ sāʔalta	سَاءَلْتُمَا sāʔaltumā	سَاءَلْتُمْ sāʔaltum
2f	سَاءَلْتِ sāʔalti		سَاءَلْتُنَّ sāʔaltunna
3m	سَاءَلَ sāʔala	سَاءَلَا sāʔalā	سَاءَلُوا sāʔalū
3f	سَاءَلَتْ sāʔalat	سَاءَلَتَا sāʔalatā	سَاءَلْنَ sāʔalna

indicative

	singular	dual	plural
1	أُسَائِلُ ʔusāʔilu	نُسَائِلُ nusāʔilu	
2m	تُسَائِلُ tusāʔilu	تُسَائِلَانِ tusāʔilāni	تُسَائِلُونَ tusāʔilūna
2f	تُسَائِلِينَ tusāʔilīna		تُسَائِلْنَ tusāʔilna
3m	يُسَائِلُ yusāʔilu	يُسَائِلَانِ yusāʔilāni	يُسَائِلُونَ yusāʔilūna
3f	تُسَائِلُ tusāʔilu	تُسَائِلَانِ tusāʔilāni	يُسَائِلْنَ yusāʔilna

subjunctive

	singular	dual	plural
1	أُسَائِلَ ʔusāʔila	نُسَائِلَ nusāʔila	
2m	تُسَائِلَ tusāʔila	تُسَائِلَا tusāʔilā	تُسَائِلُوا tusāʔilū
2f	تُسَائِلِي tusāʔilī		تُسَائِلْنَ tusāʔilna
3m	يُسَائِلَ yusāʔila	يُسَائِلَا yusāʔilā	يُسَائِلُوا yusāʔilū
3f	تُسَائِلَ tusāʔila	تُسَائِلَا tusāʔilā	يُسَائِلْنَ yusāʔilna

jussive

	singular	dual	plural
1	أُسَائِلْ ʔusāʔil	نُسَائِلْ nusāʔil	
2m	تُسَائِلْ tusāʔil	تُسَائِلَا tusāʔilā	تُسَائِلُوا tusāʔilū
2f	تُسَائِلِي tusāʔilī		تُسَائِلْنَ tusāʔilna
3m	يُسَائِلْ yusāʔil	يُسَائِلَا yusāʔilā	يُسَائِلُوا yusāʔilū
3f	تُسَائِلْ tusāʔil	تُسَائِلَا tusāʔilā	يُسَائِلْنَ yusāʔilna

imperative

	singular	dual	plural
2m	سَائِلْ sāʔil	سَائِلَا sāʔilā	سَائِلُوا sāʔilū
2f	سَائِلِي sāʔilī		سَائِلْنَ sāʔilna

participles

active	passive
مُسَائِل musāʔil	مُسَاءَل musāʔal

passive

perfect	imperfect
سُوئِلَ sūʔila	يُسَاءَلُ yusāʔalu

hamzated measure III

masdar: مُفَاجَأَة mufājaʔa[t]

	و	ي	ء	other
R^1	✓	✓		✓
R^2	✓	✓		✓
R^3			✓	

3s(c)
to surprise

perfect

	singular	dual	plural
1	فَاجَأْتُ fājaʔtu	فَاجَأْنَا fājaʔnā	
2m	فَاجَأْتَ fājaʔta	فَاجَأْتُمَا fājaʔtumā	فَاجَأْتُمْ fājaʔtum
2f	فَاجَأْتِ fājaʔti		فَاجَأْتُنَّ fājaʔtunna
3m	فَاجَأَ fājaʔa	فَاجَآ fājaʔā	فَاجَؤُوا fājaʔū
3f	فَاجَأَتْ fājaʔat	فَاجَأَتَا fājaʔatā	فَاجَأْنَ fājaʔna

indicative

	singular	dual	plural
1	أُفَاجِئُ ʔufājiʔu	نُفَاجِئُ nufājiʔu	
2m	تُفَاجِئُ tufājiʔu	تُفَاجِئَانِ tufājiʔāni	تُفَاجِؤُونَ tufājiʔūna
2f	تُفَاجِئِينَ tufājiʔīna		تُفَاجِئْنَ tufājiʔna
3m	يُفَاجِئُ yufājiʔu	يُفَاجِئَانِ yufājiʔāni	يُفَاجِؤُونَ yufājiʔūna
3f	تُفَاجِئُ tufājiʔu	تُفَاجِئَانِ tufājiʔāni	يُفَاجِئْنَ yufājiʔna

subjunctive

	singular	dual	plural
1	أُفَاجِئَ ʔufājiʔa	نُفَاجِئَ nufājiʔa	
2m	تُفَاجِئَ tufājiʔa	تُفَاجِئَا tufājiʔā	تُفَاجِؤُوا tufājiʔū
2f	تُفَاجِئِي tufājiʔī		تُفَاجِئْنَ tufājiʔna
3m	يُفَاجِئَ yufājiʔa	يُفَاجِئَا yufājiʔā	يُفَاجِؤُوا yufājiʔū
3f	تُفَاجِئَ tufājiʔa	تُفَاجِئَا tufājiʔā	يُفَاجِئْنَ yufājiʔna

jussive

	singular	dual	plural
1	أُفَاجِئْ ʔufājiʔ	نُفَاجِئْ nufājiʔ	
2m	تُفَاجِئْ tufājiʔ	تُفَاجِئَا tufājiʔā	تُفَاجِؤُوا tufājiʔū
2f	تُفَاجِئِي tufājiʔī		تُفَاجِئْنَ tufājiʔna
3m	يُفَاجِئْ yufājiʔ	يُفَاجِئَا yufājiʔā	يُفَاجِؤُوا yufājiʔū
3f	تُفَاجِئْ tufājiʔ	تُفَاجِئَا tufājiʔā	يُفَاجِئْنَ yufājiʔna

imperative

	singular	dual	plural
2m	فَاجِئْ fājiʔ	فَاجِئَا fājiʔā	فَاجِؤُوا fājiʔū
2f	فَاجِئِي fājiʔī		فَاجِئْنَ fājiʔna

participles

active	passive
مُفَاجِئ mufājiʔ	مُفَاجَأ mufājaʔ

passive

perfect	imperfect
فُوجِئَ fūjiʔa	يُفَاجَأُ yufājaʔu

geminate measure III

masdar: مُحَاجَّة muɧājja^{t}

	و	ي	ء	*other*
R¹				✓
R²				✓
R³				✓

3g

to debate

perfect

	singular	dual	plural
1	حَاجَجْتُ ɧājajtu	حَاجَجْنَا ɧājajnā	
2m	حَاجَجْتَ ɧājajta	حَاجَجْتُمَا ɧājajtumā	حَاجَجْتُمْ ɧājajtum
2f	حَاجَجْتِ ɧājajti		حَاجَجْتُنَّ ɧājajtunna
3m	حَاجَّ ɧājja	حَاجَّا ɧājjā	حَاجُّوا ɧājjū
3f	حَاجَّتْ ɧājjat	حَاجَّتَا ɧājjatā	حَاجَجْنَ ɧājajna

indicative

	singular	dual	plural
1	أُحَاجُّ ʔuɧājju	نُحَاجُّ nuɧājju	
2m	تُحَاجُّ tuɧājju	تُحَاجَّانِ tuɧājjāni	تُحَاجُّونَ tuɧājjūna
2f	تُحَاجِّينَ tuɧājjīna		تُحَاجِجْنَ tuɧājijna
3m	يُحَاجُّ yuɧājju	يُحَاجَّانِ yuɧājjāni	يُحَاجُّونَ yuɧājjūna
3f	تُحَاجُّ tuɧājju	تُحَاجَّانِ tuɧājjāni	يُحَاجِجْنَ yuɧājijna

subjunctive

	singular	dual	plural
1	أُحَاجَّ ʔuɧājja	نُحَاجَّ nuɧājja	
2m	تُحَاجَّ tuɧājja	تُحَاجَّا tuɧājjā	تُحَاجُّوا tuɧājjū
2f	تُحَاجِّي tuɧājī		تُحَاجِجْنَ tuɧājijna
3m	يُحَاجَّ yuɧājja	يُحَاجَّا yuɧājjā	يُحَاجُّوا yuɧājjū
3f	تُحَاجَّ tuɧājja	تُحَاجَّا tuɧājjā	يُحَاجِجْنَ yuɧājijna

jussive

	singular	dual	plural
1	أُحَاجَّ ʔuɧājja	نُحَاجَّ nuɧājja	
2m	تُحَاجَّ tuɧājja	تُحَاجَّا tuɧājjā	تُحَاجُّوا tuɧājjū
2f	تُحَاجِّي tuɧājī		تُحَاجِجْنَ tuɧājijna
3m	يُحَاجَّ yuɧājja	يُحَاجَّا yuɧājjā	يُحَاجُّوا yuɧājjū
3f	تُحَاجَّ tuɧājja	تُحَاجَّا tuɧājjā	يُحَاجِجْنَ yuɧājijna

imperative

	singular	dual	plural
2m	حَاجَّ ɧājja	حَاجَّا ɧājjā	حَاجُّوا ɧājjū
2f	حَاجِّي ɧājī		حَاجِجْنَ ɧājijna

participles

active	passive
مُحَاجّ muɧājj	مُحَاجّ muɧājj

passive

perfect	imperfect
حُوجِجَ ɧūjija	يُحَاجُّ yuɧājju

defective measure III

masdar: مُعَانَاة mu3ānā^{t}

	و	ي	ء	*other*
R¹				✓
R²	✓			✓
R³	✓	✓		

3d
to suffer

perfect

	singular	dual	plural
1	عَانَيْتُ 3ānaytu	عَانَيْنَا 3ānaynā	
2m	عَانَيْتَ 3ānayta	عَانَيْتُمَا 3ānaytumā	عَانَيْتُمْ 3ānaytum
2f	عَانَيْتِ 3ānayti		عَانَيْتُنَّ 3ānaytunna
3m	عَانَى 3ānā	عَانَيَا 3ānayā	عَانَوْا 3ānaw
3f	عَانَتْ 3ānat	عَانَتَا 3ānatā	عَانَيْنَ 3ānayna

indicative

	singular	dual	plural
1	أُعَانِي ʔu3ānī	نُعَانِي nu3ānī	
2m	تُعَانِي tu3ānī	تُعَانِيَانِ tu3āniyāni	تُعَانُونَ tu3ānūna
2f	تُعَانِينَ tu3ānīna		تُعَانِينَ tu3ānīna
3m	يُعَانِي yu3ānī	يُعَانِيَانِ yu3āniyāni	يُعَانُونَ yu3ānūna
3f	تُعَانِي tu3ānī	تُعَانِيَانِ tu3āniyāni	يُعَانِينَ yu3ānīna

subjunctive

	singular	dual	plural
1	أُعَانِيَ ʔu3āniya	نُعَانِيَ nu3āniya	
2m	تُعَانِيَ tu3āniya	تُعَانِيَا tu3āniyā	تُعَانُوا tu3ānū
2f	تُعَانِي tu3ānī		تُعَانِينَ tu3ānīna
3m	يُعَانِيَ yu3āniya	يُعَانِيَا tu3āniyā	يُعَانُوا yu3ānū
3f	تُعَانِيَ tu3āniya	تُعَانِيَا yu3āniyā	يُعَانِينَ yu3ānīna

jussive

	singular	dual	plural
1	أُعَانِ ʔu3āni	نُعَانِ nu3āni	
2m	تُعَانِ tu3āni	تُعَانِيَا tu3āniyā	تُعَانُوا tu3ānū
2f	تُعَانِي tu3ānī		تُعَانِينَ tu3ānīna
3m	يُعَانِ yu3āni	يُعَانِيَا tu3āniyā	يُعَانُوا yu3ānū
3f	تُعَانِ tu3āni	تُعَانِيَا yu3āniyā	يُعَانِينَ yu3ānīna

imperative

	singular	dual	plural
2m	عَانِ 3āni	عَانِيَا 3āniyā	عَانُوا 3ānū
2f	عَانِي 3ānī		عَانِينَ 3ānīna

participles

active	passive
مُعَانٍ mu3ān(in)	مُعَانًى mu3ān(an)

passive

perfect	imperfect
عُونِيَ 3ūniya	يُعَانَى yu3ānā

hamzated defective meas. III

masdar: مُؤَاتَاة muʔātā^t

	و	ي	ء	other
R¹			✓	
R²				✓
R³	✓	✓		

3d(a)

to give

perfect

	singular	dual	plural
1	آتَيْتُ ʔātaytu	آتَيْنَا ʔātaynā	
2m	آتَيْتَ ʔātayta	آتَيْتُمَا ʔātaytumā	آتَيْتُمْ ʔātaytum
2f	آتَيْتِ ʔātayti		آتَيْتُنَّ ʔātaytunna
3m	آتَى ʔātā	آتَيَا ʔātayā	آتَوْا ʔātaw
3f	آتَتْ ʔātat	آتَتَا ʔātatā	آتَيْنَ ʔātayna

indicative

	singular	dual	plural
1	أُؤَاتِي ʔuʔātī	نُؤَاتِي nuʔātī	
2m	تُؤَاتِي tuʔātī	تُؤَاتِيَانِ tuʔātiyāni	تُؤَاتُونَ tuʔātūna
2f	تُؤَاتِينَ tuʔātīna		تُؤَاتِينَ tuʔātīna
3m	يُؤَاتِي yuʔātī	يُؤَاتِيَانِ yuʔātiyāni	يُؤَاتُونَ yuʔātūna
3f	تُؤَاتِي tuʔātī	تُؤَاتِيَانِ tuʔātiyāni	يُؤَاتِينَ yuʔātīna

subjunctive

	singular	dual	plural
1	أُؤَاتِيَ ʔuʔātiya	نُؤَاتِيَ nuʔātiya	
2m	تُؤَاتِيَ tuʔātiya	تُؤَاتِيَا tuʔātiyā	تُؤَاتُوا tuʔātū
2f	تُؤَاتِي tuʔātī		تُؤَاتِينَ tuʔātīna
3m	يُؤَاتِيَ yuʔātiya	يُؤَاتِيَا tuʔātiyā	يُؤَاتُوا yuʔātū
3f	تُؤَاتِيَ tuʔātiya	تُؤَاتِيَا yuʔātiyā	يُؤَاتِينَ yuʔātīna

jussive

	singular	dual	plural
1	أُؤَاتِ ʔuʔāti	نُؤَاتِ nuʔāti	
2m	تُؤَاتِ tuʔāti	تُؤَاتِيَا tuʔātiyā	تُؤَاتُوا tuʔātū
2f	تُؤَاتِي tuʔātī		تُؤَاتِينَ tuʔātīna
3m	يُؤَاتِ yuʔāti	يُؤَاتِيَا tuʔātiyā	يُؤَاتُوا yuʔātū
3f	تُؤَاتِ tuʔāti	تُؤَاتِيَا yuʔātiyā	يُؤَاتِينَ yuʔātīna

imperative

	singular	dual	plural
2m	آتِ ʔāti	آتِيَا ʔātiyā	آتُوا ʔātū
2f	آتِي ʔātī		آتِينَ ʔātīna

participles

active	passive
مُؤَاتٍ muʔāt(in)	مُؤَاتًى muʔāt(an)

passive

perfect	imperfect
أُوتِيَ ʔūtiya	يُؤَاتَى yufātā

sound measure IV

masdar: إِصْبَاح ʔiṣbāḥ

	و	ي	ء	other
R^1				✓
R^2				✓
R^3				✓

4s

to become

perfect

	singular	dual	plural
1	أَصْبَحْتُ ʔaṣbaḥtu	أَصْبَحْنَا ʔaṣbaḥnā	
2m	أَصْبَحْتَ ʔaṣbaḥta	أَصْبَحْتُمَا ʔaṣbaḥtumā	أَصْبَحْتُمْ ʔaṣbaḥtum
2f	أَصْبَحْتِ ʔaṣbaḥti		أَصْبَحْتُنَّ ʔaṣbaḥtunna
3m	أَصْبَحَ ʔaṣbaḥa	أَصْبَحَا ʔaṣbaḥā	أَصْبَحُوا ʔaṣbaḥū
3f	أَصْبَحَتْ ʔaṣbaḥat	أَصْبَحَتَا ʔaṣbaḥatā	أَصْبَحْنَ ʔaṣbaḥna

indicative

	singular	dual	plural
1	أُصْبِحُ ʔuṣbiḥu	نُصْبِحُ nuṣbiḥu	
2m	تُصْبِحُ tuṣbiḥu	تُصْبِحَانِ tuṣbiḥāni	تُصْبِحُونَ tuṣbiḥūna
2f	تُصْبِحِينَ tuṣbiḥīna		تُصْبِحْنَ tuṣbiḥna
3m	يُصْبِحُ yuṣbiḥu	يُصْبِحَانِ yuṣbiḥāni	يُصْبِحُونَ yuṣbiḥūna
3f	تُصْبِحُ tuṣbiḥu	تُصْبِحَانِ tuṣbiḥāni	يُصْبِحْنَ yuṣbiḥna

subjunctive

	singular	dual	plural
1	أُصْبِحَ ʔuṣbiḥa	نُصْبِحَ nuṣbiḥa	
2m	تُصْبِحَ tuṣbiḥa	تُصْبِحَا tuṣbiḥā	تُصْبِحُوا tuṣbiḥū
2f	تُصْبِحِي tuṣbiḥī		تُصْبِحْنَ tuṣbiḥna
3m	يُصْبِحَ yuṣbiḥa	يُصْبِحَا yuṣbiḥā	يُصْبِحُوا yuṣbiḥū
3f	تُصْبِحَ tuṣbiḥa	تُصْبِحَا tuṣbiḥā	يُصْبِحْنَ yuṣbiḥna

jussive

	singular	dual	plural
1	أُصْبِحْ ʔuṣbiḥ	نُصْبِحْ nuṣbiḥ	
2m	تُصْبِحْ tuṣbiḥ	تُصْبِحَا tuṣbiḥā	تُصْبِحُوا tuṣbiḥū
2f	تُصْبِحِي tuṣbiḥī		تُصْبِحْنَ tuṣbiḥna
3m	يُصْبِحْ yuṣbiḥ	يُصْبِحَا yuṣbiḥā	يُصْبِحُوا yuṣbiḥū
3f	تُصْبِحْ tuṣbiḥ	تُصْبِحَا tuṣbiḥā	يُصْبِحْنَ yuṣbiḥna

imperative

	singular	dual	plural
2m	أَصْبِحْ ʔaṣbiḥ	أَصْبِحَا ʔaṣbiḥā	أَصْبِحُوا ʔaṣbiḥū
2f	أَصْبِحِي ʔaṣbiḥī		أَصْبِحْنَ ʔaṣbiḥna

participles

active	passive
مُصْبِح muṣbiḥ	مُصْبَح muṣbaḥ

passive

perfect	imperfect
أُصْبِحَ ʔuṣbiḥa	يُصْبَحُ yuṣbaḥu

hamzated measure IV

masdar: إِيثَار ʔīṯār

	و	ي	ء	*other*
R^1			✓	
R^2				✓
R^3				✓

4s(a)
to prefer

perfect

	singular	dual	plural
1	آثَرْتُ ʔāṯartu	آثَرْنَا ʔāṯarnā	
2m	آثَرْتَ ʔāṯarta	آثَرْتُمَا ʔāṯartumā	آثَرْتُمْ ʔāṯartum
2f	آثَرْتِ ʔāṯarti		آثَرْتُنَّ ʔāṯartunna
3m	آثَرَ ʔāṯara	آثَرَا ʔāṯarā	آثَرُوا ʔāṯarū
3f	آثَرَتْ ʔāṯarat	آثَرَتَا ʔāṯaratā	آثَرْنَ ʔāṯarna

indicative

	singular	dual	plural
1	أُؤْثِرُ ʔuʔṯiru	نُؤْثِرُ nuʔṯiru	
2m	تُؤْثِرُ tuʔṯiru	تُؤْثِرَانِ tuʔṯirāni	تُؤْثِرُونَ tuʔṯirūna
2f	تُؤْثِرِينَ tuʔṯirīna		تُؤْثِرْنَ tuʔṯirna
3m	يُؤْثِرُ yuʔṯiru	يُؤْثِرَانِ yuʔṯirāni	يُؤْثِرُونَ yuʔṯirūna
3f	تُؤْثِرُ tuʔṯiru	تُؤْثِرَانِ tuʔṯirāni	يُؤْثِرْنَ yuʔṯirna

subjunctive

	singular	dual	plural
1	أُؤْثِرَ ʔuʔṯira	نُؤْثِرَ nuʔṯira	
2m	تُؤْثِرَ tuʔṯira	تُؤْثِرَا tuʔṯirā	تُؤْثِرُوا tuʔṯirū
2f	تُؤْثِرِي tuʔṯirī		تُؤْثِرْنَ tuʔṯirna
3m	يُؤْثِرَ yuʔṯira	يُؤْثِرَا yuʔṯirā	يُؤْثِرُوا yuʔṯirū
3f	تُؤْثِرَ tuʔṯira	تُؤْثِرَا tuʔṯirā	يُؤْثِرْنَ yuʔṯirna

jussive

	singular	dual	plural
1	أُؤْثِرْ ʔuʔṯir	نُؤْثِرْ nuʔṯir	
2m	تُؤْثِرْ tuʔṯir	تُؤْثِرَا tuʔṯirā	تُؤْثِرُوا tuʔṯirū
2f	تُؤْثِرِي tuʔṯirī		تُؤْثِرْنَ tuʔṯirna
3m	يُؤْثِرْ yuʔṯir	يُؤْثِرَا yuʔṯirā	يُؤْثِرُوا yuʔṯirū
3f	تُؤْثِرْ tuʔṯir	تُؤْثِرَا tuʔṯirā	يُؤْثِرْنَ yuʔṯirna

imperative

	singular	dual	plural
2m	آثِرْ ʔāṯir	آثِرَا ʔāṯirā	آثِرُوا ʔāṯirū
2f	آثِرِي ʔāṯirī		آثِرْنَ ʔāṯirna

participles

active	passive
مُؤْثِر muʔṯir	مُؤْثَر muʔṯar

passive

perfect	imperfect
أُوثِرَ ʔūṯira	يُؤْثَرُ yuʔṯaru

hamzated measure IV

masdar: إِكْآب ʔikʔāb

	و	ي	ء	other
R^1				✓
R^2			✓	
R^3				✓

4s(b)

to depress

perfect

	singular	dual	plural
1	أَكْأَبْتُ ʔakʔabtu	أَكْأَبْنَا ʔakʔabnā	
2m	أَكْأَبْتَ ʔakʔabta	أَكْأَبْتُمَا ʔakʔabtumā	أَكْأَبْتُمْ ʔakʔabtum
2f	أَكْأَبْتِ ʔakʔabti		أَكْأَبْتُنَّ ʔakʔabtunna
3m	أَكْأَبَ ʔakʔaba	أَكْأَبَا ʔakʔabā	أَكْأَبُوا ʔakʔabū
3f	أَكْأَبَتْ ʔakʔabat	أَكْأَبَتَا ʔakʔabatā	أَكْأَبْنَ ʔakʔabna

indicative

	singular	dual	plural
1	أُكْئِبُ ʔukʔibu	نُكْئِبُ nukʔibu	
2m	تُكْئِبُ tukʔibu	تُكْئِبَانِ tukʔibāni	تُكْئِبُونَ tukʔibūna
2f	تُكْئِبِينَ tukʔibīna		تُكْئِبْنَ tukʔibna
3m	يُكْئِبُ yukʔibu	يُكْئِبَانِ yukʔibāni	يُكْئِبُونَ yukʔibūna
3f	تُكْئِبُ tukʔibu	تُكْئِبَانِ tukʔibāni	يُكْئِبْنَ yukʔibna

subjunctive

	singular	dual	plural
1	أُكْئِبَ ʔukʔiba	نُكْئِبَ nukʔiba	
2m	تُكْئِبَ tukʔiba	تُكْئِبَا tukʔibā	تُكْئِبُوا tukʔibū
2f	تُكْئِبِي tukʔibī		تُكْئِبْنَ tukʔibna
3m	يُكْئِبَ yukʔiba	يُكْئِبَا yukʔibā	يُكْئِبُوا yukʔibū
3f	تُكْئِبَ tukʔiba	تُكْئِبَا tukʔibā	يُكْئِبْنَ yukʔibna

jussive

	singular	dual	plural
1	أُكْئِبْ ʔukʔib	نُكْئِبْ nukʔib	
2m	تُكْئِبْ tukʔib	تُكْئِبَا tukʔibā	تُكْئِبُوا tukʔibū
2f	تُكْئِبِي tukʔibī		تُكْئِبْنَ tukʔibna
3m	يُكْئِبْ yukʔib	يُكْئِبَا yukʔibā	يُكْئِبُوا yukʔibū
3f	تُكْئِبْ tukʔib	تُكْئِبَا tukʔibā	يُكْئِبْنَ yukʔibna

imperative

	singular	dual	plural
2m	أَكْئِبْ ʔakʔib	أَكْئِبَا ʔakʔibā	أَكْئِبُوا ʔakʔibū
2f	أَكْئِبِي ʔakʔibī		أَكْئِبْنَ ʔakʔibna

participles

active	passive
مُكْئِب mukʔib	مُكْأَب mukʔab

passive

perfect	imperfect
أُكْئِبَ ʔukʔiba	يُكْأَبُ yukʔabu

hamzated measure IV	و	ي	ء	*other*
masdar: إِخْطَاء ʔixṭāʔ				
R^1				✓
R^2				✓
R^3			✓	

4s(c)

to make a mistake

perfect

	singular	dual	plural
1	أَخْطَأْتُ ʔaxṭaʔtu	أَخْطَأْنَا ʔaxṭaʔnā	
2m	أَخْطَأْتَ ʔaxṭaʔta	أَخْطَأْتُمَا ʔaxṭaʔtumā	أَخْطَأْتُمْ ʔaxṭaʔtum
2f	أَخْطَأْتِ ʔaxṭaʔti		أَخْطَأْتُنَّ ʔaxṭaʔtunna
3m	أَخْطَأَ ʔaxṭaʔa	أَخْطَآ ʔaxṭaʔā	أَخْطَؤُوا ʔaxṭaʔū
3f	أَخْطَأَتْ ʔaxṭaʔat	أَخْطَأَتَا ʔaxṭaʔatā	أَخْطَأْنَ ʔaxṭaʔna

indicative

	singular	dual	plural
1	أُخْطِئُ ʔuxṭiʔu	نُخْطِئُ nuxṭiʔu	
2m	تُخْطِئُ tuxṭiʔu	تُخْطِئَانِ tuxṭiʔāni	تُخْطِئُونَ tuxṭiʔūna
2f	تُخْطِئِينَ tuxṭiʔīna		تُخْطِئْنَ tuxṭiʔna
3m	يُخْطِئُ yuxṭiʔu	يُخْطِئَانِ yuxṭiʔāni	يُخْطِئُونَ yuxṭiʔūna
3f	تُخْطِئُ tuxṭiʔu	تُخْطِئَانِ tuxṭiʔāni	يُخْطِئْنَ yuxṭiʔna

subjunctive

	singular	dual	plural
1	أُخْطِئَ ʔuxṭiʔa	نُخْطِئَ nuxṭiʔa	
2m	تُخْطِئَ tuxṭiʔa	تُخْطِئَا tuxṭiʔā	تُخْطِئُوا tuxṭiʔū
2f	تُخْطِئِي tuxṭiʔī		تُخْطِئْنَ tuxṭiʔna
3m	يُخْطِئَ yuxṭiʔa	يُخْطِئَا yuxṭiʔā	يُخْطِئُوا yuxṭiʔū
3f	تُخْطِئَ tuxṭiʔa	تُخْطِئَا tuxṭiʔā	يُخْطِئْنَ yuxṭiʔna

jussive

	singular	dual	plural
1	أُخْطِئْ ʔuxṭiʔ	نُخْطِئْ nuxṭiʔ	
2m	تُخْطِئْ tuxṭiʔ	تُخْطِئَا tuxṭiʔā	تُخْطِئُوا tuxṭiʔū
2f	تُخْطِئِي tuxṭiʔī		تُخْطِئْنَ tuxṭiʔna
3m	يُخْطِئْ yuxṭiʔ	يُخْطِئَا yuxṭiʔā	يُخْطِئُوا yuxṭiʔū
3f	تُخْطِئْ tuxṭiʔ	تُخْطِئَا tuxṭiʔā	يُخْطِئْنَ yuxṭiʔna

imperative

	singular	dual	plural
2m	أَخْطِئْ ʔaxṭiʔ	أَخْطِئَا ʔaxṭiʔā	أَخْطِئُوا ʔaxṭiʔū
2f	أَخْطِئِي ʔaxṭiʔī		أَخْطِئْنَ ʔaxṭiʔna

participles

active	passive
مُخْطِئ muxṭiʔ	مُخْطَأ muxṭaʔ

passive

perfect	imperfect
أُخْطِئَ ʔuxṭiʔa	يُخْطَأُ yuxṭaʔu

geminate measure IV		و	ي	ء	other	**4g**
masdar: إِحْباب ʔiħbāb	R[1]				✓	**to love**
	R[2]				✓	
	R[3]				✓	

perfect

	singular	dual	plural
1	أَحْبَبْتُ ʔaħbabtu	أَحْبَبْنَا ʔaħbabnā	
2m	أَحْبَبْتَ ʔaħbabta	أَحْبَبْتُمَا ʔaħbabtumā	أَحْبَبْتُمْ ʔaħbabtum
2f	أَحْبَبْتِ ʔaħbabti		أَحْبَبْتُنَّ ʔaħbabtunna
3m	أَحَبَّ ʔaħabba	أَحَبَّا ʔaħabbā	أَحَبُّوا ʔaħabbū
3f	أَحَبَّتْ ʔaħabbat	أَحَبَّتَا ʔaħabbatā	أَحْبَبْنَ ʔaħbabna

indicative

	singular	dual	plural
1	أُحِبُّ ʔuħibbu	نُحِبُّ nuħħibu	
2m	تُحِبُّ tuħibbu	تُحِبَّانِ tuħibbāni	تُحِبُّونَ tuħibbūna
2f	تُحِبِّينَ tuħibbīna		تُحْبِبْنَ tuħbibna
3m	يُحِبُّ yuħibbu	يُحِبَّانِ yuħibbāni	يُحِبُّونَ yuħibbūna
3f	تُحِبُّ tuħibbu	تُحِبَّانِ tuħibbāni	يُحْبِبْنَ yuħbibna

subjunctive

	singular	dual	plural
1	أُحِبَّ ʔuħibba	نُحِبَّ nuħibba	
2m	تُحِبَّ tuħibba	تُحِبَّا tuħibbā	تُحِبُّوا tuħibbū
2f	تُحِبِّي tuħibbī		تُحْبِبْنَ tuħbibna
3m	يُحِبَّ yuħibba	يُحِبَّا yuħibbā	يُحِبُّوا yuħibbū
3f	تُحِبَّ tuħibba	تُحِبَّا tuħibbā	يُحْبِبْنَ yuħbibna

jussive

	singular	dual	plural
1	أُحِبَّ ʔuħibba	نُحِبَّ nuħibba	
2m	تُحِبَّ tuħibba	تُحِبَّا tuħibbā	تُحِبُّوا tuħibbū
2f	تُحِبِّي tuħibbī		تُحْبِبْنَ tuħbibna
3m	يُحِبَّ yuħibba	يُحِبَّا yuħibbā	يُحِبُّوا yuħibbū
3f	تُحِبَّ tuħibba	تُحِبَّا tuħibbā	يُحْبِبْنَ yuħbibna

imperative

	singular	dual	plural
2m	أَحِبَّ ʔaħibba	أَحِبَّا ʔaħibbā	أَحِبُّوا ʔaħibbū
2f	أَحِبِّي ʔaħibbī		أَحْبِبْنَ ʔaħbibna

participles

active	passive
مُحِبّ muħibb	مُحَبّ muħabb

passive

perfect	imperfect
أُحِبَّ ʔuħibba	يُحَبُّ yuħabbu

assimilated measure IV

masdar: إيضاح ʔīḍāḥ

	و	ي	ء	other
R^1	✓			
R^2				✓
R^3				✓

4a1

to clarify

perfect

	singular	dual	plural
1	أَوْضَحْتُ ʔawḍaḥtu	أَوْضَحْنَا ʔawḍaḥnā	
2m	أَوْضَحْتَ ʔawḍaḥta	أَوْضَحْتُمَا ʔawḍaḥtumā	أَوْضَحْتُمْ ʔawḍaḥtum
2f	أَوْضَحْتِ ʔawḍaḥti		أَوْضَحْتُنَّ ʔawḍaḥtunna
3m	أَوْضَحَ ʔawḍaḥa	أَوْضَحَا ʔawḍaḥā	أَوْضَحُوا ʔawḍaḥū
3f	أَوْضَحَتْ ʔawḍaḥat	أَوْضَحَتَا ʔawḍaḥatā	أَوْضَحْنَ ʔawḍaḥna

indicative

	singular	dual	plural
1	أُوضِحُ ʔūḍiḥu	نُوضِحُ nūḍiḥu	
2m	تُوضِحُ tūḍiḥu	تُوضِحَانِ tūḍiḥāni	تُوضِحُونَ tūḍiḥūna
2f	تُوضِحِينَ tūḍiḥīna		تُوضِحْنَ tūḍiḥna
3m	يُوضِحُ yūḍiḥu	يُوضِحَانِ yūḍiḥāni	يُوضِحُونَ yūḍiḥūna
3f	تُوضِحُ tūḍiḥu	تُوضِحَانِ tūḍiḥāni	يُوضِحْنَ yūḍiḥna

subjunctive

	singular	dual	plural
1	أُوضِحَ ʔūḍiḥa	نُوضِحَ nūḍiḥa	
2m	تُوضِحَ tūḍiḥa	تُوضِحَا tūḍiḥā	تُوضِحُوا tuḍiḥū
2f	تُوضِحِي tūḍiḥī		تُوضِحْنَ tūḍiḥna
3m	يُوضِحَ yūḍiḥa	يُوضِحَا yūḍiḥā	يُوضِحُوا yūḍiḥū
3f	تُوضِحَ tūḍiḥa	تُوضِحَا tūḍiḥā	يُوضِحْنَ yūḍiḥna

jussive

	singular	dual	plural
1	أُوضِحْ ʔūḍiḥ	نُوضِحْ nūḍiḥ	
2m	تُوضِحْ tūḍiḥ	تُوضِحَا tūḍiḥā	تُوضِحُوا tūḍiḥū
2f	تُوضِحِي tūḍiḥī		تُوضِحْنَ tūḍiḥna
3m	يُوضِحْ yūḍiḥ	يُوضِحَا yūḍiḥā	يُوضِحُوا yūḍiḥū
3f	تُوضِحْ tūḍiḥ	تُوضِحَا tūḍiḥā	يُوضِحْنَ yūḍiḥna

imperative

	singular	dual	plural
2m	أَوْضِحْ ʔawḍiḥ	أَوْضِحَا ʔawḍiḥā	أَوْضِحُوا ʔawḍiḥū
2f	أَوْضِحِي ʔawḍiḥī		أَوْضِحْنَ ʔawḍiḥna

participles

active	passive
مُوضِح mūḍiḥ	مُوضَح mūḍaḥ

passive

perfect	imperfect
أُوضِحَ ʔūḍiḥa	يُوضَحُ yūḍaḥu

hamz. assimilated meas. IV		و	ي	ء	*other*	**4a1(a)**
masdar: إيماء ʔīmāʔ	*R¹*	✓				**to point**
	R²				✓	
	R³			✓		

perfect

	singular	dual	plural
1	أَوْمَأْتُ ʔawmaʔtu	أَوْمَأْنَا ʔawmaʔnā	
2m	أَوْمَأْتَ ʔawmaʔta	أَوْمَأْتُمَا ʔawmaʔtumā	أَوْمَأْتُمْ ʔawmaʔtum
2f	أَوْمَأْتِ ʔawmaʔti		أَوْمَأْتُنَّ ʔawmaʔtunna
3m	أَوْمَأَ ʔawmaʔa	أَوْمَآ ʔawmaʔā	أَوْمَؤُوا ʔawmaʔū
3f	أَوْمَأَتْ ʔawmaʔat	أَوْمَأَتَا ʔawmaʔatā	أَوْمَأْنَ ʔawmaʔna

indicative

	singular	dual	plural
1	أُومِئُ ʔūmiʔu	نُومِئُ nūmiʔu	
2m	تُومِئُ tūmiʔu	تُومِئَانِ tūmiʔāni	تُومِئُونَ tūmiʔūna
2f	تُومِئِينَ tūmiʔīna		تُومِئْنَ tūmiʔna
3m	يُومِئُ yūmiʔu	يُومِئَانِ yūmiʔāni	يُومِئُونَ yūmiʔūna
3f	تُومِئُ tūmiʔu	تُومِئَانِ tūmiʔāni	يُومِئْنَ yūmiʔna

subjunctive

	singular	dual	plural
1	أُومِئَ ʔūmiʔa	نُومِئَ nūmiʔa	
2m	تُومِئَ tūmiʔa	تُومِئَا tūmiʔā	تُومِئُوا tūmiʔūna
2f	تُومِئِي tūmiʔī		تُومِئْنَ tūmiʔna
3m	يُومِئَ yūmiʔa	يُومِئَا yūmiʔā	يُومِئُوا yūmiʔū
3f	تُومِئَ tūmiʔa	تُومِئَا tūmiʔā	يُومِئْنَ yūmiʔna

jussive

	singular	dual	plural
1	أُومِئْ ʔūmiʔ	نُومِئْ nūmiʔ	
2m	تُومِئْ tūmiʔ	تُومِئَا tūmiʔā	تُومِئُوا tūmiʔū
2f	تُومِئِي tūmiʔī		تُومِئْنَ tūmiʔna
3m	يُومِئْ yūmiʔ	يُومِئَا yūmiʔā	يُومِئُوا yūmiʔū
3f	تُومِئْ tūmiʔ	تُومِئَا tūmiʔā	يُومِئْنَ yūmiʔna

imperative

	singular	dual	plural
2m	أَومِئْ ʔawmiʔ	أَومِئَا ʔawmiʔā	أَومِئُوا ʔawmiʔū
2f	أَومِئِي ʔawmiʔī		أَومِئْنَ ʔawmiʔna

participles

active	passive
مُومِئ mūmiʔ	مُومَأ mūmaʔ

passive

perfect	imperfect
أُومِلَ ʔūmila	يُومَلُ yūmalu

assimilated measure IV

masdar: إيقاظ ʔīqāẓ

	و	ي	ء	other
R1		✓		
R2				✓
R3				✓

4a2

to wake up

perfect

	singular	dual	plural
1	أَيْقَظْتُ ʔayqaẓtu	أَيْقَظْنَا ʔayqaẓnā	
2m	أَيْقَظْتَ ʔayqaẓta	أَيْقَظْتُمَا ʔayqaẓtumā	أَيْقَظْتُمْ ʔayqaẓtum
2f	أَيْقَظْتِ ʔayqaẓti		أَيْقَظْتُنَّ ʔayqaẓtunna
3m	أَيْقَظَ ʔayqaẓa	أَيْقَظَا ʔayqaẓā	أَيْقَظُوا ʔayqaẓū
3f	أَيْقَظَتْ ʔayqaẓat	أَيْقَظَتَا ʔayqaẓatā	أَيْقَظْنَ ʔayqaẓna

indicative

	singular	dual	plural
1	أُوقِظُ ʔūqiẓu	نُوقِظُ nūqiẓu	
2m	تُوقِظُ tūqiẓu	تُوقِظَانِ tūqiẓāni	تُوقِظُونَ tūqiẓūna
2f	تُوقِظِينَ tūqiẓīna		تُوقِظْنَ tūqiẓna
3m	يُوقِظُ yūqiẓu	يُوقِظَانِ yūqiẓāni	يُوقِظُونَ yūqiẓūna
3f	تُوقِظُ tūqiẓu	تُوقِظَانِ tūqiẓāni	يُوقِظْنَ yūqiẓna

subjunctive

	singular	dual	plural
1	أُوقِظَ ʔūqiẓa	نُوقِظَ nūqiẓa	
2m	تُوقِظَ tūqiẓa	تُوقِظَا tūqiẓā	تُوقِظُوا tuqiẓū
2f	تُوقِظِي tūqiẓī		تُوقِظْنَ tūqiẓna
3m	يُوقِظَ yūqiẓa	يُوقِظَا yūqiẓā	يُوقِظُوا yūqiẓū
3f	تُوقِظَ tūqiẓa	تُوقِظَا tūqiẓā	يُوقِظْنَ yūqiẓna

jussive

	singular	dual	plural
1	أُوقِظْ ʔūqiẓ	نُوقِظْ nūqiẓ	
2m	تُوقِظْ tūqiẓ	تُوقِظَا tūqiẓā	تُوقِظُوا tūqiẓū
2f	تُوقِظِي tūqiẓī		تُوقِظْنَ tūqiẓna
3m	يُوقِظْ yūqiẓ	يُوقِظَا yūqiẓā	يُوقِظُوا yūqiẓū
3f	تُوقِظْ tūqiẓ	تُوقِظَا tūqiẓā	يُوقِظْنَ yūqiẓna

imperative

	singular	dual	plural
2m	أَيْقِظْ ʔayqiẓ	أَيْقِظَا ʔayqiẓā	أَيْقِظُوا ʔayqiẓū
2f	أَيْقِظِي ʔayqiẓī		أَيْقِظْنَ ʔayqiẓna

participles

active	passive
مُوقِظ mūqiẓ	مُوقَظ mūqaẓ

passive

perfect	imperfect
أُوقِظَ ʔūqiẓa	يُوقَظُ yūqaẓu

hollow measure IV

masdar: إِرَادَة ʔirādaᵗ

	و	ي	ء	other
R¹				✓
R²	✓	✓		
R³				✓

4h
to want

perfect

	singular	dual	plural
1	أَرَدْتُ ʔaradtu	أَرَدْنَا ʔaradnā	
2m	أَرَدْتَ ʔaradta	أَرَدْتُمَا ʔaradtumā	أَرَدْتُمْ ʔaradtum
2f	أَرَدْتِ ʔaradti		أَرَدْتُنَّ ʔaradtunna
3m	أَرَادَ ʔarāda	أَرَادَا ʔarādā	أَرَادُوا ʔarādū
3f	أَرَادَتْ ʔarādat	أَرَادَتَا ʔarādatā	أَرَدْنَ ʔaradna

indicative

	singular	dual	plural
1	أُرِيدُ ʔurīdu	نُرِيدُ nurīdu	
2m	تُرِيدُ turīdu	تُرِيدَانِ turīdāni	تُرِيدُونَ turīdūna
2f	تُرِيدِينَ turīdīna		تُرِدْنَ turidna
3m	يُرِيدُ yurīdu	يُرِيدَانِ yurīdāni	يُرِيدُونَ yurīdūna
3f	تُرِيدُ turīdu	تُرِيدَانِ turīdāni	يُرِدْنَ yuridna

subjunctive

	singular	dual	plural
1	أُرِيدَ ʔurīda	نُرِيدَ nurīda	
2m	تُرِيدَ turīda	تُرِيدَا turīdā	تُرِيدُوا turīdū
2f	تُرِيدِي turīdī		تُرِدْنَ turidna
3m	يُرِيدَ yurīda	يُرِيدَا yurīdā	يُرِيدُوا yurīdū
3f	تُرِيدَ turīda	تُرِيدَا turīdā	يُرِدْنَ yuridna

jussive

	singular	dual	plural
1	أُرِدْ ʔurid	نُرِدْ nurid	
2m	تُرِدْ turid	تُرِيدَا turīdā	تُرِيدُوا turīdū
2f	تُرِيدِي turīdī		تُرِدْنَ turidna
3m	يُرِدْ yurid	يُرِيدَا yurīdā	يُرِيدُوا yurīdū
3f	تُرِدْ turid	تُرِيدَا turīdā	يُرِدْنَ yuridna

imperative

	singular	dual	plural
2m	أَرِدْ ʔarid	أَرِيدَا ʔarīdā	أَرِيدُوا ʔarīdū
2f	أَرِيدِي ʔarīdī		أَرِدْنَ ʔaridna

participles

active	passive
مُرِيد murīd	مُرَاد murād

passive

perfect	imperfect
أُرِيدَ ʔurīda	يُرَادُ yurādu

hamzated hollow measure IV

masdar: إِسَاءَة ʔisāʔaᵗ

	و	ي	ء	*other*
R^1				✓
R^2	✓			
R^3			✓	

4h(a)

to harm

perfect

	singular	dual	plural
1	أَسَأْتُ ʔasaʔtu	أَسَأْنَا ʔasaʔnā	
2m	أَسَأْتَ ʔasaʔta	أَسَأْتُمَا ʔasaʔtumā	أَسَأْتُمْ ʔasaʔtum
2f	أَسَأْتِ ʔasaʔti		أَسَأْتُنَّ ʔasaʔtunna
3m	أَسَاءَ ʔasāʔa	أَسَاءَا ʔasāʔā	أَسَاؤُوا ʔasāʔū
3f	أَسَاءَتْ ʔasāʔat	أَسَاءَتَا ʔasāʔatā	أَسَأْنَ ʔasaʔna

indicative

	singular	dual	plural
1	أُسِيءُ ʔusīʔu	نُسِيءُ nusīʔu	
2m	تُسِيءُ tusīʔu	تُسِيئَانِ tusīʔāni	تُسِيئُونَ (تُسِيؤُونَ) tusīʔūna
2f	تُسِيئِينَ tusīʔīna		تُسِئْنَ tusiʔna
3m	يُسِيءُ yusīʔu	يُسِيئَانِ yusīʔāni	يُسِيئُونَ (يُسِيؤُونَ) yusīʔūna
3f	تُسِيءُ tusīʔu	تُسِيئَانِ tusīʔāni	يُسِئْنَ yusiʔna

subjunctive

	singular	dual	plural
1	أُسِيءَ ʔusīʔa	نُسِيءَ nusīʔa	
2m	تُسِيءَ tusīʔa	تُسِيئَا tusīʔā	تُسِيئُوا (تُسِيؤُوا) tusīʔū
2f	تُسِيئِي tusīʔī		تُسِئْنَ tusiʔna
3m	يُسِيءَ yusīʔa	يُسِيئَا yusīʔā	يُسِيئُوا (يُسِيؤُوا) yusīʔū
3f	تُسِيءَ tusīʔa	تُسِيئَا tusīʔā	يُسِئْنَ yusiʔna

jussive

	singular	dual	plural
1	أُسِئْ ʔusiʔ	نُسِئْ nusiʔ	
2m	تُسِئْ tusiʔ	تُسِيئَا tusīʔā	تُسِيئُوا (تُسِيؤُوا) tusīʔū
2f	تُسِيئِي tusīʔī		تُسِئْنَ tusiʔna
3m	يُسِئْ yusiʔ	يُسِيئَا yusīʔā	يُسِيئُوا (يُسِيؤُوا) yusīʔū
3f	تُسِئْ tusiʔ	تُسِيئَا tusīʔā	يُسِئْنَ yusiʔna

imperative

	singular	dual	plural
2m	أَسِئْ ʔasiʔ	أَسِيئَا ʔasīʔā	أَسِيئُوا (أَسِيؤُوا) ʔasīʔū
2f	أَسِيئِي ʔasīʔī		أَسِئْنَ ʔasiʔna

participles

active	passive
مُسِيء musīʔ	مُسَاء musāʔ

passive

perfect	imperfect
أُسِيءَ ʔusīʔa	يُسَاءُ yusāʔu

defective measure IV

masdar: إِعْطَاء ʔi3ṭāʔ

	و	ي	ء	other
R^1				✓
R^2		✓		✓
R^3	✓	✓		

4d
to give

perfect

	singular	dual	plural
1	أَعْطَيْتُ ʔa3ṭaytu	أَعْطَيْنَا ʔa3ṭaynā	
2m	أَعْطَيْتَ ʔa3ṭayta	أَعْطَيْتُمَا ʔa3ṭaytumā	أَعْطَيْتُمْ ʔa3ṭaytum
2f	أَعْطَيْتِ ʔa3ṭayti		أَعْطَيْتُنَّ ʔa3ṭaytunna
3m	أَعْطَى ʔa3ṭā*	أَعْطَيَا ʔa3ṭayā	أَعْطَوْا ʔa3ṭaw
3f	أَعْطَتْ ʔa3ṭat	أَعْطَتَا ʔa3ṭatā	أَعْطَيْنَ ʔa3ṭayna

indicative

	singular	dual	plural
1	أُعْطِي ʔu3ṭī	نُعْطِي nu3ṭī	
2m	تُعْطِي tu3ṭī	تُعْطِيَانِ tu3ṭiyāni	تُعْطُونَ tu3ṭūna
2f	تُعْطِينَ tu3ṭīna		تُعْطِينَ tu3ṭīna
3m	يُعْطِي yu3ṭī	يُعْطِيَانِ yu3ṭiyāni	يُعْطُونَ yu3ṭūna
3f	تُعْطِي tu3ṭī	تُعْطِيَانِ tu3ṭiyāni	يُعْطِينَ yu3ṭīna

subjunctive

	singular	dual	plural
1	أُعْطِيَ ʔu3ṭiya	نُعْطِيَ nu3ṭiya	
2m	تُعْطِيَ tu3ṭiya	تُعْطِيَا tu3ṭiyā	تُعْطُوا tu3ṭū
2f	تُعْطِي tu3ṭī		تُعْطِينَ tu3ṭīna
3m	يُعْطِيَ yu3ṭiya	يُعْطِيَا yu3ṭiyā	يُعْطُوا yu3ṭūna
3f	تُعْطِيَ tu3ṭiya	تُعْطِيَا tu3ṭiyā	يُعْطِينَ yu3ṭīna

jussive

	singular	dual	plural
1	أُعْطِ ʔu3ṭi	نُعْطِ nu3ṭi	
2m	تُعْطِ tu3ṭi	تُعْطِيَا tu3ṭiyā	تُعْطُوا tu3ṭū
2f	تُعْطِي tu3ṭī		تُعْطِينَ tu3ṭīna
3m	يُعْطِ yu3ṭi	يُعْطِيَا yu3ṭiyā	يُعْطُوا yu3ṭūna
3f	تُعْطِ tu3ṭi	تُعْطِيَا tu3ṭiyā	يُعْطِينَ yu3ṭīna

imperative

	singular	dual	plural
2m	أَعْطِ ʔa3ṭi	أَعْطِيَا ʔa3ṭiyā	أَعْطُوا ʔa3ṭū
2f	أَعْطِي ʔa3ṭī		أَعْطِينَ ʔa3ṭīna

participles

active	passive
مُعْطٍ mu3ṭ(in)	مُعْطًى mu3ṭ(an)

passive

perfect	imperfect
أُعْطِيَ ʔu3ṭiya	يُعْطَى yu3ṭā

* The verb أحيا ʔaḥyā (*revive*) is irregular in that it takes ا instead of ى in the third person singular perfect form.

hamzated defective meas. IV

masdar: إِيوَاء ʔīwāʔ

	و	ي	ء	*other*
R^1			✓	
R^2	✓			✓
R^3	✓	✓		

4d(a)
to shelter

perfect

	singular	dual	plural
1	آوَيْتُ ʔāwaytu	آوَيْنَا ʔāwaynā	
2m	آوَيْتَ ʔāwayta	آوَيْتُمَا ʔāwaytumā	آوَيْتُمْ ʔāwaytum
2f	آوَيْتِ ʔāwayti		آوَيْتُنَّ ʔāwaytunna
3m	آوَى ʔāwā	آوَيَا ʔāwayā	آوَوْا ʔāwaw
3f	آوَتْ ʔāwat	آوَتَا ʔāwatā	آوَيْنَ ʔāwayna

indicative

	singular	dual	plural
1	أُووِي ʔūwī	نُؤْوِي nuʔwī	
2m	تُؤْوِي tuʔwī	تُؤْوِيَانِ tuʔwiyāni	تُؤْوُونَ tuʔwūna
2f	تُؤْوِينَ tuʔwīna		تُؤْوِينَ tuʔwīna
3m	يُؤْوِي yuʔwī	يُؤْوِيَانِ yuʔwiyāni	يُؤْوُونَ yuʔwūna
3f	تُؤْوِي tuʔwī	تُؤْوِيَانِ tuʔwiyāni	يُؤْوِينَ yuʔwīna

subjunctive

	singular	dual	plural
1	أُووِيَ ʔūwiya	نُؤْوِيَ nuʔwiya	
2m	تُؤْوِيَ tuʔwiya	تُؤْوِيَا tuʔwiyā	تُؤْوُوا tuʔwū
2f	تُؤْوِي tuʔwī		تُؤْوِينَ tuʔwīna
3m	يُؤْوِيَ yuʔwiya	يُؤْوِيَا yuʔwiyā	يُؤْوُوا yuʔwūna
3f	تُؤْوِيَ tuʔwiya	تُؤْوِيَا tuʔwiyā	يُؤْوِينَ yuʔwīna

jussive

	singular	dual	plural
1	أُووِ ʔūwi	نُؤْوِ nuʔwi	
2m	تُؤْوِ tuʔwi	تُؤْوِيَا tuʔwiyā	تُؤْوُوا tuʔwū
2f	تُؤْوِي tuʔwī		تُؤْوِينَ tuʔwīna
3m	يُؤْوِ yuʔwi	يُؤْوِيَا yuʔwiyā	يُؤْوُوا yuʔwūna
3f	تُؤْوِ tuʔwi	تُؤْوِيَا tuʔwiyā	يُؤْوِينَ yuʔwīna

imperative

	singular	dual	plural
2m	آوِ ʔāwi	آوِيَا ʔāwiyā	آوُوا ʔāwū
2f	آوِي ʔāwī		آوِينَ ʔāwīna

participles

active	passive
مُؤْوٍ muʔw(in)	مُؤْوًى muʔw(an)

passive

perfect	imperfect
أُووِيَ ʔūwiya	يُؤْوَى yuʔwā

hollow defective measure IV

masdar: إيحَاء ʔīɧāʔ

	و	ي	ء	*other*
R^1	✓			
R^2				✓
R^3	✓	✓		

4d(b)

to imply

perfect

	singular	dual	plural
1	أَوْحَيْتُ ʔawɧaytu	أَوْحَيْنَا ʔawɧaynā	
2m	أَوْحَيْتَ ʔawɧayta	أَوْحَيْتُمَا ʔawɧaytumā	أَوْحَيْتُمْ ʔawɧaytum
2f	أَوْحَيْتِ ʔawɧayti		أَوْحَيْتُنَّ ʔawɧaytunna
3m	أَوْحَى ʔawɧā	أَوْحَيَا ʔawɧayā	أَوْحَوْا ʔawɧaw
3f	أَوْحَتْ ʔawɧat	أَوْحَتَا ʔawɧatā	أَوْحَيْنَ ʔawɧayna

indicative

	singular	dual	plural
1	أُوحِي ʔūɧī	نُوحِي nūɧī	
2m	تُوحِي tūɧī	تُوحِيَانِ tūɧiyāni	تُوحُونَ tūɧūna
2f	تُوحِينَ tūɧīna		تُوحِينَ tūɧīna
3m	يُوحِي yūɧī	يُوحِيَانِ yūɧiyāni	يُوحُونَ yūɧūna
3f	تُوحِي tūɧī	تُوحِيَانِ tūɧiyāni	يُوحِينَ yūɧīna

subjunctive

	singular	dual	plural
1	أُوحِيَ ʔūɧiya	نُوحِيَ nūɧiya	
2m	تُوحِيَ tūɧiya	تُوحِيَا tūɧiyā	تُوحُوا tūɧū
2f	تُوحِي tūɧī		تُوحِينَ tūɧīna
3m	يُوحِيَ yūɧiya	يُوحِيَا yūɧiyā	يُوحُوا yūɧūna
3f	تُوحِيَ tūɧiya	تُوحِيَا tūɧiyā	يُوحِينَ yūɧīna

jussive

	singular	dual	plural
1	أُوحِ ʔūɧi	نُوحِ nūɧi	
2m	تُوحِ tūɧi	تُوحِيَا tūɧiyā	تُوحُوا tūɧū
2f	تُوحِي tūɧī		تُوحِينَ tūɧīna
3m	يُوحِ yūɧi	يُوحِيَا yūɧiyā	يُوحُوا yūɧūna
3f	تُوحِ tūɧi	تُوحِيَا tūɧiyā	يُوحِينَ yūɧīna

imperative

	singular	dual	plural
2m	أَوْحِ ʔawɧi	أَوْحِيَا ʔawɧiyā	أَوْحُوا ʔawɧū
2f	أَوْحِي ʔawɧī		أَوْحِينَ ʔawɧīna

participles

active	passive
مُوحٍ mūɧ(in)	مُوحًى mūɧ(an)

passive

perfect	imperfect
أُوحِيَ ʔūɧiya	يُوحَى yūɧā

irregular defective measure IV		و	ي	ء	other	**4d(c)**
masdar: إِرَاءَة ʔirāʔaᵗ	R^1				✓	to show
	R^2			✓		
	R^3		✓			

perfect

	singular	dual	plural
1	أَرَيْتُ ʔaraytu	أَرَيْنَا ʔaraynā	
2m	أَرَيْتَ ʔarayta	أَرَيْتُمَا ʔaraytumā	أَرَيْتُمْ ʔaraytum
2f	أَرَيْتِ ʔarayti		أَرَيْتُنَّ ʔaraytunna
3m	أَرَى ʔarā	أَرَيَا ʔarayā	أَرَوْا ʔaraw
3f	أَرَتْ ʔarat	أَرَتَا ʔaratā	أَرَيْنَ ʔarayna

indicative

	singular	dual	plural
1	أُرِي ʔurī	نُرِي nurī	
2m	تُرِي turī	تُرِيَانِ turiyāni	تُرُونَ turūna
2f	تُرِينَ turīna		تُرِينَ turīna
3m	يُرِي yurī	يُرِيَانِ yuriyāni	يُرُونَ yurūna
3f	تُرِي turī	تُرِيَانِ turiyāni	يُرِينَ yurīna

subjunctive

	singular	dual	plural
1	أُرِيَ ʔuriya	نُرِيَ nuriya	
2m	تُرِيَ turiya	تُرِيَا turiyā	تُرُوا turū
2f	تُرِي turī		تُرِينَ turīna
3m	يُرِيَ yuriya	يُرِيَا yuriyā	يُرُوا yurūna
3f	تُرِيَ turiya	تُرِيَا turiyā	يُرِينَ yurīna

jussive

	singular	dual	plural
1	أُرِ ʔuri	نُرِ nuri	
2m	تُرِ turi	تُرِيَا turiyā	تُرُوا turū
2f	تُرِي turī		تُرِينَ turīna
3m	يُرِ yuri	يُرِيَا yuriyā	يُرُوا yurūna
3f	تُرِ turi	تُرِيَا turiyā	يُرِينَ yurīna

imperative

	singular	dual	plural
2m	أَرِ ʔari	أَرِيَا ʔariyā	أَرُوا ʔarū
2f	أَرِي ʔarī		أَرِينَ ʔarīna

participles

active	passive
مُرٍ mur(in)	مُرًى mur(an)

passive

perfect	imperfect
أُرِيَ ʔuriya	يُرَى yurā

* The verb أَرَى ʔarā (*show*) is irregular in that the second radical (ء) is absent in all forms.

sound measure V

masdar: تَحَدُّث taɦadduŧ

	و	ي	ء	other
R^1	✓	✓		✓
R^2	✓	✓		✓
R^3				✓

5s

to speak

perfect

	singular	dual	plural
1	تَحَدَّثْتُ taɦaddaŧtu	تَحَدَّثْنَا taɦaddaŧnā	
2m	تَحَدَّثْتَ taɦaddaŧta	تَحَدَّثْتُمَا taɦaddaŧtumā	تَحَدَّثْتُمْ taɦaddaŧtum
2f	تَحَدَّثْتِ taɦaddaŧti		تَحَدَّثْتُنَّ taɦaddaŧtunna
3m	تَحَدَّثَ taɦaddaŧa	تَحَدَّثَا taɦaddaŧā	تَحَدَّثُوا taɦaddaŧū
3f	تَحَدَّثَتْ taɦaddaŧat	تَحَدَّثَتَا taɦaddaŧatā	تَحَدَّثْنَ taɦaddaŧna

indicative

	singular	dual	plural
1	أَتَحَدَّثُ ʔataɦaddaŧu	نَتَحَدَّثُ nataɦaddaŧu	
2m	تَتَحَدَّثُ tataɦaddaŧu	تَتَحَدَّثَانِ tataɦaddaŧāni	تَتَحَدَّثُونَ tataɦaddaŧūna
2f	تَتَحَدَّثِينَ tataɦaddaŧīna		تَتَحَدَّثْنَ tataɦaddaŧna
3m	يَتَحَدَّثُ yataɦaddaŧu	يَتَحَدَّثَانِ yataɦaddaŧāni	يَتَحَدَّثُونَ yataɦaddaŧūna
3f	تَتَحَدَّثُ tataɦaddaŧu	تَتَحَدَّثَانِ tataɦaddaŧāni	يَتَحَدَّثْنَ yataɦaddaŧna

subjunctive

	singular	dual	plural
1	أَتَحَدَّثَ ʔataɦaddaŧa	نَتَحَدَّثَ nataɦaddaŧa	
2m	تَتَحَدَّثَ tataɦaddaŧa	تَتَحَدَّثَا tataɦaddaŧā	تَتَحَدَّثُوا tataɦaddaŧū
2f	تَتَحَدَّثِي tataɦaddaŧī		تَتَحَدَّثْنَ tataɦaddaŧna
3m	يَتَحَدَّثَ yataɦaddaŧa	يَتَحَدَّثَا yataɦaddaŧā	يَتَحَدَّثُوا yataɦaddaŧū
3f	تَتَحَدَّثَ tataɦaddaŧa	تَتَحَدَّثَا tataɦaddaŧā	يَتَحَدَّثْنَ yataɦaddaŧna

jussive

	singular	dual	plural
1	أَتَحَدَّثْ ʔataɦaddaŧ	نَتَحَدَّثْ nataɦaddaŧ	
2m	تَتَحَدَّثْ tataɦaddaŧ	تَتَحَدَّثَا tataɦaddaŧā	تَتَحَدَّثُوا tataɦaddaŧū
2f	تَتَحَدَّثِي tataɦaddaŧī		تَتَحَدَّثْنَ tataɦaddaŧna
3m	يَتَحَدَّثْ yataɦaddaŧ	يَتَحَدَّثَا yataɦaddaŧā	يَتَحَدَّثُوا yataɦaddaŧū
3f	تَتَحَدَّثْ tataɦaddaŧ	تَتَحَدَّثَا tataɦaddaŧā	يَتَحَدَّثْنَ yataɦaddaŧna

imperative

	singular	dual	plural
2m	تَحَدَّثْ taɦaddaŧ	تَحَدَّثَا taɦaddaŧā	تَحَدَّثُوا taɦaddaŧū
2f	تَحَدَّثِي taɦaddaŧī		تَحَدَّثْنَ taɦaddaŧna

participles

active	passive
مُتَحَدِّث mutaɦaddiŧ	مُتَحَدَّث mutaɦaddaŧ

passive

perfect	imperfect
تُحُدِّثَ tuɦuddiŧa	يُتَحَدَّثُ yutaɦaddaŧu

hamzated measure V

masdar: تَأَخُّر taʔaxxur

	و	ي	ء	*other*
R^1			✓	
R^2	✓	✓		✓
R^3				✓

5s(a)
to be late

perfect

	singular	dual	plural
1	تَأَخَّرْتُ taʔaxxartu	تَأَخَّرْنَا taʔaxxarnā	
2m	تَأَخَّرْتَ taʔaxxarta	تَأَخَّرْتُمَا taʔaxxartumā	تَأَخَّرْتُمْ taʔaxxartum
2f	تَأَخَّرْتِ taʔaxxarti		تَأَخَّرْتُنَّ taʔaxxartunna
3m	تَأَخَّرَ taʔaxxara	تَأَخَّرَا taʔaxxarā	تَأَخَّرُوا taʔaxxarū
3ʔ	تَأَخَّرَتْ taʔaxxarat	تَأَخَّرَتَا taʔaxxaratā	تَأَخَّرْنَ taʔaxxarna

indicative

	singular	dual	plural
1	أَتَأَخَّرُ ʔataʔaxxaru	نَتَأَخَّرُ nataʔaxxaru	
2m	تَتَأَخَّرُ tataʔaxxaru	تَتَأَخَّرَانِ tataʔaxxarāni	تَتَأَخَّرُونَ tataʔaxxarūna
2f	تَتَأَخَّرِينَ tataʔaxxarīna		تَتَأَخَّرْنَ tataʔaxxarna
3m	يَتَأَخَّرُ yataʔaxxaru	يَتَأَخَّرَانِ yataʔaxxarāni	يَتَأَخَّرُونَ yataʔaxxarūna
3ʔ	تَتَأَخَّرُ tataʔaxxaru	تَتَأَخَّرَانِ tataʔaxxarāni	يَتَأَخَّرْنَ yataʔaxxarna

subjunctive

	singular	dual	plural
1	أَتَأَخَّرَ ʔataʔaxxara	نَتَأَخَّرَ nataʔaxxara	
2m	تَتَأَخَّرَ tataʔaxxara	تَتَأَخَّرَا tataʔaxxarā	تَتَأَخَّرُوا tataʔaxxarū
2f	تَتَأَخَّرِي tataʔaxxarī		تَتَأَخَّرْنَ tataʔaxxarna
3m	يَتَأَخَّرَ yataʔaxxara	يَتَأَخَّرَا yataʔaxxarā	يَتَأَخَّرُوا yataʔaxxarū
3ʔ	تَتَأَخَّرَ tataʔaxxara	تَتَأَخَّرَا tataʔaxxarā	يَتَأَخَّرْنَ yataʔaxxarna

jussive

	singular	dual	plural
1	أَتَأَخَّرْ ʔataʔaxxar	نَتَأَخَّرْ nataʔaxxar	
2m	تَتَأَخَّرْ tataʔaxxar	تَتَأَخَّرَا tataʔaxxarā	تَتَأَخَّرُوا tataʔaxxarū
2f	تَتَأَخَّرِي tataʔaxxarī		تَتَأَخَّرْنَ tataʔaxxarna
3m	يَتَأَخَّرْ yataʔaxxar	يَتَأَخَّرَا yataʔaxxarā	يَتَأَخَّرُوا yataʔaxxarū
3ʔ	تَتَأَخَّرْ tataʔaxxar	تَتَأَخَّرَا tataʔaxxarā	يَتَأَخَّرْنَ yataʔaxxarna

imperative

	singular	dual	plural
2m	تَأَخَّرْ taʔaxxar	تَأَخَّرَا taʔaxxarā	تَأَخَّرُوا taʔaxxarū
2f	تَأَخَّرِي taʔaxxarī		تَأَخَّرْنَ taʔaxxarna

participles

active	passive
مُتَأَخِّر mutaʔaxxir	مُتَأَخَّر mutaʔaxxar

passive

perʔect	imperʔect
تُؤُخِّرَ tuʔuxxira	يُتَأَخَّرُ yutaʔaxxaru

hamzated measure V **masdar:** تَرَؤُّس taraʔʔus		و	ي	ء	*other*	**5s(b)** **to head**
	R¹	✓	✓		✓	
	R²			✓		
	R³				✓	

perfect

	singular	dual	plural
1	تَرَأَّسْتُ taraʔʔastu	تَرَأَّسْنَا taraʔʔasnā	
2m	تَرَأَّسْتَ taraʔʔasta	تَرَأَّسْتُمَا taraʔʔastumā	تَرَأَّسْتُمْ taraʔʔastum
2f	تَرَأَّسْتِ taraʔʔasti		تَرَأَّسْتُنَّ taraʔʔastunna
3m	تَرَأَّسَ taraʔʔasa	تَرَأَّسَا taraʔʔasā	تَرَأَّسُوا taraʔʔasū
3f	تَرَأَّسَتْ taraʔʔasat	تَرَأَّسَتَا taraʔʔasatā	تَرَأَّسْنَ taraʔʔasna

indicative

	singular	dual	plural
1	أَتَرَأَّسُ ʔataraʔʔasu	نَتَرَأَّسُ nataraʔʔasu	
2m	تَتَرَأَّسُ tataraʔʔasu	تَتَرَأَّسَانِ tataraʔʔasāni	تَتَرَأَّسُونَ tataraʔʔasūna
2f	تَتَرَأَّسِينَ tataraʔʔasīna		تَتَرَأَّسْنَ tataraʔʔasna
3m	يَتَرَأَّسُ yataraʔʔasu	يَتَرَأَّسَانِ yataraʔʔasāni	يَتَرَأَّسُونَ yataraʔʔasūna
3f	تَتَرَأَّسُ tataraʔʔasu	تَتَرَأَّسَانِ tataraʔʔasāni	يَتَرَأَّسْنَ yataraʔʔasna

subjunctive

	singular	dual	plural
1	أَتَرَأَّسَ ʔataraʔʔasa	نَتَرَأَّسَ nataraʔʔasa	
2m	تَتَرَأَّسَ tataraʔʔasa	تَتَرَأَّسَا tataraʔʔasā	تَتَرَأَّسُوا tataraʔʔasū
2f	تَتَرَأَّسِي tataraʔʔasī		تَتَرَأَّسْنَ tataraʔʔasna
3m	يَتَرَأَّسَ yataraʔʔasa	يَتَرَأَّسَا yataraʔʔasā	يَتَرَأَّسُوا yataraʔʔasū
3f	تَتَرَأَّسَ tataraʔʔasa	تَتَرَأَّسَا tataraʔʔasā	يَتَرَأَّسْنَ yataraʔʔasna

jussive

	singular	dual	plural
1	أَتَرَأَّسْ ʔataraʔʔas	نَتَرَأَّسْ nataraʔʔas	
2m	تَتَرَأَّسْ tataraʔʔas	تَتَرَأَّسَا tataraʔʔasā	تَتَرَأَّسُوا tataraʔʔasū
2f	تَتَرَأَّسِي tataraʔʔasī		تَتَرَأَّسْنَ tataraʔʔasna
3m	يَتَرَأَّسْ yataraʔʔas	يَتَرَأَّسَا yataraʔʔasā	يَتَرَأَّسُوا yataraʔʔasū
3f	تَتَرَأَّسْ tataraʔʔas	تَتَرَأَّسَا tataraʔʔasā	يَتَرَأَّسْنَ yataraʔʔasna

imperative

	singular	dual	plural
2m	تَرَأَّسْ taraʔʔas	تَرَأَّسَا taraʔʔasā	تَرَأَّسُوا taraʔʔasū
2f	تَرَأَّسِي taraʔʔasī		تَرَأَّسْنَ taraʔʔasna

participles

active	passive
مُتَرَئِّس mutaraʔʔis	مُتَرَأَّس mutaraʔʔas

passive

perfect	imperfect
تُرُئِّسَ turuʔʔisa	يُتَرَأَّسُ yutaraʔʔasu

hamzated measure V

masdar: تَنَبُّؤ tanabbuʔ

	و	ي	ء	other
R^1	✓	✓		✓
R^2	✓	✓		✓
R^3			✓	

5s(c)
to predict

perfect

	singular	dual	plural
1	تَنَبَّأْتُ tanabbaʔtu	تَنَبَّأْنَا tanabbaʔnā	
2m	تَنَبَّأْتَ tanabbaʔta	تَنَبَّأْتُمَا tanabbaʔtumā	تَنَبَّأْتُمْ tanabbaʔtum
2f	تَنَبَّأْتِ tanabbaʔti		تَنَبَّأْتُنَّ tanabbaʔtunna
3m	تَنَبَّأَ tanabbaʔa	تَنَبَّآ tanabbaʔā	تَنَبَّؤُوا tanabbaʔū
3f	تَنَبَّأَتْ tanabbaʔat	تَنَبَّأَتَا tanabbaʔatā	تَنَبَّأْنَ tanabbaʔna

indicative

	singular	dual	plural
1	أَتَنَبَّأُ ʔatanabbaʔu	نَتَنَبَّأُ natanabbaʔu	
2m	تَتَنَبَّأُ tatanabbaʔu	تَتَنَبَّآنِ tatanabbaʔāni	تَتَنَبَّؤُونَ tatanabbaʔūna
2f	تَتَنَبَّئِينَ tatanabbaʔīna		تَتَنَبَّأْنَ tatanabbaʔna
3m	يَتَنَبَّأُ yatanabbaʔu	يَتَنَبَّآنِ yatanabbaʔāni	يَتَنَبَّؤُونَ yatanabbaʔūna
3f	تَتَنَبَّأُ tatanabbaʔu	تَتَنَبَّآنِ tatanabbaʔāni	يَتَنَبَّأْنَ yatanabbaʔna

subjunctive

	singular	dual	plural
1	أَتَنَبَّأَ ʔatanabbaʔa	نَتَنَبَّأَ natanabbaʔa	
2m	تَتَنَبَّأَ tatanabbaʔa	تَتَنَبَّآ tatanabbaʔā	تَتَنَبَّؤُوا tatanabbaʔū
2f	تَتَنَبَّئِي tatanabbaʔī		تَتَنَبَّأْنَ tatanabbaʔna
3m	يَتَنَبَّأَ yatanabbaʔa	يَتَنَبَّآ yatanabbaʔā	يَتَنَبَّؤُوا yatanabbaʔū
3f	تَتَنَبَّأَ tatanabbaʔa	تَتَنَبَّآ tatanabbaʔā	يَتَنَبَّأْنَ yatanabbaʔna

jussive

	singular	dual	plural
1	أَتَنَبَّأْ ʔatanabbaʔ	نَتَنَبَّأْ natanabbaʔ	
2m	تَتَنَبَّأْ tatanabbaʔ	تَتَنَبَّآ tatanabbaʔā	تَتَنَبَّؤُوا tatanabbaʔū
2f	تَتَنَبَّئِي tatanabbaʔī		تَتَنَبَّأْنَ tatanabbaʔna
3m	يَتَنَبَّأْ yatanabbaʔ	يَتَنَبَّآ yatanabbaʔā	يَتَنَبَّؤُوا yatanabbaʔū
3f	تَتَنَبَّأْ tatanabbaʔ	تَتَنَبَّآ tatanabbaʔā	يَتَنَبَّأْنَ yatanabbaʔna

imperative

	singular	dual	plural
2m	تَنَبَّأْ tanabbaʔ	تَنَبَّآ tanabbaʔā	تَنَبَّؤُوا tanabbaʔū
2f	تَنَبَّئِي tanabbaʔī		تَنَبَّأْنَ tanabbaʔna

participles

active	passive
مُتَنَبِّئ mutanabbiʔ	مُتَنَبَّأ mutanabbaʔ

passive

perfect	imperfect
تُنُبِّئَ tunubbiʔa	يُتَنَبَّأُ yutanabbaʔu

defective measure V

masdar: تَمَنٍّ tamann(in)

	و	ي	ء	other
R^1	✓	✓		✓
R^2	✓	✓		✓
R^3	✓	✓		

5d
to hope

perfect

	singular	dual	plural
1	تَمَنَّيْتُ tamannaytu	تَمَنَّيْنَا tamannaynā	
2m	تَمَنَّيْتَ tamannayta	تَمَنَّيْتُمَا tamannaytumā	تَمَنَّيْتُمْ tamannaytum
2f	تَمَنَّيْتِ tamannayti		تَمَنَّيْتُنَّ tamannaytunna
3m	تَمَنَّى tamannā	تَمَنَّيَا tamannayā	تَمَنَّوْا tamannaw
3f	تَمَنَّتْ tamannat	تَمَنَّتَا tamannatā	تَمَنَّيْنَ tamannayna

indicative

	singular	dual	plural
1	أَتَمَنَّى ʔatamannā	نَتَمَنَّى natamannā	
2m	تَتَمَنَّى tatamannā	تَتَمَنَّيَانِ tatamannayāni	تَتَمَنَّوْنَ tatamannawna
2f	تَتَمَنَّيْنَ tatamannayna		تَتَمَنَّيْنَ tatamannayna
3m	يَتَمَنَّى yatamannā	يَتَمَنَّيَانِ yatamannayāni	يَتَمَنَّوْنَ yatamannawna
3f	تَتَمَنَّى tatamannā	تَتَمَنَّيَانِ tatamannayāni	يَتَمَنَّيْنَ yatamannayna

subjunctive

	singular	dual	plural
1	أَتَمَنَّى ʔatamannā	نَتَمَنَّى natamannā	
2m	تَتَمَنَّى tatamannā	تَتَمَنَّيَا tatamannayā	تَتَمَنَّوْا tatamannaw
2f	تَتَمَنَّيْ tatamannay		تَتَمَنَّيْنَ tatamannayna
3m	يَتَمَنَّى yatamannā	يَتَمَنَّيَا yatamannayā	يَتَمَنَّوْا yatamannaw
3f	تَتَمَنَّى tatamannā	تَتَمَنَّيَا tatamannayā	يَتَمَنَّيْنَ yatamannayna

jussive

	singular	dual	plural
1	أَتَمَنَّ ʔatamanna	نَتَمَنَّ natamanna	
2m	تَتَمَنَّ tatamanna	تَتَمَنَّيَا tatamannayā	تَتَمَنَّوْا tatamannaw
2f	تَتَمَنَّيْ tatamannay		تَتَمَنَّيْنَ tatamannayna
3m	يَتَمَنَّ yatamanna	يَتَمَنَّيَا yatamannayā	يَتَمَنَّوْا yatamannaw
3f	تَتَمَنَّ tatamanna	تَتَمَنَّيَا tatamannayā	يَتَمَنَّيْنَ yatamannayna

imperative

	singular	dual	plural
2m	تَمَنَّ tamanna	تَمَنَّيَا tamannayā	تَمَنَّوْا tamannaw
2f	تَمَنَّيْ tamannay		تَمَنَّيْنَ tamannayna

participles

active	passive
مُتَمَنٍّ mutamann(in)	مُتَمَنًّى mutamann(an)

passive

perfect	imperfect
تُمُنِّيَ tumunniya	يُتَمَنَّى yutamannā

hamzated defective meas. V

masdar: تَأَنٍّ taʔann(in)

	و	ي	ء	other
R^1			✓	
R^2	✓	✓		✓
R^3	✓	✓		

5d(a)

to take one's time

perfect

	singular	dual	plural
1	تَأَنَّيْتُ taʔannaytu	تَأَنَّيْنَا taʔannaynā	
2m	تَأَنَّيْتَ taʔannayta	تَأَنَّيْتُمَا taʔannaytumā	تَأَنَّيْتُمْ taʔannaytum
2f	تَأَنَّيْتِ taʔannayti		تَأَنَّيْتُنَّ taʔannaytunna
3m	تَأَنَّى taʔannā	تَأَنَّيَا taʔannayā	تَأَنَّوْا taʔannaw
3f	تَأَنَّتْ taʔannat	تَأَنَّتَا taʔannatā	تَأَنَّيْنَ taʔannayna

indicative

	singular	dual	plural
1	أَتَأَنَّى ʔataʔannā	نَتَأَنَّى nataʔannā	
2m	تَتَأَنَّى tataʔannā	تَتَأَنَّيَانِ tataʔannayāni	تَتَأَنَّوْنَ tataʔannawna
2f	تَتَأَنَّيْنَ tataʔannayna		تَتَأَنَّيْنَ tataʔannayna
3m	يَتَأَنَّى yataʔannā	يَتَأَنَّيَانِ yataʔannayāni	يَتَأَنَّوْنَ yataʔannawna
3f	تَتَأَنَّى tataʔannā	تَتَأَنَّيَانِ tataʔannayāni	يَتَأَنَّيْنَ yataʔannayna

subjunctive

	singular	dual	plural
1	أَتَأَنَّى ʔataʔannā	نَتَأَنَّى nataʔannā	
2m	تَتَأَنَّى tataʔannā	تَتَأَنَّيَا tataʔannayā	تَتَأَنَّوْا tataʔannaw
2f	تَتَأَنَّيْ tataʔannay		تَتَأَنَّيْنَ tataʔannayna
3m	يَتَأَنَّى yataʔannā	يَتَأَنَّيَا yataʔannayā	يَتَأَنَّوْا yataʔannaw
3f	تَتَأَنَّى tataʔannā	تَتَأَنَّيَا tataʔannayā	يَتَأَنَّيْنَ yataʔannayna

jussive

	singular	dual	plural
1	أَتَأَنَّ ʔataʔanna	نَتَأَنَّ nataʔanna	
2m	تَتَأَنَّ tataʔanna	تَتَأَنَّيَا tataʔannayā	تَتَأَنَّوْا tataʔannaw
2f	تَتَأَنَّيْ tataʔannay		تَتَأَنَّيْنَ tataʔannayna
3m	يَتَأَنَّ yataʔanna	يَتَأَنَّيَا yataʔannayā	يَتَأَنَّوْا yataʔannaw
3f	تَتَأَنَّ tataʔanna	تَتَأَنَّيَا tataʔannayā	يَتَأَنَّيْنَ yataʔannayna

imperative

	singular	dual	plural
2m	تَأَنَّ taʔanna	تَأَنَّيَا taʔannayā	تَأَنَّوْا taʔannaw
2f	تَأَنَّيْ taʔannay		تَأَنَّيْنَ taʔannayna

participles

active	passive
مُتَأَنٍّ mutaʔann(in)	مُتَأَنًّى mutaʔann(an)

passive

perfect	imperfect
تُؤُنِّيَ tuʔunniya	يُتَأَنَّى yutaʔannā

sound measure VI

masdar: تَنَاوُل tanāwul

	و	ي	ء	*other*
R¹	✓	✓		✓
R²	✓	✓		✓
R³				✓

6s
to deal with

perfect

	singular	dual	plural
1	تَنَاوَلْتُ tanāwaltu	تَنَاوَلْنَا tanāwalnā	
2m	تَنَاوَلْتَ tanāwalta	تَنَاوَلْتُمَا tanāwaltumā	تَنَاوَلْتُمْ tanāwaltum
2f	تَنَاوَلْتِ tanāwalti		تَنَاوَلْتُنَّ tanāwaltunna
3m	تَنَاوَلَ tanāwala	تَنَاوَلَا tanāwalā	تَنَاوَلُوا tanāwalū
3f	تَنَاوَلَتْ tanāwalat	تَنَاوَلَتَا tanāwalatā	تَنَاوَلْنَ tanāwalna

indicative

	singular	dual	plural
1	أَتَنَاوَلُ ʔatanāwalu	نَتَنَاوَلُ natanāwalu	
2m	تَتَنَاوَلُ tatanāwalu	تَتَنَاوَلَانِ tatanāwalāni	تَتَنَاوَلُونَ tatanāwalūna
2f	تَتَنَاوَلِينَ tatanāwalīna		تَتَنَاوَلْنَ tatanāwalna
3m	يَتَنَاوَلُ yatanāwalu	يَتَنَاوَلَانِ yatanāwalāni	يَتَنَاوَلُونَ yatanāwalūna
3f	تَتَنَاوَلُ tatanāwalu	تَتَنَاوَلَانِ tatanāwalāni	يَتَنَاوَلْنَ yatanāwalna

subjunctive

	singular	dual	plural
1	أَتَنَاوَلَ ʔatanāwala	نَتَنَاوَلَ natanāwala	
2m	تَتَنَاوَلَ tatanāwala	تَتَنَاوَلَا tatanāwalā	تَتَنَاوَلُوا tatanāwalū
2f	تَتَنَاوَلِي tatanāwalī		تَتَنَاوَلْنَ tatanāwalna
3m	يَتَنَاوَلَ yatanāwala	يَتَنَاوَلَا yatanāwalā	يَتَنَاوَلُوا yatanāwalū
3f	تَتَنَاوَلَ tatanāwala	تَتَنَاوَلَا tatanāwalā	يَتَنَاوَلْنَ yatanāwalna

jussive

	singular	dual	plural
1	أَتَنَاوَلْ ʔatanāwal	نَتَنَاوَلْ natanāwal	
2m	تَتَنَاوَلْ tatanāwal	تَتَنَاوَلَا tatanāwalā	تَتَنَاوَلُوا tatanāwalū
2f	تَتَنَاوَلِي tatanāwalī		تَتَنَاوَلْنَ tatanāwalna
3m	يَتَنَاوَلْ yatanāwal	يَتَنَاوَلَا yatanāwalā	يَتَنَاوَلُوا yatanāwalū
3f	تَتَنَاوَلْ tatanāwal	تَتَنَاوَلَا tatanāwalā	يَتَنَاوَلْنَ yatanāwalna

imperative

	singular	dual	plural
2m	تَنَاوَلْ tanāwal	تَنَاوَلَا tanāwalā	تَنَاوَلُوا tanāwalū
2f	تَنَاوَلِي tanāwalī		تَنَاوَلْنَ tanāwalna

participles

active	passive
مُتَنَاوِل mutanāwil	مُتَنَاوَل mutanāwal

passive

perfect	imperfect
تُنُووِلَ tunūwila	يُتَنَاوَلُ yutanāwalu

hamzated measure VI **masdar:** تَآمُر taʔāmur		و	ي	ء	other	**6s(a)** **to conspire**
	R^1			✓		
	R^2	✓	✓		✓	
	R^3				✓	

perfect

	singular	dual	plural
1	تَآمَرْتُ taʔāmartu	تَآمَرْنَا taʔāmarnā	
2m	تَآمَرْتَ taʔāmarta	تَآمَرْتُمَا taʔāmartumā	تَآمَرْتُمْ taʔāmartum
2f	تَآمَرْتِ taʔāmarti		تَآمَرْتُنَّ taʔāmartunna
3m	تَآمَرَ taʔāmara	تَآمَرَا taʔāmarā	تَآمَرُوا taʔāmarū
3f	تَآمَرَتْ taʔāmarat	تَآمَرَتَا taʔāmaratā	تَآمَرْنَ taʔāmarna

indicative

	singular	dual	plural
1	أَتَآمَرُ ʔataʔāmaru	نَتَآمَرُ nataʔāmaru	
2m	تَتَآمَرُ tataʔāmaru	تَتَآمَرَانِ tataʔāmarāni	تَتَآمَرُونَ tataʔāmarūna
2f	تَتَآمَرِينَ tataʔāmarīna		تَتَآمَرْنَ tataʔāmarna
3m	يَتَآمَرُ yataʔāmaru	يَتَآمَرَانِ yataʔāmarāni	يَتَآمَرُونَ yataʔāmarūna
3f	تَتَآمَرُ tataʔāmaru	تَتَآمَرَانِ tataʔāmarāni	يَتَآمَرْنَ yataʔāmarna

subjunctive

	singular	dual	plural
1	أَتَآمَرَ ʔataʔāmara	نَتَآمَرَ nataʔāmara	
2m	تَتَآمَرَ tataʔāmara	تَتَآمَرَا tataʔāmarā	تَتَآمَرُوا tataʔāmarū
2f	تَتَآمَرِي tataʔāmarī		تَتَآمَرْنَ tataʔāmarna
3m	يَتَآمَرَ yataʔāmara	يَتَآمَرَا yataʔāmarā	يَتَآمَرُوا yataʔāmarū
3f	تَتَآمَرَ tataʔāmara	تَتَآمَرَا tataʔāmarā	يَتَآمَرْنَ yataʔāmarna

jussive

	singular	dual	plural
1	أَتَآمَرْ ʔataʔāmar	نَتَآمَرْ nataʔāmar	
2m	تَتَآمَرْ tataʔāmar	تَتَآمَرَا tataʔāmarā	تَتَآمَرُوا tataʔāmarū
2f	تَتَآمَرِي tataʔāmarī		تَتَآمَرْنَ tataʔāmarna
3m	يَتَآمَرْ yataʔāmar	يَتَآمَرَا yataʔāmarā	يَتَآمَرُوا yataʔāmarū
3f	تَتَآمَرْ tataʔāmar	تَتَآمَرَا tataʔāmarā	يَتَآمَرْنَ yataʔāmarna

imperative

	singular	dual	plural
2m	تَآمَرْ taʔāmar	تَآمَرَا taʔāmarā	تَآمَرُوا taʔāmarū
2f	تَآمَرِي taʔāmarī		تَآمَرْنَ taʔāmarna

participles

active	passive
مُتَآمِر mutaʔāmir	مُتَآمَر mutaʔāmar

passive

perfect	imperfect
تُؤُومِرَ tuʔūmira	يُتَآمَرُ yutaʔāmaru

hamzated measure VI

masdar: تَسَاؤُل tasāʔul

	و	ي	ء	other
R^1	✓	✓		✓
R^2			✓	
R^3				✓

6s(b)

to wonder

perfect

	singular	dual	plural
1	تَسَاءَلْتُ tasāʔaltu	تَسَاءَلْنَا tasāʔalnā	
2m	تَسَاءَلْتَ tasāʔalta	تَسَاءَلْتُمَا tasāʔaltumā	تَسَاءَلْتُمْ tasāʔaltum
2f	تَسَاءَلْتِ tasāʔalti		تَسَاءَلْتُنَّ tasāʔaltunna
3m	تَسَاءَلَ tasāʔala	تَسَاءَلَا tasāʔalā	تَسَاءَلُوا tasāʔalū
3f	تَسَاءَلَتْ tasāʔalat	تَسَاءَلَتَا tasāʔalatā	تَسَاءَلْنَ tasāʔalna

indicative

	singular	dual	plural
1	أَتَسَاءَلُ ʔatasāʔalu	نَتَسَاءَلُ natasāʔalu	
2m	تَتَسَاءَلُ tatasāʔalu	تَتَسَاءَلَانِ tatasāʔalāni	تَتَسَاءَلُونَ tatasāʔalūna
2f	تَتَسَاءَلِينَ tatasāʔalīna		تَتَسَاءَلْنَ tatasāʔalna
3m	يَتَسَاءَلُ yatasāʔalu	يَتَسَاءَلَانِ yatasāʔalāni	يَتَسَاءَلُونَ yatasāʔalūna
3f	تَتَسَاءَلُ tatasāʔalu	تَتَسَاءَلَانِ tatasāʔalāni	يَتَسَاءَلْنَ yatasāʔalna

subjunctive

	singular	dual	plural
1	أَتَسَاءَلَ ʔatasāʔala	نَتَسَاءَلَ natasāʔala	
2m	تَتَسَاءَلَ tatasāʔala	تَتَسَاءَلَا tatasāʔalā	تَتَسَاءَلُوا tatasāʔalū
2f	تَتَسَاءَلِي tatasāʔalī		تَتَسَاءَلْنَ tatasāʔalna
3m	يَتَسَاءَلَ yatasāʔala	يَتَسَاءَلَا yatasāʔalā	يَتَسَاءَلُوا yatasāʔalū
3f	تَتَسَاءَلَ tatasāʔala	تَتَسَاءَلَا tatasāʔalā	يَتَسَاءَلْنَ yatasāʔalna

jussive

	singular	dual	plural
1	أَتَسَاءَلْ ʔatasāʔal	نَتَسَاءَلْ natasāʔal	
2m	تَتَسَاءَلْ tatasāʔal	تَتَسَاءَلَا tatasāʔalā	تَتَسَاءَلُوا tatasāʔalū
2f	تَتَسَاءَلِي tatasāʔalī		تَتَسَاءَلْنَ tatasāʔalna
3m	يَتَسَاءَلْ yatasāʔal	يَتَسَاءَلَا yatasāʔalā	يَتَسَاءَلُوا yatasāʔalū
3f	تَتَسَاءَلْ tatasāʔal	تَتَسَاءَلَا tatasāʔalā	يَتَسَاءَلْنَ yatasāʔalna

imperative

	singular	dual	plural
2m	تَسَاءَلْ tasāʔal	تَسَاءَلَا tasāʔalā	تَسَاءَلُوا tasāʔalū
2f	تَسَاءَلِي tasāʔalī		تَسَاءَلْنَ tasāʔalna

participles

active	passive
مُتَسَائِل mutasāʔil	مُتَسَاءَل mutasāʔal

passive

perfect	imperfect
تُسُوئِلَ tusūʔila	يُتَسَاءَلُ yutasāʔalu

geminate measure VI

masdar: تَضَادّ taḍādd

	و	ي	ء	other
R^1				✓
R^2				✓
R^3				✓

6g

to contradict each other

perfect

	singular	dual	plural
1	تَضَادَدْتُ taḍādadtu	تَضَادَدْنَا taḍādadnā	
2m	تَضَادَدْتَ taḍādadta	تَضَادَدْتُمَا taḍādadtumā	تَضَادَدْتُمْ taḍādadtum
2f	تَضَادَدْتِ taḍādadti		تَضَادَدْتُنَّ taḍādadtunna
3m	تَضَادَّ taḍādda	تَضَادَّا taḍāddā	تَضَادُّوا taḍāddū
3f	تَضَادَّتْ taḍāddat	تَضَادَّتَا taḍāddatā	تَضَادَدْنَ taḍādadna

indicative

	singular	dual	plural
1	أَتَضَادُّ ʔataḍāddu	نَتَضَادُّ nataḍāddu	
2m	تَتَضَادُّ tataḍāddu	تَتَضَادَّانِ tataḍāddāni	تَتَضَادُّونَ tataḍāddūna
2f	تَتَضَادِّينَ tataḍāddīna		تَتَضَادَدْنَ tataḍādadna
3m	يَتَضَادُّ yataḍāddu	يَتَضَادَّانِ yataḍāddāni	يَتَضَادُّونَ yataḍāddūna
3f	تَتَضَادُّ tataḍāddu	تَتَضَادَّانِ tataḍāddāni	يَتَضَادَدْنَ yataḍādadna

subjunctive

	singular	dual	plural
1	أَتَضَادَّ ʔataḍādda	نَتَضَادَّ nataḍādda	
2m	تَتَضَادَّ tataḍādda	تَتَضَادَّا tataḍāddā	تَتَضَادُّوا tataḍāddū
2f	تَتَضَادِّي tataḍāddī		تَتَضَادَدْنَ tataḍādadna
3m	يَتَضَادَّ yataḍādda	يَتَضَادَّا yataḍāddā	يَتَضَادُّوا yataḍāddū
3f	تَتَضَادَّ tataḍādda	تَتَضَادَّا tataḍāddā	يَتَضَادَدْنَ yataḍādadna

jussive

	singular	dual	plural
1	أَتَضَادَّ ʔataḍādda	نَتَضَادَّ nataḍādda	
2m	تَتَضَادَّ tataḍādda	تَتَضَادَّا tataḍāddā	تَتَضَادُّوا tataḍāddū
2f	تَتَضَادِّي tataḍāddī		تَتَضَادَدْنَ tataḍādadna
3m	يَتَضَادَّ yataḍādda	يَتَضَادَّا yataḍāddā	يَتَضَادُّوا yataḍāddū
3f	تَتَضَادَّ tataḍādda	تَتَضَادَّا tataḍāddā	يَتَضَادَدْنَ yataḍādadna

imperative

	singular	dual	plural
2m	تَضَادَّ taḍādda	تَضَادَّا taḍāddā	تَضَادُّوا taḍāddū
2f	تَضَادِّي taḍāddī		تَضَادَدْنَ taḍādadna

participles

active	passive
مُتَضَادّ mutaḍādd	مُتَضَادّ mutaḍādd

passive

perfect	imperfect
تُضُودِدَ tuḍūdida	يُتَضَادُّ yutaḍāddu

defective measure VI

masdar: تَوَالٍ tawāl(in)

	و	ي	ء	other
R^1	✓	✓		✓
R^2	✓	✓		✓
R^3	✓	✓		

6d
to follow in succession

perfect

	singular	dual	plural
1	تَوَالَيْتُ tawālaytu	تَوَالَيْنَا tawālaynā	
2m	تَوَالَيْتَ tawālayta	تَوَالَيْتُمَا tawālaytumā	تَوَالَيْتُمْ tawālaytum
2f	تَوَالَيْتِ tawālayti		تَوَالَيْتُنَّ tawālaytunna
3m	تَوَالَى tawālā	تَوَالَيَا tawālayā	تَوَالَوْا tawālaw
3f	تَوَالَتْ tawālat	تَوَالَتَا tawālatā	تَوَالَيْنَ tawālayna

indicative

	singular	dual	plural
1	أَتَوَالَى ʔatawālā	نَتَوَالَى natawālā	
2m	تَتَوَالَى tatawālā	تَتَوَالَيَانِ tatawālayāni	تَتَوَالَوْنَ tatawālawna
2f	تَتَوَالَيْنَ tatawālayna		تَتَوَالَيْنَ tatawālayna
3m	يَتَوَالَى yatawālā	يَتَوَالَيَانِ yatawālayāni	يَتَوَالَوْنَ yatawālawna
3f	تَتَوَالَى tatawālā	تَتَوَالَيَانِ tatawālayāni	يَتَوَالَيْنَ yatawālayna

subjunctive

	singular	dual	plural
1	أَتَوَالَى ʔatawālā	نَتَوَالَى natawālā	
2m	تَتَوَالَى tatawālā	تَتَوَالَيَا tatawālayā	تَتَوَالَوْا tatawālaw
2f	تَتَوَالَيْ tatawālay		تَتَوَالَيْنَ tatawālayna
3m	يَتَوَالَى yatawālā	يَتَوَالَيَا yatawālayā	يَتَوَالَوْا yatawālaw
3f	تَتَوَالَى tatawālā	تَتَوَالَيَا tatawālayā	يَتَوَالَيْنَ yatawāʔayna

jussive

	singular	dual	plural
1	أَتَوَالَ ʔatawāla	نَتَوَالَ natawāla	
2m	تَتَوَالَ tatawāla	تَتَوَالَيَا tatawālayā	تَتَوَالَوْا tatawālaw
2f	تَتَوَالَيْ tatawālay		تَتَوَالَيْنَ tatawālayna
3m	يَتَوَالَ yatawāla	يَتَوَالَيَا yatawālayā	يَتَوَالَوْا yatawālaw
3f	تَتَوَالَ tatawāla	تَتَوَالَيَا tatawālayā	يَتَوَالَيْنَ yatawālayna

imperative

	singular	dual	plural
2m	تَوَالَ tawāla	تَوَالَيَا tawālayā	تَوَالَوْا tawālaw
2f	تَوَالَيْ tawālay		تَوَالَيْنَ tawālayna

participles

active	passive
مُتَوَالٍ mutawāl(in)	مُتَوَالًى mutawāl(an)

passive

perfect	imperfect
تُوُولِيَ tuwūliya	يُتَوَالَى yutawālā

hamzated defective meas. VI		و	ي	ء	*other*	**6d(a)**
masdar: تَآخٍ taʔāx(in)	*R¹*			✓		**to fraternize**
	R²	✓	✓		✓	
	R³	✓	✓			

perfect

	singular	dual	plural
1	تَآخَيْتُ taʔāxaytu	تَآخَيْنَا taʔāxaynā	
2m	تَآخَيْتَ taʔāxayta	تَآخَيْتُمَا taʔāxaytumā	تَآخَيْتُمْ taʔāxaytum
2ff	تَآخَيْتِ taʔāxayti		تَآخَيْتُنَّ taʔāxaytunna
3m	تَآخَى taʔāxā	تَآخَيَا taʔāxayā	تَآخَوْا taʔāxaw
3f	تَآخَتْ taʔāxat	تَآخَتَا taʔāxatā	تَآخَيْنَ taʔāxayna

indicative

	singular	dual	plural
1	أَتَآخَى ʔataʔāxā	نَتَآخَى nataʔāxā	
2m	تَتَآخَى tataʔāxā	تَتَآخَيَانِ tataʔāxayāni	تَتَآخَوْنَ tataʔāxawna
2ff	تَتَآخَيْنَ tataʔāxayna		تَتَآخَيْنَ tataʔāxayna
3m	يَتَآخَى yataʔāxā	يَتَآخَيَانِ yataʔāxayāni	يَتَآخَوْنَ yataʔāxawna
3f	تَتَآخَى tataʔāxā	تَتَآخَيَانِ tataʔāxayāni	يَتَآخَيْنَ yataʔāxayna

subjunctive

	singular	dual	plural
1	أَتَآخَى ʔataʔāxā	نَتَآخَى nataʔāxā	
2m	تَتَآخَى tataʔāxā	تَتَآخَيَا tataʔāxayā	تَتَآخَوْا tataʔāxaw
2f	تَتَآخَيْ tataʔāxay		تَتَآخَيْنَ tataʔāxayna
3m	يَتَآخَى yataʔāxā	يَتَآخَيَا yataʔāxayā	يَتَآخَوْا yataʔāxaw
3f	تَتَآخَى tataʔāxā	تَتَآخَيَا tataʔāxayā	يَتَآخَيْنَ yataʔāʔayna

jussive

	singular	dual	plural
1	أَتَآخَ ʔataʔāxa	نَتَآخَ nataʔāxa	
2m	تَتَآخَ tataʔāxa	تَتَآخَيَا tataʔāxayā	تَتَآخَوْا tataʔāxaw
2f	تَتَآخَيْ tataʔāxay		تَتَآخَيْنَ tataʔāxayna
3m	يَتَآخَ yataʔāxa	يَتَآخَيَا yataʔāxayā	يَتَآخَوْا yataʔāxaw
3f	تَتَآخَ tataʔāxa	تَتَآخَيَا tataʔāxayā	يَتَآخَيْنَ yataʔāxayna

imperative

	singular	dual	plural
2m	تَآخَ taʔāxa	تَآخَيَا taʔāxayā	تَآخَوْا taʔāxaw
2f	تَآخَيْ taʔāxay		تَآخَيْنَ taʔāxayna

participles

active	passive
مُتَآخٍ mutaʔāx(in)	مُتَآخًى mutaʔāx(an)

passive

perʔect	imperʔect
تُؤُوخِيَ tuʔūxiya	يُتَآخَى yutaʔāxā

sound measure VII		و	ي	ء	*other*	**7s**
masdar: اِنْطِلَاق inṭilāq	*R¹*				✓	**to depart**
	R²				✓	
	R³				✓	

perfect

	singular	dual	plural
1	اِنْطَلَقْتُ inṭalaqtu	اِنْطَلَقْنَا inṭalaqnā	
2m	اِنْطَلَقْتَ inṭalaqta	اِنْطَلَقْتُمَا inṭalaqtumā	اِنْطَلَقْتُمْ inṭalaqtum
2f	اِنْطَلَقْتِ inṭalaqti		اِنْطَلَقْتُنَّ inṭalaqtunna
3m	اِنْطَلَقَ inṭalaqa	اِنْطَلَقَا inṭalaqā	اِنْطَلَقُوا inṭalaqū
3f	اِنْطَلَقَتْ inṭalaqat	اِنْطَلَقَتَا inṭalaqatā	اِنْطَلَقْنَ inṭalaqna

indicative

	singular	dual	plural
1	أَنْطَلِقُ ʔanṭaliqu	نَنْطَلِقُ nanṭaliqu	
2m	تَنْطَلِقُ tanṭaliqu	تَنْطَلِقَانِ tanṭaliqāni	تَنْطَلِقُونَ tanṭaliqūna
2f	تَنْطَلِقِينَ tanṭaliqīna		تَنْطَلِقْنَ tanṭaliqna
3m	يَنْطَلِقُ yanṭaliqu	يَنْطَلِقَانِ yanṭaliqāni	يَنْطَلِقُونَ yanṭaliqūna
3f	تَنْطَلِقُ tanṭaliqu	تَنْطَلِقَانِ tanṭaliqāni	يَنْطَلِقْنَ yanṭaliqna

subjunctive

	singular	dual	plural
1	أَنْطَلِقَ ʔanṭaliqa	نَنْطَلِقَ nanṭaliqa	
2m	تَنْطَلِقَ tanṭaliqa	تَنْطَلِقَا tanṭaliqā	تَنْطَلِقُوا tanṭaliqū
2f	تَنْطَلِقِي tanṭaliqī		تَنْطَلِقْنَ tanṭaliqna
3m	يَنْطَلِقَ yanṭaliqa	يَنْطَلِقَا yanṭaliqā	يَنْطَلِقُوا yanṭaliqū
3f	تَنْطَلِقَ tanṭaliqa	تَنْطَلِقَا tanṭaliqā	يَنْطَلِقْنَ yanṭaliqna

jussive

	singular	dual	plural
1	أَنْطَلِقْ ʔanṭaliq	نَنْطَلِقْ nanṭaliq	
2m	تَنْطَلِقْ tanṭaliq	تَنْطَلِقَا tanṭaliqā	تَنْطَلِقُوا tanṭaliqū
2f	تَنْطَلِقِي tanṭaliqī		تَنْطَلِقْنَ tanṭaliqna
3m	يَنْطَلِقْ yanṭaliq	يَنْطَلِقَا yanṭaliqā	يَنْطَلِقُوا yanṭaliqū
3f	تَنْطَلِقْ tanṭaliq	تَنْطَلِقَا tanṭaliqā	يَنْطَلِقْنَ yanṭaliqna

imperative

	singular	dual	plural
2m	اِنْطَلِقْ inṭaliq	اِنْطَلِقَا inṭaliqā	اِنْطَلِقُوا inṭaliqū
2f	اِنْطَلِقِي inṭaliqī		اِنْطَلِقْنَ inṭaliqna

participles

active
مُنْطَلِق munṭaliq

hamzated measure VII

masdar: إِنْكِفَاء inkifāʔ

	و	ي	ء	other
R^1				✓
R^2				✓
R^3			✓	

7s(a)

to retreat

perfect

	singular	dual	plural
1	إِنْكَفَأْتُ inkafaʔtu	إِنْكَفَأْنَا inkafaʔnā	
2m	إِنْكَفَأْتَ inkafaʔta	إِنْكَفَأْتُمَا inkafaʔtumā	إِنْكَفَأْتُمْ inkafaʔtum
2f	إِنْكَفَأْتِ inkafaʔti		إِنْكَفَأْتُنَّ inkafaʔtunna
3m	إِنْكَفَأَ inkafaʔa	إِنْكَفَآ inkafaʔā	إِنْكَفَؤُوا inkafaʔū
3f	إِنْكَفَأَتْ inkafaʔat	إِنْكَفَأَتَا inkafaʔatā	إِنْكَفَأْنَ inkafaʔna

indicative

	singular	dual	plural
1	أَنْكَفِئُ ʔankafiʔu	نَنْكَفِئُ nankafiʔu	
2m	تَنْكَفِئُ tankafiʔu	تَنْكَفِئَانِ tankafiʔāni	تَنْكَفِئُونَ tankafiʔūna
2f	تَنْكَفِئِينَ tankafiʔīna		تَنْكَفِئْنَ tankafiʔna
3m	يَنْكَفِئُ yankafiʔu	يَنْكَفِئَانِ yankafiʔāni	يَنْكَفِئُونَ yankafiʔūna
3f	تَنْكَفِئُ tankafiʔu	تَنْكَفِئَانِ tankafiʔāni	يَنْكَفِئْنَ yankafiʔna

subjunctive

	singular	dual	plural
1	أَنْكَفِئَ ʔankafiʔa	نَنْكَفِئَ nankafiʔa	
2m	تَنْكَفِئَ tankafiʔa	تَنْكَفِئَا tankafiʔā	تَنْكَفِئُوا tankafiʔū
2f	تَنْكَفِئِي tankafiʔī		تَنْكَفِئْنَ tankafiʔna
3m	يَنْكَفِئَ yankafiʔa	يَنْكَفِئَا yankafiʔā	يَنْكَفِئُوا yankafiʔū
3f	تَنْكَفِئَ tankafiʔa	تَنْكَفِئَا tankafiʔā	يَنْكَفِئْنَ yankafiʔna

jussive

	singular	dual	plural
1	أَنْكَفِئْ ʔankafiʔ	نَنْكَفِئْ nankafiʔ	
2m	تَنْكَفِئْ tankafiʔ	تَنْكَفِئَا tankafiʔā	تَنْكَفِئُوا tankafiʔū
2f	تَنْكَفِئِي tankafiʔī		تَنْكَفِئْنَ tankafiʔna
3m	يَنْكَفِئْ yankafiʔ	يَنْكَفِئَا yankafiʔā	يَنْكَفِئُوا yankafiʔū
3f	تَنْكَفِئْ tankafiʔ	تَنْكَفِئَا tankafiʔā	يَنْكَفِئْنَ yankafiʔna

imperative

	singular	dual	plural
2m	إِنْكَفِئْ inkafiʔ	إِنْكَفِئَا inkafiʔā	إِنْكَفِئُوا inkafiʔū
2f	إِنْكَفِئِي inkafiʔī		إِنْكَفِئْنَ inkafiʔna

participles

active
مُنْكَفِئ munkafiʔ

geminate measure VII

masdar: اِنْضِمَام inḍimām

	و	ي	ء	other
R[1]				✓
R[2]				✓
R[3]				✓

7g
to join

perfect

	singular	dual	plural
1	اِنْضَمَمْتُ inḍamamtu	اِنْضَمَمْنَا inḍamamnā	
2m	اِنْضَمَمْتَ inḍamamta	اِنْضَمَمْتُمَا inḍamamtumā	اِنْضَمَمْتُمْ inḍamamtum
2f	اِنْضَمَمْتِ inḍamamti		اِنْضَمَمْتُنَّ inḍamamtunna
3m	اِنْضَمَّ inḍamma	اِنْضَمَّا inḍammā	اِنْضَمُّوا inḍammū
3f	اِنْضَمَّتْ inḍammat	اِنْضَمَّتَا inḍammatā	اِنْضَمَمْنَ inḍamamna

indicative

	singular	dual	plural
1	أَنْضَمُّ ʔanḍammu	نَنْضَمُّ nanḍammu	
2m	تَنْضَمُّ tanḍammu	تَنْضَمَّانِ tanḍammāni	تَنْضَمُّونَ tanḍammūna
2f	تَنْضَمِّينَ tanḍammīna		تَنْضَمِمْنَ tanḍamimna
3m	يَنْضَمُّ yanḍammu	يَنْضَمَّانِ yanḍammāni	يَنْضَمُّونَ yanḍammūna
3f	تَنْضَمُّ tanḍammu	تَنْضَمَّانِ tanḍammāni	يَنْضَمِمْنَ yanḍamimna

subjunctive

	singular	dual	plural
1	أَنْضَمَّ ʔanḍamma	نَنْضَمَّ nanḍamma	
2m	تَنْضَمَّ tanḍamma	تَنْضَمَّا tanḍammā	تَنْضَمُّوا tanḍammū
2f	تَنْضَمِّي tanḍammī		تَنْضَمِمْنَ tanḍamimna
3m	يَنْضَمَّ yanḍamma	يَنْضَمَّا yanḍammā	يَنْضَمُّوا yanḍammū
3f	تَنْضَمَّ tanḍamma	تَنْضَمَّا tanḍammā	يَنْضَمِمْنَ yanḍamimna

jussive

	singular	dual	plural
1	أَنْضَمَّ ʔanḍamma	نَنْضَمَّ nanḍamma	
2m	تَنْضَمَّ tanḍamma	تَنْضَمَّا tanḍammā	تَنْضَمُّوا tanḍammū
2f	تَنْضَمِّي tanḍammī		تَنْضَمِمْنَ tanḍamimna
3m	يَنْضَمَّ yanḍamma	يَنْضَمَّا yanḍammā	يَنْضَمُّوا yanḍammū
3f	تَنْضَمَّ tanḍamma	تَنْضَمَّا tanḍammā	يَنْضَمِمْنَ yanḍamimna

imperative

	singular	dual	plural
2m	اِنْضَمَّ inḍamma	اِنْضَمَّا inḍammā	اِنْضَمُّوا inḍammū
2f	اِنْضَمِّي inḍammī		اِنْضَمِمْنَ inḍamimna

participles

active
مُنْضَمّ munḍamm

hollow measure VII

masdar: اِنْهِيَار inhiyār

	و	ي	ء	*other*
R^1				✓
R^2	✓	✓		
R^3				✓

7h

to collapse

perfect

	singular	dual	plural
1	اِنْهَرْتُ inhartu	اِنْهَرْنَا inharnā	
2m	اِنْهَرْتَ inharta	اِنْهَرْتُمَا inhartumā	اِنْهَرْتُمْ inhartum
2f	اِنْهَرْتِ inharti		اِنْهَرْتُنَّ inhartunna
3m	اِنْهَارَ inhāra	اِنْهَارَا inhārā	اِنْهَارُوا inhārū
3f	اِنْهَارَتْ inhārat	اِنْهَارَتَا inhāratā	اِنْهَرْنَ inharna

indicative

	singular	dual	plural
1	أَنْهَارُ ʔanhāru	نَنْهَارُ nanhāru	
2m	تَنْهَارُ tanhāru	تَنْهَارَانِ tanhārāni	تَنْهَارُونَ tanhārūna
2f	تَنْهَارِينَ tanhārīna		تَنْهَرْنَ tanharna
3m	يَنْهَارُ yanhāru	يَنْهَارَانِ yanhārāni	يَنْهَارُونَ yanhārūna
3f	تَنْهَارُ tanhāru	تَنْهَارَانِ tanhārāni	يَنْهَرْنَ yanharna

subjunctive

	singular	dual	plural
1	أَنْهَارَ ʔanhāra	نَنْهَارَ nanhāra	
2m	تَنْهَارَ tanhāra	تَنْهَارَا tanhārā	تَنْهَارُوا tanhārū
2f	تَنْهَارِي tanhārī		تَنْهَرْنَ tanharna
3m	يَنْهَارَ yanhāra	يَنْهَارَا yanhārā	يَنْهَارُوا yanhārū
3f	تَنْهَارَ tanhāra	تَنْهَارَا tanhārā	يَنْهَرْنَ yanharna

jussive

	singular	dual	plural
1	أَنْهَرْ ʔanhar	نَنْهَرْ nanhar	
2m	تَنْهَرْ tanhar	تَنْهَارَا tanhārā	تَنْهَارُوا tanhārū
2f	تَنْهَارِي tanhārī		تَنْهَرْنَ tanharna
3m	يَنْهَرْ yanhar	يَنْهَارَا yanhārā	يَنْهَارُوا yanhārū
3f	تَنْهَرْ tanhar	تَنْهَارَا tanhārā	يَنْهَرْنَ yanharna

imperative

	singular	dual	plural
2m	اِنْهَرْ inhar	اِنْهَارَا inhārā	اِنْهَارُوا inhārū
2f	اِنْهَارِي inhārī		اِنْهَرْنَ inharna

participles

active
مُنْهَار munhār

defective measure I **masdar: إِنْحِنَاء** inɧināʔ		و	ي	ء	*other*	**7d** **to bend**
	R[1]				✓	
	R[2]				✓	
	R[3]	✓	✓			

perfect

	singular	dual	plural
1	إِنْحَنَيْتُ inɧanaytu	إِنْحَنَيْنَا inɧanaynā	
2m	إِنْحَنَيْتَ inɧanayta	إِنْحَنَيْتُمَا inɧanaytumā	إِنْحَنَيْتُمْ inɧanaytum
2f	إِنْحَنَيْتِ inɧanayti		إِنْحَنَيْتُنَّ inɧanaytunna
3m	إِنْحَنَى inɧanā	إِنْحَنَيَا inɧanayā	إِنْحَنَوْا inɧanaw
3f	إِنْحَنَتْ inɧanat	إِنْحَنَتَا inɧanatā	إِنْحَنَيْنَ inɧanayna

indicative

	singular	dual	plural
1	أَنْحَنِي ʔanɧanī	نَنْحَنِي nanɧanī	
2m	تَنْحَنِي tanɧanī	تَنْحَنِيَانِ tanɧaniyāni	تَنْحَنُونَ tanɧanūna
2f	تَنْحَنِينَ tanɧanīna		تَنْحَنِينَ tanɧanīna
3m	يَنْحَنِي yanɧanī	يَنْحَنِيَانِ yanɧaniyāni	يَنْحَنُونَ yanɧanūna
3f	تَنْحَنِي tanɧanī	تَنْحَنِيَانِ tanɧaniyāni	يَنْحَنِينَ yanɧanīna

subjunctive

	singular	dual	plural
1	أَنْحَنِيَ ʔanɧaniya	نَنْحَنِيَ nanɧaniya	
2m	تَنْحَنِيَ tanɧaniya	تَنْحَنِيَا tanɧaniyā	تَنْحَنُوا tanɧanū
2f	تَنْحَنِي tanɧanī		تَنْحَنِينَ tanɧanīna
3m	يَنْحَنِيَ yanɧaniya	يَنْحَنِيَا yanɧaniyā	يَنْحَنُوا yanɧanū
3f	تَنْحَنِيَ tanɧaniya	تَنْحَنِيَا tanɧaniyā	يَنْحَنِينَ yanɧanīna

jussive

	singular	dual	plural
1	أَنْحَنِ ʔanɧani	نَنْحَنِ nanɧani	
2m	تَنْحَنِ tanɧani	تَنْحَنِيَا tanɧaniyā	تَنْحَنُوا tanɧanū
2f	تَنْحَنِي tanɧanī		تَنْحَنِينَ tanɧanīna
3m	يَنْحَنِ yanɧani	يَنْحَنِيَا yanɧaniyā	يَنْحَنُوا yanɧanū
3f	تَنْحَنِ tanɧani	تَنْحَنِيَا tanɧaniyā	يَنْحَنِينَ yanɧanīna

imperative

	singular	dual	plural
2m	إِنْحَنِ inɧani	إِنْحَنِيَا inɧaniyā	إِنْحَنُوا inɧanū
2f	إِنْحَنِي inɧanī		إِنْحَنِينَ inɧanīna

participles

active
مُنْحَنٍ munɧan(in)

sound measure VIII

masdar: اِعْتِبَار i3tibār

	و	ي	ء	other
R^1				✓
R^2				✓
R^3				✓

8s
to consider

perfect

	singular	dual	plural
1	اِعْتَبَرْتُ i3tabartu	اِعْتَبَرْنَا i3tabarnā	
2m	اِعْتَبَرْتَ i3tabarta	اِعْتَبَرْتُمَا i3tabartumā	اِعْتَبَرْتُمْ i3tabartum
2f	اِعْتَبَرْتِ i3tabarti		اِعْتَبَرْتُنَّ i3tabartunna
3m	اِعْتَبَرَ i3tabara	اِعْتَبَرَا i3tabarā	اِعْتَبَرُوا i3tabarū
3f	اِعْتَبَرَتْ i3tabarat	اِعْتَبَرَتَا i3tabaratā	اِعْتَبَرْنَ i3tabarna

indicative

	singular	dual	plural
1	أَعْتَبِرُ ʔa3tabiru	نَعْتَبِرُ na3tabiru	
2m	تَعْتَبِرُ ta3tabiru	تَعْتَبِرَانِ ta3tabirāni	تَعْتَبِرُونَ ta3tabirūna
2f	تَعْتَبِرِينَ ta3tabirīna		تَعْتَبِرْنَ ta3tabirna
3m	يَعْتَبِرُ ya3tabiru	يَعْتَبِرَانِ ya3tabirāni	يَعْتَبِرُونَ ya3tabirūna
3f	تَعْتَبِرُ ta3tabiru	تَعْتَبِرَانِ ta3tabirāni	يَعْتَبِرْنَ ya3tabirna

subjunctive

	singular	dual	plural
1	أَعْتَبِرَ ʔa3tabira	نَعْتَبِرَ na3tabira	
2m	تَعْتَبِرَ ta3tabira	تَعْتَبِرَا ta3tabirā	تَعْتَبِرُوا ta3tabirū
2f	تَعْتَبِرِي ta3tabirī		تَعْتَبِرْنَ ta3tabirna
3m	يَعْتَبِرَ ya3tabira	يَعْتَبِرَا ya3tabirā	يَعْتَبِرُوا ya3tabirū
3f	تَعْتَبِرَ ta3tabira	تَعْتَبِرَا ta3tabirā	يَعْتَبِرْنَ ya3tabirna

jussive

	singular	dual	plural
1	أَعْتَبِرْ ʔa3tabir	نَعْتَبِرْ na3tabir	
2m	تَعْتَبِرْ ta3tabir	تَعْتَبِرَا ta3tabirā	تَعْتَبِرُوا ta3tabirū
2f	تَعْتَبِرِي ta3tabirī		تَعْتَبِرْنَ ta3tabirna
3m	يَعْتَبِرْ ya3tabir	يَعْتَبِرَا ya3tabirā	يَعْتَبِرُوا ya3tabirū
3f	تَعْتَبِرْ ta3tabir	تَعْتَبِرَا ta3tabirā	يَعْتَبِرْنَ ya3tabirna

imperative

	singular	dual	plural
2m	اِعْتَبِرْ i3tabir	اِعْتَبِرَا i3tabirā	اِعْتَبِرُوا i3tabirū
2f	اِعْتَبِرِي i3tabirī		اِعْتَبِرْنَ i3tabirna

participles

active	passive
مُعْتَبِر mu3tabir	مُعْتَبَر mu3tabar

passive

perfect	imperfect
أُعْتُبِرَ u3tubira	يُعْتَبَرُ yu3tabaru

hamzated measure VIII

masdar: إِئْتِلَاف iʔtilāf

	و	ي	ء	other
R^1			✓	
R^2				✓
R^3				✓

8s(a)

to form a coalition

perfect

	singular	dual	plural
1	اِئْتَلَفْتُ iʔtalaftu	اِئْتَلَفْنَا iʔtalafnā	
2m	اِئْتَلَفْتَ iʔtalafta	اِئْتَلَفْتُمَا iʔtalaftumā	اِئْتَلَفْتُمْ iʔtalaftum
2f	اِئْتَلَفْتِ iʔtalafti		اِئْتَلَفْتُنَّ iʔtalaftunna
3m	اِئْتَلَفَ iʔtalafa	اِئْتَلَفَا iʔtalafā	اِئْتَلَفُوا iʔtalafū
3f	اِئْتَلَفَتْ iʔtalafat	اِئْتَلَفَتَا iʔtalafatā	اِئْتَلَفْنَ iʔtalafna

indicative

	singular	dual	plural
1	آتَلِفُ ʔātalifu	نَأْتَلِفُ naʔtalifu	
2m	تَأْتَلِفُ taʔtalifu	تَأْتَلِفَانِ taʔtalifāni	تَأْتَلِفُونَ taʔtalifūna
2f	تَأْتَلِفِينَ taʔtalifīna		تَأْتَلِفْنَ taʔtalifna
3m	يَأْتَلِفُ yaʔtalifu	يَأْتَلِفَانِ yaʔtalifāni	يَأْتَلِفُونَ yaʔtalifūna
3f	تَأْتَلِفُ taʔtalifu	تَأْتَلِفَانِ taʔtalifāni	يَأْتَلِفْنَ yaʔtalifna

subjunctive

	singular	dual	plural
1	آتَلِفَ ʔātalifa	نَأْتَلِفَ naʔtalifa	
2m	تَأْتَلِفَ taʔtalifa	تَأْتَلِفَا taʔtalifā	تَأْتَلِفُوا taʔtalifū
2f	تَأْتَلِفِي taʔtalifī		تَأْتَلِفْنَ taʔtalifna
3m	يَأْتَلِفَ yaʔtalifa	يَأْتَلِفَا yaʔtalifā	يَأْتَلِفُوا yaʔtalifū
3f	تَأْتَلِفَ taʔtalifa	تَأْتَلِفَا taʔtalifā	يَأْتَلِفْنَ yaʔtalifna

jussive

	singular	dual	plural
1	آتَلِفْ ʔātalif	نَأْتَلِفْ naʔtalif	
2m	تَأْتَلِفْ taʔtalif	تَأْتَلِفَا taʔtalifā	تَأْتَلِفُوا taʔtalifū
2f	تَأْتَلِفِي taʔtalifī		تَأْتَلِفْنَ taʔtalifna
3m	يَأْتَلِفْ yaʔtalif	يَأْتَلِفَا yaʔtalifā	يَأْتَلِفُوا yaʔtalifū
3f	تَأْتَلِفْ taʔtalif	تَأْتَلِفَا taʔtalifā	يَأْتَلِفْنَ yaʔtalifna

imperative

	singular	dual	plural
2m	اِئْتَلِفْ iʔtalif	اِئْتَلِفَا iʔtalifā	اِئْتَلِفُوا iʔtalifū
2f	اِئْتَلِفِي iʔtalifī		اِئْتَلِفْنَ iʔtalifna

participles

active	passive
مُؤْتَلِف muʔtalif	مُؤْتَلَف muʔtalaf

passive

perfect	imperfect
أُوْتُلِفَ uʔtulifa	يُؤْتَلَفُ yuʔtalafu

hamzated measure VIII

masdar: اِكْتِئَاب iktiʔāb

	و	ي	ء	other
R^1				✓
R^2			✓	
R^3				✓

8s(b) to become depressed

perfect

	singular	dual	plural
1	اِكْتَأَبْتُ iktaʔabtu	اِكْتَأَبْنَا iktaʔabnā	
2m	اِكْتَأَبْتَ iktaʔabta	اِكْتَأَبْتُمَا iktaʔabtumā	اِكْتَأَبْتُمْ iktaʔabtum
2f	اِكْتَأَبْتِ iktaʔabti		اِكْتَأَبْتُنَّ iktaʔabtunna
3m	اِكْتَأَبَ iktaʔaba	اِكْتَأَبَا iktaʔabā	اِكْتَأَبُوا iktaʔabū
3f	اِكْتَأَبَتْ iktaʔabat	اِكْتَأَبَتَا iktaʔabatā	اِكْتَأَبْنَ iktaʔabna

indicative

	singular	dual	plural
1	أَكْتَئِبُ ʔaktaʔibu	نَكْتَئِبُ naktaʔibu	
2m	تَكْتَئِبُ taktaʔibu	تَكْتَئِبَانِ taktaʔibāni	تَكْتَئِبُونَ taktaʔibūna
2f	تَكْتَئِبِينَ taktaʔibīna		تَكْتَئِبْنَ taktaʔibna
3m	يَكْتَئِبُ yaktaʔibu	يَكْتَئِبَانِ yaktaʔibāni	يَكْتَئِبُونَ yaktaʔibūna
3f	تَكْتَئِبُ taktaʔibu	تَكْتَئِبَانِ taktaʔibāni	يَكْتَئِبْنَ yaktaʔibna

subjunctive

	singular	dual	plural
1	أَكْتَئِبَ ʔaktaʔiba	نَكْتَئِبَ naktaʔiba	
2m	تَكْتَئِبَ taktaʔiba	تَكْتَئِبَا taktaʔibā	تَكْتَئِبُوا taktaʔibū
2f	تَكْتَئِبِي taktaʔibī		تَكْتَئِبْنَ taktaʔibna
3m	يَكْتَئِبَ yaktaʔiba	يَكْتَئِبَا yaktaʔibā	يَكْتَئِبُوا yaktaʔibū
3f	تَكْتَئِبَ taktaʔiba	تَكْتَئِبَا taktaʔibā	يَكْتَئِبْنَ yaktaʔibna

jussive

	singular	dual	plural
1	أَكْتَئِبْ ʔaktaʔib	نَكْتَئِبْ naktaʔib	
2m	تَكْتَئِبْ taktaʔib	تَكْتَئِبَا taktaʔibā	تَكْتَئِبُوا taktaʔibū
2f	تَكْتَئِبِي taktaʔibī		تَكْتَئِبْنَ taktaʔibna
3m	يَكْتَئِبْ yaktaʔib	يَكْتَئِبَا yaktaʔibā	يَكْتَئِبُوا yaktaʔibū
3f	تَكْتَئِبْ taktaʔib	تَكْتَئِبَا taktaʔibā	يَكْتَئِبْنَ yaktaʔibna

imperative

	singular	dual	plural
2m	اِكْتَئِبْ iktaʔib	اِكْتَئِبَا iktaʔibā	اِكْتَئِبُوا iktaʔibū
2f	اِكْتَئِبِي iktaʔibī		اِكْتَئِبْنَ iktaʔibna

participles

active	passive
مُكْتَئِب muktaʔib	مُكْتَأَب muktaʔab

passive

perfect	imperfect
اُكْتُئِبَ uktuʔiba	يُكْتَأَبُ yuktaʔabu

hamzated measure VIII

masdar: اِبْتِدَاء ibtidāʔ

	و	ي	ء	other
R^1				✓
R^2				✓
R^3			✓	

8s(c)
to begin

perfect

	singular	dual	plural
1	اِبْتَدَأْتُ ibtadaʔtu	اِبْتَدَأْنَا ibtadaʔnā	
2m	اِبْتَدَأْتَ ibtadaʔta	اِبْتَدَأْتُمَا ibtadaʔtumā	اِبْتَدَأْتُمْ ibtadaʔtum
2f	اِبْتَدَأْتِ ibtadaʔti		اِبْتَدَأْتُنَّ ibtadaʔtunna
3m	اِبْتَدَأَ ibtadaʔa	اِبْتَدَآ ibtadaʔā	اِبْتَدَؤُوا (اِبْتَدَأُوا) ibtadaʔū
3f	اِبْتَدَأَتْ ibtadaʔat	اِبْتَدَأَتَا ibtadaʔatā	اِبْتَدَأْنَ ibtadaʔna

indicative

	singular	dual	plural
1	أَبْتَدِئُ ʔabtadiʔu	نَبْتَدِئُ nabtadiʔu	
2m	تَبْتَدِئُ tabtadiʔu	تَبْتَدِئَانِ tabtadiʔāni	تَبْتَدِئُونَ tabtadiʔūna
2f	تَبْتَدِئِينَ tabtadiʔīna		تَبْتَدِئْنَ tabtadiʔna
3m	يَبْتَدِئُ yabtadiʔu	يَبْتَدِئَانِ yabtadiʔāni	يَبْتَدِئُونَ yabtadiʔūna
3f	تَبْتَدِئُ tabtadiʔu	تَبْتَدِئَانِ tabtadiʔāni	يَبْتَدِئْنَ yabtadiʔna

subjunctive

	singular	dual	plural
1	أَبْتَدِئَ ʔabtadiʔa	نَبْتَدِئَ nabtadiʔa	
2m	تَبْتَدِئَ tabtadiʔa	تَبْتَدِئَا tabtadiʔā	تَبْتَدِئُوا tabtadiʔū
2f	تَبْتَدِئِي tabtadiʔī		تَبْتَدِئْنَ tabtadiʔna
3m	يَبْتَدِئَ yabtadiʔa	يَبْتَدِئَا yabtadiʔā	يَبْتَدِئُوا yabtadiʔū
3f	تَبْتَدِئَ tabtadiʔa	تَبْتَدِئَا tabtadiʔā	يَبْتَدِئْنَ yabtadiʔna

jussive

	singular	dual	plural
1	أَبْتَدِئْ ʔabtadiʔ	نَبْتَدِئْ nabtadiʔ	
2m	تَبْتَدِئْ tabtadiʔ	تَبْتَدِئَا tabtadiʔā	تَبْتَدِئُوا tabtadiʔū
2f	تَبْتَدِئِي tabtadiʔī		تَبْتَدِئْنَ tabtadiʔna
3m	يَبْتَدِئْ yabtadiʔ	يَبْتَدِئَا yabtadiʔā	يَبْتَدِئُوا yabtadiʔū
3f	تَبْتَدِئْ tabtadiʔ	تَبْتَدِئَا tabtadiʔā	يَبْتَدِئْنَ yabtadiʔna

imperative

	singular	dual	plural
2m	اِبْتَدِئْ ibtadiʔ	اِبْتَدِئَا ibtadiʔā	اِبْتَدِئُوا ibtadiʔū
2f	اِبْتَدِئِي ibtadiʔī		اِبْتَدِئْنَ ibtadiʔna

participles

active	passive
مُبْتَدِئ mubtadiʔ	مُبْتَدَأ mubtadaʔ

passive

perfect	imperfect
أُبْتُدِئَ ubtudiʔa	يُبْتَدَأُ yubtadaʔu

geminate measure VIII		و	ي	ء	other	**8g1**
masdar: اِهْتِمَام ihtimām	R^1				✓	to be interested
	R^2				✓	
	R^3				✓	

perfect

	singular	dual	plural
1	اِهْتَمَمْتُ ihtamamtu	اِهْتَمَمْنَا ihtamamnā	
2m	اِهْتَمَمْتَ ihtamamta	اِهْتَمَمْتُمَا ihtamamtumā	اِهْتَمَمْتُمْ ihtamamtum
2f	اِهْتَمَمْتِ ihtamamti		اِهْتَمَمْتُنَّ ihtamamtunna
3m	اِهْتَمَّ ihtamma	اِهْتَمَّا ihtammā	اِهْتَمُّوا ihtammū
3f	اِهْتَمَّتْ ihtammat	اِهْتَمَّتَا ihtammatā	اِهْتَمَمْنَ ihtamamna

indicative

	singular	dual	plural
1	أَهْتَمُّ ʔahtammu	نَهْتَمُّ nahtammu	
2m	تَهْتَمُّ tahtammu	تَهْتَمَّانِ tahtammāni	تَهْتَمُّونَ tahtammūna
2f	تَهْتَمِّينَ tahtammīna		تَهْتَمِمْنَ tahtamimna
3m	يَهْتَمُّ yahtammu	يَهْتَمَّانِ yahtammāni	يَهْتَمُّونَ yahtammūna
3f	تَهْتَمُّ tahtammu	تَهْتَمَّانِ tahtammāni	يَهْتَمِمْنَ yahtamimna

subjunctive

	singular	dual	plural
1	أَهْتَمَّ ʔahtamma	نَهْتَمَّ nahtamma	
2m	تَهْتَمَّ tahtamma	تَهْتَمَّا tahtammā	تَهْتَمُّوا tahtammū
2f	تَهْتَمِّي tahtammī		تَهْتَمِمْنَ tahtamimna
3m	يَهْتَمَّ yahtamma	يَهْتَمَّا yahtammā	يَهْتَمُّوا yahtammū
3f	تَهْتَمَّ tahtamma	تَهْتَمَّا tahtammā	يَهْتَمِمْنَ yahtamimna

jussive

	singular	dual	plural
1	أَهْتَمَّ ʔahtamma	نَهْتَمَّ nahtamma	
2m	تَهْتَمَّ tahtamma	تَهْتَمَّا tahtammā	تَهْتَمُّوا tahtammū
2f	تَهْتَمِّي tahtammī		تَهْتَمِمْنَ tahtamimna
3m	يَهْتَمَّ yahtamma	يَهْتَمَّا yahtammā	يَهْتَمُّوا yahtammū
3f	تَهْتَمَّ tahtamma	تَهْتَمَّا tahtammā	يَهْتَمِمْنَ yahtamimna

imperative

	singular	dual	plural
2m	اِهْتَمَّ ihtamma	اِهْتَمَّا ihtammā	اِهْتَمُّوا ihtammū
2f	اِهْتَمِّي ihtammī		اِهْتَمِمْنَ ihtamimna

participles

active	passive
مُهْتَمّ muhtamm	مُهْتَمّ muhtamm

passive

perfect	imperfect
أُهْتُمَّ uhtumma	يُهْتَمُّ yuhtammu

assimilated gem. meas. VIII		و	ي	ء	*other*	**8g2**
masdar: اِضْطِرَار iḍṭirār	***R¹***				ض	**to force**
	R²				✓	
	R³				✓	

perfect

	singular	dual	plural
1	اِضْطَرَرْتُ iḍṭarartu	اِضْطَرَرْنَا iḍṭararnā	
2m	اِضْطَرَرْتَ iḍṭararta	اِضْطَرَرْتُمَا iḍṭarartumā	اِضْطَرَرْتُمْ iḍṭarartum
2f	اِضْطَرَرْتِ iḍṭararti		اِضْطَرَرْتُنَّ iḍṭarartunna
3m	اِضْطَرَّ iḍṭarra	اِضْطَرَّا iḍṭarrā	اِضْطَرُّوا iḍṭarrū
3f	اِضْطَرَّتْ iḍṭarrat	اِضْطَرَّتَا iḍṭarratā	اِضْطَرَرْنَ iḍṭararna

indicative

	singular	dual	plural
1	أَضْطَرُّ ʔaḍṭarru	نَضْطَرُّ naḍṭarru	
2m	تَضْطَرُّ taḍṭarru	تَضْطَرَّانِ taḍṭarrāni	تَضْطَرُّونَ taḍṭarrūna
2f	تَضْطَرِّينَ taḍṭarrīna		تَضْطَرِرْنَ taḍṭarirna
3m	يَضْطَرُّ yaḍṭarru	يَضْطَرَّانِ yaḍṭarrāni	يَضْطَرُّونَ yaḍṭarrūna
3f	تَضْطَرُّ taḍṭarru	تَضْطَرَّانِ taḍṭarrāni	يَضْطَرِرْنَ yaḍṭarirna

subjunctive

	singular	dual	plural
1	أَضْطَرَّ ʔaḍṭarra	نَضْطَرَّ naḍṭarra	
2m	تَضْطَرَّ taḍṭarra	تَضْطَرَّا taḍṭarrā	تَضْطَرُّوا taḍṭarrū
2f	تَضْطَرِّي taḍṭarrī		تَضْطَرِرْنَ taḍṭarirna
3m	يَضْطَرَّ yaḍṭarra	يَضْطَرَّا yaḍṭarrā	يَضْطَرُّوا yaḍṭarrū
3f	تَضْطَرَّ taḍṭarra	تَضْطَرَّا taḍṭarrā	يَضْطَرِرْنَ yaḍṭarirna

jussive

	singular	dual	plural
1	أَضْطَرَّ ʔaḍṭarra	نَضْطَرَّ naḍṭarra	
2m	تَضْطَرَّ taḍṭarra	تَضْطَرَّا taḍṭarrā	تَضْطَرُّوا taḍṭarrū
2f	تَضْطَرِّي taḍṭarrī		تَضْطَرِرْنَ taḍṭarirna
3m	يَضْطَرَّ yaḍṭarra	يَضْطَرَّا yaḍṭarrā	يَضْطَرُّوا yaḍṭarrū
3f	تَضْطَرَّ taḍṭarra	تَضْطَرَّا taḍṭarrā	يَضْطَرِرْنَ yaḍṭarirna

imperative

	singular	dual	plural
2m	اِضْطَرَّ iḍṭarra	اِضْطَرَّا iḍṭarrā	اِضْطَرُّوا iḍṭarrū
2f	اِضْطَرِّي iḍṭarrī		اِضْطَرِرْنَ iḍṭarirna

participles

active	passive
مُضْطَرّ muḍṭarr	مُضْطَرّ muḍṭarr

passive

perfect	imperfect
اُضْطُرَّ uḍṭurra	يُضْطَرُّ yuḍṭarru

assimilated measure VIII

masdar: اِتِّصَال ittiṣāl

	و	ي	ء	other
R^1	✓		(✓)	ت
R^2				✓
R^3				✓

8a1
to contact

perfect

	singular	dual	plural
1	اِتَّصَلْتُ ittaṣaltu	اِتَّصَلْنَا ittaṣalnā	
2m	اِتَّصَلْتَ ittaṣalta	اِتَّصَلْتُمَا ittaṣaltumā	اِتَّصَلْتُمْ ittaṣaltum
2f	اِتَّصَلْتِ ittaṣalti		اِتَّصَلْتُنَّ ittaṣaltunna
3m	اِتَّصَلَ ittaṣala	اِتَّصَلَا ittaṣalā	اِتَّصَلُوا ittaṣalū
3f	اِتَّصَلَتْ ittaṣalat	اِتَّصَلَتَا ittaṣalatā	اِتَّصَلْنَ ittaṣalna

indicative

	singular	dual	plural
1	أَتَّصِلُ ʔattaṣilu	نَتَّصِلُ nattaṣilu	
2m	تَتَّصِلُ tattaṣilu	تَتَّصِلَانِ tattaṣilāni	تَتَّصِلُونَ tattaṣilūna
2f	تَتَّصِلِينَ tattaṣilīna		تَتَّصِلْنَ tattaṣilna
3m	يَتَّصِلُ yattaṣilu	يَتَّصِلَانِ yattaṣilāni	يَتَّصِلُونَ yattaṣilūna
3f	تَتَّصِلُ tattaṣilu	تَتَّصِلَانِ tattaṣilāni	يَتَّصِلْنَ yattaṣilna

subjunctive

	singular	dual	plural
1	أَتَّصِلَ ʔattaṣila	نَتَّصِلَ nattaṣila	
2m	تَتَّصِلَ tattaṣila	تَتَّصِلَا tattaṣilā	تَتَّصِلُوا tattaṣilū
2f	تَتَّصِلِي tattaṣilī		تَتَّصِلْنَ tattaṣilna
3m	يَتَّصِلَ yattaṣila	يَتَّصِلَا yattaṣilā	يَتَّصِلُوا yattaṣilū
3f	تَتَّصِلَ tattaṣila	تَتَّصِلَا tattaṣilā	يَتَّصِلْنَ yattaṣilna

jussive

	singular	dual	plural
1	أَتَّصِلْ ʔattaṣil	نَتَّصِلْ nattaṣil	
2m	تَتَّصِلْ tattaṣil	تَتَّصِلَا tattaṣilā	تَتَّصِلُوا tattaṣilū
2f	تَتَّصِلِي tattaṣilī		تَتَّصِلْنَ tattaṣilna
3m	يَتَّصِلْ yattaṣil	يَتَّصِلَا yattaṣilā	يَتَّصِلُوا yattaṣilū
3f	تَتَّصِلْ tattaṣil	تَتَّصِلَا tattaṣilā	يَتَّصِلْنَ yattaṣilna

imperative

	singular	dual	plural
2m	اِتَّصِلْ ittaṣil	اِتَّصِلَا ittaṣilā	اِتَّصِلُوا ittaṣilū
2f	اِتَّصِلِي ittaṣilī		اِتَّصِلْنَ ittaṣilna

participles

active	passive
مُتَّصِل muttaṣil	مُتَّصَل muttaṣal

passive

perfect	imperfect
اُتُّصِلَ uttuṣila	يُتَّصَلُ yuttaṣalu

hamz. assimilated meas. VIII

masdar: اِتِّكَاء ittikāʔ

	و	ي	ء	*other*
R^1	✓			
R^2				✓
R^3			✓	

8a1(a)

to lean

perfect

	singular	dual	plural
1	اِتَّكَأْتُ ittakaʔtu	اِتَّكَأْنَا ittakaʔnā	
2m	اِتَّكَأْتَ ittakaʔta	اِتَّكَأْتُمَا ittakaʔtumā	اِتَّكَأْتُمْ ittakaʔtum
2f	اِتَّكَأْتِ ittakaʔti		اِتَّكَأْتُنَّ ittakaʔtunna
3m	اِتَّكَأَ ittakaʔa	اِتَّكَآ ittakaʔā	اِتَّكَؤُوا (اِتَّكَأُوا) ittakaʔū
3f	اِتَّكَأَتْ ittakaʔat	اِتَّكَأَتَا ittakaʔatā	اِتَّكَأْنَ ittakaʔna

indicative

	singular	dual	plural
1	أَتَّكِئُ ʔattakiʔu	نَتَّكِئُ nattakiʔu	
2m	تَتَّكِئُ tattakiʔu	تَتَّكِئَانِ tattakiʔāni	تَتَّكِئُونَ tattakiʔūna
2f	تَتَّكِئِينَ tattakiʔīna		تَتَّكِئْنَ tattakiʔna
3m	يَتَّكِئُ yattakiʔu	يَتَّكِئَانِ yattakiʔāni	يَتَّكِئُونَ yattakiʔūna
3f	تَتَّكِئُ tattakiʔu	تَتَّكِئَانِ tattakiʔāni	يَتَّكِئْنَ yattakiʔna

subjunctive

	singular	dual	plural
1	أَتَّكِئَ ʔattakiʔa	نَتَّكِئَ nattakiʔa	
2m	تَتَّكِئَ tattakiʔa	تَتَّكِئَا tattakiʔā	تَتَّكِئُوا tattakiʔū
2f	تَتَّكِئِي tattakiʔī		تَتَّكِئْنَ tattakiʔna
3m	يَتَّكِئَ yattakiʔa	يَتَّكِئَا yattakiʔā	يَتَّكِئُوا yattakiʔū
3f	تَتَّكِئَ tattakiʔa	تَتَّكِئَا tattakiʔā	يَتَّكِئْنَ yattakiʔna

jussive

	singular	dual	plural
1	أَتَّكِئْ ʔattakiʔ	نَتَّكِئْ nattakiʔ	
2m	تَتَّكِئْ tattakiʔ	تَتَّكِئَا tattakiʔā	تَتَّكِئُوا tattakiʔū
2f	تَتَّكِئِي tattakiʔī		تَتَّكِئْنَ tattakiʔna
3m	يَتَّكِئْ yattakiʔ	يَتَّكِئَا yattakiʔā	يَتَّكِئُوا yattakiʔū
3f	تَتَّكِئْ tattakiʔ	تَتَّكِئَا tattakiʔā	يَتَّكِئْنَ yattakiʔna

imperative

	singular	dual	plural
2m	اِتَّكِئْ ittakiʔ	اِتَّكِئَا ittakiʔā	اِتَّكِئُوا ittakiʔū
2f	اِتَّكِئِي ittakiʔī		اِتَّكِئْنَ ittakiʔna

participles

active	passive
مُتَّكِئ muttakiʔ	مُتَّكَأ muttakaʔ

passive

perfect	imperfect
اُتُّكِئَ uttukiʔa	يُتَّكَأُ yuttakaʔu

assimilated measure VIII

masdar: اِدِّخَار iddixār

	و	ي	ء	other
R^1				د / ذ
R^2				✓
R^3				✓

8a2
to store

perfect

	singular	dual	plural
1	اِدَّخَرْتُ iddaxartu	اِدَّخَرْنَا iddaxarnā	
2m	اِدَّخَرْتَ iddaxarta	اِدَّخَرْتُمَا iddaxartumā	اِدَّخَرْتُمْ iddaxartum
2f	اِدَّخَرْتِ iddaxarti		اِدَّخَرْتُنَّ iddaxartunna
3m	اِدَّخَرَ iddaxara	اِدَّخَرَا iddaxarā	اِدَّخَرُوا iddaxarū
3f	اِدَّخَرَتْ iddaxarat	اِدَّخَرَتَا iddaxaratā	اِدَّخَرْنَ iddaxarna

indicative

	singular	dual	plural
1	أَدَّخِرُ ʔaddaxiru	نَدَّخِرُ naddaxiru	
2m	تَدَّخِرُ taddaxiru	تَدَّخِرَانِ taddaxirāni	تَدَّخِرُونَ taddaxirūna
2f	تَدَّخِرِينَ taddaxirīna		تَدَّخِرْنَ taddaxirna
3m	يَدَّخِرُ yaddaxiru	يَدَّخِرَانِ yaddaxirāni	يَدَّخِرُونَ yaddaxirūna
3f	تَدَّخِرُ taddaxiru	تَدَّخِرَانِ taddaxirāni	يَدَّخِرْنَ yaddaxirna

subjunctive

	singular	dual	plural
1	أَدَّخِرَ ʔaddaxira	نَدَّخِرَ naddaxira	
2m	تَدَّخِرَ taddaxira	تَدَّخِرَا taddaxirā	تَدَّخِرُوا taddaxirū
2f	تَدَّخِرِي taddaxirī		تَدَّخِرْنَ taddaxirna
3m	يَدَّخِرَ yaddaxira	يَدَّخِرَا yaddaxirā	يَدَّخِرُوا yaddaxirū
3f	تَدَّخِرَ taddaxira	تَدَّخِرَا taddaxirā	يَدَّخِرْنَ yaddaxirna

jussive

	singular	dual	plural
1	أَدَّخِرْ ʔaddaxir	نَدَّخِرْ naddaxir	
2m	تَدَّخِرْ taddaxir	تَدَّخِرَا taddaxirā	تَدَّخِرُوا taddaxirū
2f	تَدَّخِرِي taddaxirī		تَدَّخِرْنَ taddaxirna
3m	يَدَّخِرْ yaddaxir	يَدَّخِرَا yaddaxirā	يَدَّخِرُوا yaddaxirū
3f	تَدَّخِرْ taddaxir	تَدَّخِرَا taddaxirā	يَدَّخِرْنَ yaddaxirna

imperative

	singular	dual	plural
2m	اِدَّخِرْ iddaxir	اِدَّخِرَا iddaxirā	اِدَّخِرُوا iddaxirū
2f	اِدَّخِرِي iddaxirī		اِدَّخِرْنَ iddaxirna

participles

active	passive
مُدَّخِر muddaxir	مُدَّخَر muddaxar

passive

perfect	imperfect
اُدُّخِرَ udduxira	يُدَّخَرُ yuddaxaru

assimilated measure VIII

masdar: اِطِّلَاع iṭṭilā3

	و	ي	ء	other
R¹				ط
R²				✓
R³				✓

8a3

to become acquainted

perfect

	singular	dual	plural
1	اِطَّلَعْتُ iṭṭala3tu	اِطَّلَعْنَا iṭṭala3nā	
2m	اِطَّلَعْتَ iṭṭala3ta	اِطَّلَعْتُمَا iṭṭala3tumā	اِطَّلَعْتُمْ iṭṭala3tum
2f	اِطَّلَعْتِ iṭṭala3ti		اِطَّلَعْتُنَّ iṭṭala3tunna
3m	اِطَّلَعَ iṭṭala3a	اِطَّلَعَا iṭṭala3ā	اِطَّلَعُوا iṭṭala3ū
3f	اِطَّلَعَتْ iṭṭala3at	اِطَّلَعَتَا iṭṭala3atā	اِطَّلَعْنَ iṭṭala3na

indicative

	singular	dual	plural
1	أَطَّلِعُ ʔaṭṭali3u	نَطَّلِعُ naṭṭali3u	
2m	تَطَّلِعُ taṭṭali3u	تَطَّلِعَانِ taṭṭali3āni	تَطَّلِعُونَ taṭṭali3ūna
2f	تَطَّلِعِينَ taṭṭali3īna		تَطَّلِعْنَ taṭṭali3na
3m	يَطَّلِعُ yaṭṭali3u	يَطَّلِعَانِ yaṭṭali3āni	يَطَّلِعُونَ yaṭṭali3ūna
3f	تَطَّلِعُ taṭṭali3u	تَطَّلِعَانِ taṭṭali3āni	يَطَّلِعْنَ yaṭṭali3na

subjunctive

	singular	dual	plural
1	أَطَّلِعَ ʔaṭṭali3a	نَطَّلِعَ naṭṭali3a	
2m	تَطَّلِعَ taṭṭali3a	تَطَّلِعَا taṭṭali3ā	تَطَّلِعُوا taṭṭali3ū
2f	تَطَّلِعِي taṭṭali3ī		تَطَّلِعْنَ taṭṭali3na
3m	يَطَّلِعَ yaṭṭali3a	يَطَّلِعَا yaṭṭali3ā	يَطَّلِعُوا yaṭṭali3ū
3f	تَطَّلِعَ taṭṭali3a	تَطَّلِعَا taṭṭali3ā	يَطَّلِعْنَ yaṭṭali3na

jussive

	singular	dual	plural
1	أَطَّلِعْ ʔaṭṭali3	نَطَّلِعْ naṭṭali3	
2m	تَطَّلِعْ taṭṭali3	تَطَّلِعَا taṭṭali3ā	تَطَّلِعُوا taṭṭali3ū
2f	تَطَّلِعِي taṭṭali3ī		تَطَّلِعْنَ taṭṭali3na
3m	يَطَّلِعْ yaṭṭali3	يَطَّلِعَا yaṭṭali3ā	يَطَّلِعُوا yaṭṭali3ū
3f	تَطَّلِعْ taṭṭali3	تَطَّلِعَا taṭṭali3ā	يَطَّلِعْنَ yaṭṭali3na

imperative

	singular	dual	plural
2m	اِطَّلِعْ iṭṭali3	اِطَّلِعَا iṭṭali3ā	اِطَّلِعُوا iṭṭali3ū
2f	اِطَّلِعِي iṭṭali3ī		اِطَّلِعْنَ iṭṭali3na

participles

active	passive
مُطَّلِع muṭṭali3	مُطَّلَع muṭṭala3

passive

perfect	imperfect
أُطُّلِعَ uṭṭuli3a	يُطَّلَعُ yuṭṭala3u

assimilated measure VIII		و	ي	ء	other	**8a4**
masdar: اِزْدِهَار izdihār	R^1				ز	**to flourish**
	R^2	✓			✓	
	R^3				✓	

perfect

	singular	dual	plural
1	اِزْدَهَرْتُ izdahartu	اِزْدَهَرْنَا izdaharnā	
2m	اِزْدَهَرْتَ izdaharta	اِزْدَهَرْتُمَا izdahartumā	اِزْدَهَرْتُمْ izdahartum
2f	اِزْدَهَرْتِ izdaharti		اِزْدَهَرْتُنَّ izdahartunna
3m	اِزْدَهَرَ izdahara	اِزْدَهَرَا izdaharā	اِزْدَهَرُوا izdaharū
3f	اِزْدَهَرَتْ izdaharat	اِزْدَهَرَتَا izdaharatā	اِزْدَهَرْنَ izdaharna

indicative

	singular	dual	plural
1	أَزْدَهِرُ ʔazdahiru	نَزْدَهِرُ nazdahiru	
2m	تَزْدَهِرُ tazdahiru	تَزْدَهِرَانِ tazdahirāni	تَزْدَهِرُونَ tazdahirūna
2f	تَزْدَهِرِينَ tazdahirīna		تَزْدَهِرْنَ tazdahirna
3m	يَزْدَهِرُ yazdahiru	يَزْدَهِرَانِ yazdahirāni	يَزْدَهِرُونَ yazdahirūna
3f	تَزْدَهِرُ tazdahiru	تَزْدَهِرَانِ tazdahirāni	يَزْدَهِرْنَ yazdahirna

subjunctive

	singular	dual	plural
1	أَزْدَهِرَ ʔazdahira	نَزْدَهِرَ nazdahira	
2m	تَزْدَهِرَ tazdahira	تَزْدَهِرَا tazdahirā	تَزْدَهِرُوا tazdahirū
2f	تَزْدَهِرِي tazdahirī		تَزْدَهِرْنَ tazdahirna
3m	يَزْدَهِرَ yazdahira	يَزْدَهِرَا yazdahirā	يَزْدَهِرُوا yazdahirū
3f	تَزْدَهِرَ tazdahira	تَزْدَهِرَا tazdahirā	يَزْدَهِرْنَ yazdahirna

jussive

	singular	dual	plural
1	أَزْدَهِرْ ʔazdahir	نَزْدَهِرْ nazdahir	
2m	تَزْدَهِرْ tazdahir	تَزْدَهِرَا tazdahirā	تَزْدَهِرُوا tazdahirū
2f	تَزْدَهِرِي tazdahirī		تَزْدَهِرْنَ tazdahirna
3m	يَزْدَهِرْ yazdahir	يَزْدَهِرَا yazdahirā	يَزْدَهِرُوا yazdahirū
3f	تَزْدَهِرْ tazdahir	تَزْدَهِرَا tazdahirā	يَزْدَهِرْنَ yazdahirna

imperative

	singular	dual	plural
2m	اِزْدَهِرْ izdahir	اِزْدَهِرَا izdahirā	اِزْدَهِرُوا izdahirū
2f	اِزْدَهِرِي izdahirī		اِزْدَهِرْنَ izdahirna

participles

active	passive
مُزْدَهِر muzdahir	مُزْدَهَر muzdahar

passive

perfect	imperfect
أُزْدُهِرَ uzduhira	يُزْدَهَرُ yuzdaharu

assimilated measure VIII

masdar: اِصْطِحَاب iṣṭiɦāb

	و	ي	ء	other
R^1				ص
R^2				✓
R^3				✓

8a5
to accompany

perfect

	singular	dual	plural
1	اِصْطَحَبْتُ iṣṭaɦabtu	اِصْطَحَبْنَا iṣṭaɦabnā	
2m	اِصْطَحَبْتَ iṣṭaɦabta	اِصْطَحَبْتُمَا iṣṭaɦabtumā	اِصْطَحَبْتُمْ iṣṭaɦabtum
2f	اِصْطَحَبْتِ iṣṭaɦabti		اِصْطَحَبْتُنَّ iṣṭaɦabtunna
3m	اِصْطَحَبَ iṣṭaɦaba	اِصْطَحَبَا iṣṭaɦabā	اِصْطَحَبُوا iṣṭaɦabū
3f	اِصْطَحَبَتْ iṣṭaɦabat	اِصْطَحَبَتَا iṣṭaɦabatā	اِصْطَحَبْنَ iṣṭaɦabna

indicative

	singular	dual	plural
1	أَصْطَحِبُ ʔaṣṭaɦibu	نَصْطَحِبُ naṣṭaɦibu	
2m	تَصْطَحِبُ taṣṭaɦibu	تَصْطَحِبَانِ taṣṭaɦibāni	تَصْطَحِبُونَ taṣṭaɦibūna
2f	تَصْطَحِبِينَ taṣṭaɦibīna		تَصْطَحِبْنَ taṣṭaɦibna
3m	يَصْطَحِبُ yaṣṭaɦibu	يَصْطَحِبَانِ yaṣṭaɦibāni	يَصْطَحِبُونَ yaṣṭaɦibūna
3f	تَصْطَحِبُ taṣṭaɦibu	تَصْطَحِبَانِ taṣṭaɦibāni	يَصْطَحِبْنَ yaṣṭaɦibna

subjunctive

	singular	dual	plural
1	أَصْطَحِبَ ʔaṣṭaɦiba	نَصْطَحِبَ naṣṭaɦiba	
2m	تَصْطَحِبَ taṣṭaɦiba	تَصْطَحِبَا taṣṭaɦibā	تَصْطَحِبُوا taṣṭaɦibū
2f	تَصْطَحِبِي taṣṭaɦibī		تَصْطَحِبْنَ taṣṭaɦibna
3m	يَصْطَحِبَ yaṣṭaɦiba	يَصْطَحِبَا yaṣṭaɦibā	يَصْطَحِبُوا yaṣṭaɦibū
3f	تَصْطَحِبَ taṣṭaɦiba	تَصْطَحِبَا taṣṭaɦibā	يَصْطَحِبْنَ yaṣṭaɦibna

jussive

	singular	dual	plural
1	أَصْطَحِبْ ʔaṣṭaɦib	نَصْطَحِبْ naṣṭaɦib	
2m	تَصْطَحِبْ taṣṭaɦib	تَصْطَحِبَا taṣṭaɦibā	تَصْطَحِبُوا taṣṭaɦibū
2f	تَصْطَحِبِي taṣṭaɦibī		تَصْطَحِبْنَ taṣṭaɦibna
3m	يَصْطَحِبْ yaṣṭaɦib	يَصْطَحِبَا yaṣṭaɦibā	يَصْطَحِبُوا yaṣṭaɦibū
3f	تَصْطَحِبْ taṣṭaɦib	تَصْطَحِبَا taṣṭaɦibā	يَصْطَحِبْنَ yaṣṭaɦibna

imperative

	singular	dual	plural
2m	اِصْطَحِبْ iṣṭaɦib	اِصْطَحِبَا iṣṭaɦibā	اِصْطَحِبُوا iṣṭaɦibū
2f	اِصْطَحِبِي iṣṭaɦibī		اِصْطَحِبْنَ iṣṭaɦibna

participles

active	passive
مُصْطَحِب muṣṭaɦib	مُصْطَحَب muṣṭaɦab

passive

perfect	imperfect
اُصْطُحِبَ uṣṭuɦiba	يُصْطَحَبُ yuṣṭaɦabu

assimilated measure VIII		و	ي	ء	other	**8a6**
masdar: اِضْطِرَاب idṭirāb	R^1				ض	to be disturbed
	R^2				✓	
	R^3				✓	

perfect

	singular	dual	plural
1	اِضْطَرَبْتُ idṭarabtu	اِضْطَرَبْنَا idṭarabnā	
2m	اِضْطَرَبْتَ idṭarabta	اِضْطَرَبْتُمَا idṭarabtumā	اِضْطَرَبْتُمْ idṭarabtum
2f	اِضْطَرَبْتِ idṭarabti		اِضْطَرَبْتُنَّ idṭarabtunna
3m	اِضْطَرَبَ idṭaraba	اِضْطَرَبَا idṭarabā	اِضْطَرَبُوا idṭarabū
3f	اِضْطَرَبَتْ idṭarabat	اِضْطَرَبَتَا idṭarabatā	اِضْطَرَبْنَ idṭarabna

indicative

	singular	dual	plural
1	أَضْطَرِبُ ʔadṭaribu	نَضْطَرِبُ nadṭaribu	
2m	تَضْطَرِبُ tadṭaribu	تَضْطَرِبَانِ tadṭaribāni	تَضْطَرِبُونَ tadṭaribūna
2f	تَضْطَرِبِينَ tadṭaribīna		تَضْطَرِبْنَ tadṭaribna
3m	يَضْطَرِبُ yadṭaribu	يَضْطَرِبَانِ yadṭaribāni	يَضْطَرِبُونَ yadṭaribūna
3f	تَضْطَرِبُ tadṭaribu	تَضْطَرِبَانِ tadṭaribāni	يَضْطَرِبْنَ yadṭaribna

subjunctive

	singular	dual	plural
1	أَضْطَرِبَ ʔadṭariba	نَضْطَرِبَ nadṭariba	
2m	تَضْطَرِبَ tadṭariba	تَضْطَرِبَا tadṭaribā	تَضْطَرِبُوا tadṭaribū
2f	تَضْطَرِبِي tadṭaribī		تَضْطَرِبْنَ tadṭaribna
3m	يَضْطَرِبَ yadṭariba	يَضْطَرِبَا yadṭaribā	يَضْطَرِبُوا yadṭaribū
3f	تَضْطَرِبَ tadṭariba	تَضْطَرِبَا tadṭaribā	يَضْطَرِبْنَ yadṭaribna

jussive

	singular	dual	plural
1	أَضْطَرِبْ ʔadṭarib	نَضْطَرِبْ nadṭarib	
2m	تَضْطَرِبْ tadṭarib	تَضْطَرِبَا tadṭaribā	تَضْطَرِبُوا tadṭaribū
2f	تَضْطَرِبِي tadṭaribī		تَضْطَرِبْنَ tadṭaribna
3m	يَضْطَرِبْ yadṭarib	يَضْطَرِبَا yadṭaribā	يَضْطَرِبُوا yadṭaribū
3f	تَضْطَرِبْ tadṭarib	تَضْطَرِبَا tadṭaribā	يَضْطَرِبْنَ yadṭaribna

imperative

	singular	dual	plural
2m	اِضْطَرِبْ idṭarib	اِضْطَرِبَا idṭaribā	اِضْطَرِبُوا idṭaribū
2f	اِضْطَرِبِي idṭaribī		اِضْطَرِبْنَ idṭaribna

participles

active	passive
مُضْطَرِب mudṭarib	مُضْطَرَب mudṭarab

passive

perfect	imperfect
اُضْطُرِبَ udṭuriba	يُضْطَرَبُ yudṭarabu

hollow measure VIII

masdar: اِحْتِيَاج iḥtiyāj

	و	ي	ء	*other*
R^1				✓
R^2	✓	✓		
R^3				✓

8h1
to need

perfect

	singular	dual	plural
1	اِحْتَجْتُ iḥtajtu	اِحْتَجْنَا iḥtajnā	
2m	اِحْتَجْتَ iḥtajta	اِحْتَجْتُمَا iḥtajtumā	اِحْتَجْتُمْ iḥtajtum
2f	اِحْتَجْتِ iḥtajti		اِحْتَجْتُنَّ iḥtajtunna
3m	اِحْتَاجَ iḥtāja	اِحْتَاجَا iḥtājā	اِحْتَاجُوا iḥtājū
3f	اِحْتَاجَتْ iḥtājat	اِحْتَاجَتَا iḥtājatā	اِحْتَجْنَ iḥtajna

indicative

	singular	dual	plural
1	أَحْتَاجُ ʔaḥtāju	نَحْتَاجُ naḥtāju	
2m	تَحْتَاجُ taḥtāju	تَحْتَاجَانِ taḥtājāni	تَحْتَاجُونَ taḥtājūna
2f	تَحْتَاجِينَ taḥtājīna		تَحْتَجْنَ taḥtajna
3m	يَحْتَاجُ yaḥtāju	يَحْتَاجَانِ yaḥtājāni	يَحْتَاجُونَ yaḥtājūna
3f	تَحْتَاجُ taḥtāju	تَحْتَاجَانِ taḥtājāni	يَحْتَجْنَ yaḥtajna

subjunctive

	singular	dual	plural
1	أَحْتَاجَ ʔaḥtāja	نَحْتَاجَ naḥtāja	
2m	تَحْتَاجَ taḥtāja	تَحْتَاجَا taḥtājā	تَحْتَاجُوا taḥtājū
2f	تَحْتَاجِي taḥtājī		تَحْتَجْنَ taḥtajna
3m	يَحْتَاجَ yaḥtāja	يَحْتَاجَا yaḥtājā	يَحْتَاجُوا yaḥtājū
3f	تَحْتَاجَ taḥtāja	تَحْتَاجَا taḥtājā	يَحْتَجْنَ yaḥtajna

jussive

	singular	dual	plural
1	أَحْتَجْ ʔaḥtaj	نَحْتَجْ naḥtaj	
2m	تَحْتَجْ taḥtaj	تَحْتَاجَا taḥtājā	تَحْتَاجُوا taḥtājū
2f	تَحْتَاجِي taḥtājī		تَحْتَجْنَ taḥtajna
3m	يَحْتَجْ yaḥtaj	يَحْتَاجَا yaḥtājā	يَحْتَاجُوا yaḥtājū
3f	تَحْتَجْ taḥtaj	تَحْتَاجَا taḥtājā	يَحْتَجْنَ yaḥtajna

imperative

	singular	dual	plural
2m	اِحْتَجْ iḥtaj	اِحْتَاجَا iḥtājā	اِحْتَاجُوا iḥtājū
2f	اِحْتَاجِي iḥtājī		اِحْتَجْنَ iḥtajna

participles

active	passive
مُحْتَاج muḥtāj	مُحْتَاج muḥtāj

passive

perfect	imperfect
اُحْتِيجَ uḥtīja	يُحْتَاجُ yuḥtāju

hamzated hollow measure VIII

masdar: اِسْتِيَاء istiyāʔ

	و	ي	ء	*other*
R¹				✓
R²	✓	✓		
R³			✓	

8h1(a)

to be displeased

perfect

	singular	dual	plural
1	اِسْتَأْتُ istaʔtu	اِسْتَأْنَا istaʔnā	
2m	اِسْتَأْتَ istaʔta	اِسْتَأْتُمَا istaʔtumā	اِسْتَأْتُمْ istaʔtum
2f	اِسْتَأْتِ istaʔti		اِسْتَأْتُنَّ istaʔtunna
3m	اِسْتَاءَ istāʔa	اِسْتَاءَا istāʔā	اِسْتَاؤُوا (اِسْتَاءُوا) istāʔū
3f	اِسْتَاءَتْ istāʔat	اِسْتَاءَتَا istāʔatā	اِسْتَأْنَ istaʔna

indicative

	singular	dual	plural
1	أَسْتَاءُ ʔastāʔu	نَسْتَاءُ nastāʔu	
2m	تَسْتَاءُ tastāʔu	تَسْتَاءَانِ tastāʔāni	تَسْتَاؤُونَ (تَسْتَاءُونَ) tastāʔūna
2f	تَسْتَائِينَ tastāʔīna		تَسْتَأْنَ tastaʔna
3m	يَسْتَاءُ yastāʔu	يَسْتَاءَانِ yastāʔāni	يَسْتَاؤُونَ (يَسْتَاءُونَ) yastāʔūna
3f	تَسْتَاءُ tastāʔu	تَسْتَاءَانِ tastāʔāni	يَسْتَأْنَ yastaʔna

subjunctive

	singular	dual	plural
1	أَسْتَاءَ ʔastāʔu	نَسْتَاءَ nastāʔu	
2m	تَسْتَاءَ tastāʔu	تَسْتَاءَا tastāʔā	تَسْتَاؤُوا (تَسْتَاءُوا) tastāʔū
2f	تَسْتَائِي tastāʔīna		تَسْتَأْنَ tastaʔna
3m	يَسْتَاءَ yastāʔu	يَسْتَاءَا yastāʔā	يَسْتَاؤُوا (يَسْتَاءُوا) yastāʔū
3f	تَسْتَاءَ tastāʔu	تَسْتَاءَا tastāʔā	يَسْتَأْنَ yastaʔna

jussive

	singular	dual	plural
1	أَسْتَأْ ʔastaʔ	نَسْتَأْ nastaʔ	
2m	تَسْتَأْ tastaʔ	تَسْتَاءَا tastāʔā	تَسْتَاؤُوا (تَسْتَاءُوا) tastāʔū
2f	تَسْتَائِي tastāʔī		تَسْتَأْنَ tastaʔna
3m	يَسْتَأْ yastaʔ	يَسْتَاءَا yastāʔā	يَسْتَاؤُوا (يَسْتَاءُوا) yastāʔū
3f	تَسْتَأْ tastaʔ	تَسْتَاءَا tastāʔā	يَسْتَأْنَ yastaʔna

imperative

	singular	dual	plural
2m	اِسْتَأْ tastaʔ	اِسْتَاءَا tastāʔā	اِسْتَاؤُوا (اِسْتَاءُوا) tastāʔū
2f	اِسْتَائِي tastāʔī		اِسْتَأْنَ tastaʔna

participles

active
مُسْتَاء mustāʔ

assimilated hollow meas. VIII

masdar: اِزْدِيَاد izdiyād

	و	ي	ء	*other*
R^1				ز
R^2	✓	✓		
R^3				✓

8h2

to increase

perfect

	singular	dual	plural
1	اِزْدَدْتُ izdadtu	اِزْدَدْنَا izdadnā	
2m	اِزْدَدْتَ izdadta	اِزْدَدْتُمَا izdadtumā	اِزْدَدْتُمْ izdadtum
2f	اِزْدَدْتِ izdadti		اِزْدَدْتُنَّ izdadtunna
3m	اِزْدَادَ izdāda	اِزْدَادَا izdādā	اِزْدَادُوا izdādū
3f	اِزْدَادَتْ izdādat	اِزْدَادَتَا izdādatā	اِزْدَدْنَ izdadna

indicative

	singular	dual	plural
1	أَزْدَادُ ʔazdādu	نَزْدَادُ nazdādu	
2m	تَزْدَادُ tazdādu	تَزْدَادَانِ tazdādāni	تَزْدَادُونَ tazdādūna
2f	تَزْدَادِينَ tazdādīna		تَزْدَدْنَ tazdadna
3m	يَزْدَادُ yazdādu	يَزْدَادَانِ yazdādāni	يَزْدَادُونَ yazdādūna
3f	تَزْدَادُ tazdādu	تَزْدَادَانِ tazdādāni	يَزْدَدْنَ yazdadna

subjunctive

	singular	dual	plural
1	أَزْدَادَ ʔazdāda	نَزْدَادَ nazdāda	
2m	تَزْدَادَ tazdāda	تَزْدَادَا tazdādā	تَزْدَادُوا tazdādū
2f	تَزْدَادِي tazdādī		تَزْدَدْنَ tazdadna
3m	يَزْدَادَ yazdāda	يَزْدَادَا yazdādā	يَزْدَادُوا yazdādū
3f	تَزْدَادَ tazdāda	تَزْدَادَا tazdādā	يَزْدَدْنَ yazdadna

jussive

	singular	dual	plural
1	أَزْدَدْ ʔazdad	نَزْدَدْ nazdad	
2m	تَزْدَدْ tazdad	تَزْدَادَا tazdādā	تَزْدَادُوا tazdādū
2f	تَزْدَادِي tazdādī		تَزْدَدْنَ tazdadna
3m	يَزْدَدْ yazdad	يَزْدَادَا yazdādā	يَزْدَادُوا yazdādū
3f	تَزْدَدْ tazdad	تَزْدَادَا tazdādā	يَزْدَدْنَ yazdadna

imperative

	singular	dual	plural
2m	اِزْدَدْ izdad	اِزْدَادَا izdādā	اِزْدَادُوا izdādū
2f	اِزْدَادِي izdādī		اِزْدَدْنَ izdadna

participles

active	passive
مُزْدَادٌ muzdād	مُزْدَادٌ muzdād

passive

perfect	imperfect
أُزْدِيدَ uzdīda	يُزْدَادُ yuzdādu

assimilated hollow meas. VIII

masdar: اِصْطِيَاد iṣṭiyād

	و	ي	ء	other
R¹				ص
R²	✓	✓		
R³				✓

8h3
to hunt

perfect

	singular	dual	plural
1	اِصْطَدْتُ iṣṭadtu	اِصْطَدْنَا iṣṭadnā	
2m	اِصْطَدْتَ iṣṭadta	اِصْطَدْتُمَا iṣṭadtumā	اِصْطَدْتُمْ iṣṭadtum
2f	اِصْطَدْتِ iṣṭadti		اِصْطَدْتُنَّ iṣṭadtunna
3m	اِصْطَادَ iṣṭāda	اِصْطَادَا iṣṭādā	اِصْطَادُوا iṣṭādū
3f	اِصْطَادَتْ iṣṭādat	اِصْطَادَتَا iṣṭādatā	اِصْطَدْنَ iṣṭadna

indicative

	singular	dual	plural
1	أَصْطَادُ ʔaṣṭādu	نَصْطَادُ naṣṭādu	
2m	تَصْطَادُ taṣṭādu	تَصْطَادَانِ taṣṭādāni	تَصْطَادُونَ taṣṭādūna
2f	تَصْطَادِينَ taṣṭādīna		تَصْطَدْنَ taṣṭadna
3m	يَصْطَادُ yaṣṭādu	يَصْطَادَانِ yaṣṭādāni	يَصْطَادُونَ yaṣṭādūna
3f	تَصْطَادُ taṣṭādu	تَصْطَادَانِ taṣṭādāni	يَصْطَدْنَ yaṣṭadna

subjunctive

	singular	dual	plural
1	أَصْطَادَ ʔaṣṭāda	نَصْطَادَ naṣṭāda	
2m	تَصْطَادَ taṣṭāda	تَصْطَادَا taṣṭādā	تَصْطَادُوا taṣṭādū
2f	تَصْطَادِي taṣṭādī		تَصْطَدْنَ taṣṭadna
3m	يَصْطَادَ yaṣṭāda	يَصْطَادَا yaṣṭādā	يَصْطَادُوا yaṣṭādū
3f	تَصْطَادَ taṣṭāda	تَصْطَادَا taṣṭādā	يَصْطَدْنَ yaṣṭadna

jussive

	singular	dual	plural
1	أَصْطَدْ ʔaṣṭad	نَصْطَدْ naṣṭad	
2m	تَصْطَدْ taṣṭad	تَصْطَادَا taṣṭādā	تَصْطَادُوا taṣṭādū
2f	تَصْطَادِي taṣṭādī		تَصْطَدْنَ taṣṭadna
3m	يَصْطَدْ yaṣṭad	يَصْطَادَا yaṣṭādā	يَصْطَادُوا yaṣṭādū
3f	تَصْطَدْ taṣṭad	تَصْطَادَا taṣṭādā	يَصْطَدْنَ yaṣṭadna

imperative

	singular	dual	plural
2m	اِصْطَدْ iṣṭad	اِصْطَادَا iṣṭādā	اِصْطَادُوا iṣṭādū
2f	اِصْطَادِي iṣṭādī		اِصْطَدْنَ iṣṭadna

participles

active	passive
مُصْطَاد muṣṭād	مُصْطَاد muṣṭād

passive

perfect	imperfect
اُصْطِيدَ uṣṭīda	يُصْطَادُ yuṣṭādu

defective measure VIII

masdar: اِنْتِهَاء intihāʔ

	و	ي	ء	other
R^1				✓
R^2				✓
R^3	✓	✓		

8d1
to end

perfect

	singular	dual	plural
1	اِنْتَهَيْتُ intahaytu	اِنْتَهَيْنَا intahaynā	
2m	اِنْتَهَيْتَ intahayta	اِنْتَهَيْتُمَا intahaytumā	اِنْتَهَيْتُمْ intahaytum
2f	اِنْتَهَيْتِ intahayti		اِنْتَهَيْتُنَّ intahaytunna
3m	اِنْتَهَى intahā	اِنْتَهَيَا intahayā	اِنْتَهَوْا intahaw
3f	اِنْتَهَتْ intahat	اِنْتَهَتَا intahatā	اِنْتَهَيْنَ intahayna

indicative

	singular	dual	plural
1	أَنْتَهِي ʔantahī	نَنْتَهِي nantahī	
2m	تَنْتَهِي tantahī	تَنْتَهِيَانِ tantahiyāni	تَنْتَهُونَ tantahūna
2f	تَنْتَهِينَ tantahīna		تَنْتَهِينَ tantahīna
3m	يَنْتَهِي yantahī	يَنْتَهِيَانِ yantahiyāni	يَنْتَهُونَ yantahūna
3f	تَنْتَهِي tantahī	تَنْتَهِيَانِ tantahiyāni	يَنْتَهِينَ yantahīna

subjunctive

	singular	dual	plural
1	أَنْتَهِيَ ʔantahiya	نَنْتَهِيَ nantahiya	
2m	تَنْتَهِيَ tantahiya	تَنْتَهِيَا tantahiyā	تَنْتَهُوا tantahū
2f	تَنْتَهِي tantahī		تَنْتَهِينَ tantahīna
3m	يَنْتَهِيَ yantahiya	يَنْتَهِيَا yantahiyā	يَنْتَهُوا yantahū
3f	تَنْتَهِيَ tantahiya	تَنْتَهِيَا tantahiyā	يَنْتَهِينَ yantahīna

jussive

	singular	dual	plural
1	أَنْتَهِ ʔantahi	نَنْتَهِ nantahi	
2m	تَنْتَهِ tantahi	تَنْتَهِيَا tantahiyā	تَنْتَهُوا tantahū
2f	تَنْتَهِي tantahī		تَنْتَهِينَ tantahīna
3m	يَنْتَهِ yantahi	يَنْتَهِيَا yantahiyā	يَنْتَهُوا yantahū
3f	تَنْتَهِ tantahi	تَنْتَهِيَا tantahiyā	يَنْتَهِينَ yantahīna

imperative

	singular	dual	plural
2m	اِنْتَهِ intahi	اِنْتَهِيَا intahiyā	اِنْتَهُوا intahū
2f	اِنْتَهِي intahī		اِنْتَهِينَ intahīna

participles

active	passive
مُنْتَهٍ muntah(in)	مُنْتَهًى muntah(an)

passive

perfect	imperfect
أُنْتُهِيَ untuhiya	يُنْتَهَى yuntahā

assimilated defect. meas. VIII		و	ي	ء	other	**8d2**
masdar: اِتِّقاء ittiqāʔ	*R¹*				ت	to beware
	R²				✓	
	R³	✓	✓			

perfect

	singular	dual	plural
1	اِتَّقَيْتُ ittaqaytu	اِتَّقَيْنا ittaqaynā	
2m	اِتَّقَيْتَ ittaqayta	اِتَّقَيْتُما ittaqaytumā	اِتَّقَيْتُمْ ittaqaytum
2f	اِتَّقَيْتِ ittaqayti		اِتَّقَيْتُنَّ ittaqaytunna
3m	اِتَّقَى ittaqā	اِتَّقَيا ittaqayā	اِتَّقَوْا ittaqaw
3f	اِتَّقَتْ ittaqat	اِتَّقَتا ittaqatā	اِتَّقَيْنَ ittaqayna

indicative

	singular	dual	plural
1	أَتَّقِي ʔattaqī	نَتَّقِي nattaqī	
2m	تَتَّقِي tattaqī	تَتَّقِيانِ tattaqiyāni	تَتَّقُونَ tattaqūna
2f	تَتَّقِينَ tattaqīna		تَتَّقِينَ tattaqīna
3m	يَتَّقِي yattaqī	يَتَّقِيانِ yattaqiyāni	يَتَّقُونَ yattaqūna
3f	تَتَّقِي tattaqī	تَتَّقِيانِ tattaqiyāni	يَتَّقِينَ yattaqīna

subjunctive

	singular	dual	plural
1	أَتَّقِيَ ʔattaqiya	نَتَّقِيَ nattaqiya	
2m	تَتَّقِيَ tattaqiya	تَتَّقِيا tattaqiyā	تَتَّقُوا tattaqū
2f	تَتَّقِي tattaqī		تَتَّقِينَ tattaqīna
3m	يَتَّقِيَ yattaqiya	يَتَّقِيا yattaqiyā	يَتَّقُوا yattaqū
3f	تَتَّقِيَ tattaqiya	تَتَّقِيا tattaqiyā	يَتَّقِينَ yattaqīna

jussive

	singular	dual	plural
1	أَتَّقِ ʔattaqi	نَتَّقِ nattaqi	
2m	تَتَّقِ tattaqi	تَتَّقِيا tattaqiyā	تَتَّقُوا tattaqū
2f	تَتَّقِي tattaqī		تَتَّقِينَ tattaqīna
3m	يَتَّقِ yattaqi	يَتَّقِيا yattaqiyā	يَتَّقُوا yattaqū
3f	تَتَّقِ tattaqi	تَتَّقِيا tattaqiyā	يَتَّقِينَ yattaqīna

imperative

	singular	dual	plural
2m	اِتَّقِ ittaqi	اِتَّقِيا ittaqiyā	اِتَّقُوا ittaqū
2f	اِتَّقِي ittaqī		اِتَّقِينَ ittaqīna

participles

active	passive
مُتَّقٍ muttaq(in)	مُتَّقًى muttaq(an)

passive

perfect	imperfect
اُتُّقِيَ uttuqiya	يُتَّقَى yuttaqā

assimilated defect. meas. VIII		و	ي	ء	*other*	**8d3**
masdar: اِدِّعَاء iddi3ā?	***R¹***				د	**to allege**
	R²				✓	
	R³	✓	✓			

perfect

	singular	dual	plural
1	اِدَّعَيْتُ idda3aytu	اِدَّعَيْنَا idda3aynā	
2m	اِدَّعَيْتَ idda3ayta	اِدَّعَيْتُمَا idda3aytumā	اِدَّعَيْتُمْ idda3aytum
2f	اِدَّعَيْتِ idda3ayti		اِدَّعَيْتُنَّ idda3aytunna
3m	اِدَّعَى idda3ā	اِدَّعَيَا idda3ayā	اِدَّعَوْا idda3aw
3f	اِدَّعَتْ idda3at	اِدَّعَتَا idda3atā	اِدَّعَيْنَ idda3ayna

indicative

	singular	dual	plural
1	أَدَّعِي ?adda3ī	نَدَّعِي nadda3ī	
2m	تَدَّعِي tadda3ī	تَدَّعِيَانِ tadda3iyāni	تَدَّعُونَ tadda3ūna
2f	تَدَّعِينَ tadda3īna		تَدَّعِينَ tadda3īna
3m	يَدَّعِي yadda3ī	يَدَّعِيَانِ yadda3iyāni	يَدَّعُونَ yadda3ūna
3f	تَدَّعِي tadda3ī	تَدَّعِيَانِ tadda3iyāni	يَدَّعِينَ yadda3īna

subjunctive

	singular	dual	plural
1	أَدَّعِيَ ?adda3iya	نَدَّعِيَ nadda3iya	
2m	تَدَّعِيَ tadda3iya	تَدَّعِيَا tadda3iyā	تَدَّعُوا tadda3ū
2f	تَدَّعِي tadda3ī		تَدَّعِينَ tadda3īna
3m	يَدَّعِيَ yadda3iya	يَدَّعِيَا yadda3iyā	يَدَّعُوا yadda3ū
3f	تَدَّعِيَ tadda3iya	تَدَّعِيَا tadda3iyā	يَدَّعِينَ yadda3īna

jussive

	singular	dual	plural
1	أَدَّعِ ?adda3i	نَدَّعِ nadda3i	
2m	تَدَّعِ tadda3i	تَدَّعِيَا tadda3iyā	تَدَّعُوا tadda3ū
2f	تَدَّعِي tadda3ī		تَدَّعِينَ tadda3īna
3m	يَدَّعِ yadda3i	يَدَّعِيَا yadda3iyā	يَدَّعُوا yadda3ū
3f	تَدَّعِ tadda3i	تَدَّعِيَا tadda3iyā	يَدَّعِينَ yadda3īna

imperative

	singular	dual	plural
2m	اِدَّعِ idda3i	اِدَّعِيَا idda3iyā	اِدَّعُوا idda3ū
2f	اِدَّعِي idda3ī		اِدَّعِينَ idda3īna

participles

active	passive
مُدَّعٍ mudda3(in)	مُدَّعًى mudda3(an)

passive

perfect	imperfect
اُدُّعِيَ uddu3iya	يُدَّعَى yudda3ā

assimilated defect. meas. VIII		و	ي	ء	other	8d4
masdar: اِصْطِفَاء iṣṭifāʔ	R^1				ص	to choose
	R^2				✓	
	R^3	✓	✓			

perfect

	singular	dual	plural
1	اِصْطَفَيْتُ iṣṭafaytu	اِصْطَفَيْنَا iṣṭafaynā	
2m	اِصْطَفَيْتَ iṣṭafayta	اِصْطَفَيْتُمَا iṣṭafaytumā	اِصْطَفَيْتُمْ iṣṭafaytum
2f	اِصْطَفَيْتِ iṣṭafayti		اِصْطَفَيْتُنَّ iṣṭafaytunna
3m	اِصْطَفَى iṣṭafā	اِصْطَفَيَا iṣṭafayā	اِصْطَفَوْا iṣṭafaw
3f	اِصْطَفَتْ iṣṭafat	اِصْطَفَتَا iṣṭafatā	اِصْطَفَيْنَ iṣṭafayna

indicative

	singular	dual	plural
1	أَصْطَفِي ʔaṣṭafī	نَصْطَفِي naṣṭafī	
2m	تَصْطَفِي taṣṭafī	تَصْطَفِيَانِ taṣṭafiyāni	تَصْطَفُونَ taṣṭafūna
2f	تَصْطَفِينَ taṣṭafīna		تَصْطَفِينَ taṣṭafīna
3m	يَصْطَفِي yaṣṭafī	يَصْطَفِيَانِ yaṣṭafiyāni	يَصْطَفُونَ yaṣṭafūna
3f	تَصْطَفِي taṣṭafī	تَصْطَفِيَانِ taṣṭafiyāni	يَصْطَفِينَ yaṣṭafīna

subjunctive

	singular	dual	plural
1	أَصْطَفِيَ ʔaṣṭafiya	نَصْطَفِيَ naṣṭafiya	
2m	تَصْطَفِيَ taṣṭafiya	تَصْطَفِيَا taṣṭafiyā	تَصْطَفُوا taṣṭafū
2f	تَصْطَفِي taṣṭafī		تَصْطَفِينَ taṣṭafīna
3m	يَصْطَفِيَ yaṣṭafiya	يَصْطَفِيَا yaṣṭafiyā	يَصْطَفُوا yaṣṭafū
3f	تَصْطَفِيَ taṣṭafiya	تَصْطَفِيَا taṣṭafiyā	يَصْطَفِينَ yaṣṭafīna

jussive

	singular	dual	plural
1	أَصْطَفِ ʔaṣṭafi	نَصْطَفِ naṣṭafi	
2m	تَصْطَفِ taṣṭafi	تَصْطَفِيَا taṣṭafiyā	تَصْطَفُوا taṣṭafū
2f	تَصْطَفِي taṣṭafī		تَصْطَفِينَ taṣṭafīna
3m	يَصْطَفِ yaṣṭafi	يَصْطَفِيَا yaṣṭafiyā	يَصْطَفُوا yaṣṭafū
3f	تَصْطَفِ taṣṭafi	تَصْطَفِيَا taṣṭafiyā	يَصْطَفِينَ yaṣṭafīna

imperative

	singular	dual	plural
2m	اِصْطَفِ iṣṭafi	اِصْطَفِيَا iṣṭafiyā	اِصْطَفُوا iṣṭafū
2f	اِصْطَفِي iṣṭafī		اِصْطَفِينَ iṣṭafīna

participles

active	passive
مُصْطَفٍ muṣṭaf(in)	مُصْطَفًى muṣṭaf(an)

passive

perfect	imperfect
اُصْطُفِيَ uṣṭufiya	يُصْطَفَى yuṣṭafā

sound measure IX

masdar: اِحْمِرَار iɧmirār

	و	ي	ء	other
R[1]				✓
R[2]	✓	✓		✓
R[3]				✓

9s

to turn red

perfect

	singular	dual	plural
1	اِحْمَرَرْتُ iɧmarartu	اِحْمَرَرْنَا iɧmararnā	
2m	اِحْمَرَرْتَ iɧmararta	اِحْمَرَرْتُمَا iɧmarartumā	اِحْمَرَرْتُمْ iɧmarartum
2f	اِحْمَرَرْتِ iɧmararti		اِحْمَرَرْتُنَّ iɧmarartunna
3m	اِحْمَرَّ iɧmarra	اِحْمَرَّا iɧmarrā	اِحْمَرُّوا iɧmarrū
3f	اِحْمَرَّتْ iɧmarrat	اِحْمَرَّتَا iɧmarratā	اِحْمَرَرْنَ iɧmararna

indicative

	singular	dual	plural
1	أَحْمَرُّ ʔaɧmarru	نَحْمَرُّ naɧmarru	
2m	تَحْمَرُّ taɧmarru	تَحْمَرَّانِ taɧmarrāni	تَحْمَرُّونَ taɧmarrūna
2f	تَحْمَرِّينَ taɧmarrīna		تَحْمَرِرْنَ taɧmarirna
3m	يَحْمَرُّ yaɧmarru	يَحْمَرَّانِ yaɧmarrāni	يَحْمَرُّونَ yaɧmarrūna
3f	تَحْمَرُّ taɧmarru	تَحْمَرَّانِ taɧmarrāni	يَحْمَرِرْنَ yaɧmarirna

subjunctive

	singular	dual	plural
1	أَحْمَرَّ ʔaɧmarra	نَحْمَرَّ naɧmarra	
2m	تَحْمَرَّ taɧmarru	تَحْمَرَّا taɧmarrā	تَحْمَرُّوا taɧmarrū
2f	تَحْمَرِّي taɧmarrī		تَحْمَرِرْنَ taɧmarirna
3m	يَحْمَرَّ yaɧmarra	يَحْمَرَّا yaɧmarrā	يَحْمَرُّوا yaɧmarrū
3f	تَحْمَرَّ taɧmarra	تَحْمَرَّا taɧmarrā	يَحْمَرِرْنَ yaɧmarirna

jussive

	singular	dual	plural
1	أَحْمَرِرْ ʔaɧmarir	نَحْمَرِرْ naɧmarir	
2m	تَحْمَرِرْ taɧmarir	تَحْمَرَّا taɧmarrā	تَحْمَرُّوا taɧmarrū
2f	تَحْمَرِّي taɧmarrī		تَحْمَرِرْنَ taɧmarirna
3m	يَحْمَرِرْ yaɧmarir	يَحْمَرَّا yaɧmarrā	يَحْمَرُّوا yaɧmarrū
3f	تَحْمَرِرْ taɧmarir	تَحْمَرَّا taɧmarrā	يَحْمَرِرْنَ yaɧmarirna

imperative

	singular	dual	plural
2m	اِحْمَرِرْ iɧmarir	اِحْمَرَّا iɧmarrā	اِحْمَرُّوا iɧmarrū
2f	اِحْمَرِّي iɧmarrī		اِحْمَرِرْنَ iɧmarirna

participles

active
مُحْمَرّ muɧmarr

sound measure X

gerund*: اِسْتِخْدَام istixdām

	و	ي	ء	other
R1	✓	✓		✓
R2				✓
R3				✓

10s
to use

perfect

	singular	dual	plural
1	اِسْتَخْدَمْتُ istaxdamtu	اِسْتَخْدَمْنَا istaxdamnā	
2m	اِسْتَخْدَمْتَ istaxdamta	اِسْتَخْدَمْتُمَا istaxdamtumā	اِسْتَخْدَمْتُمْ istaxdamtum
2f	اِسْتَخْدَمْتِ istaxdamti		اِسْتَخْدَمْتُنَّ istaxdamtunna
3m	اِسْتَخْدَمَ istaxdama	اِسْتَخْدَمَا istaxdamā	اِسْتَخْدَمُوا istaxdamū
3f	اِسْتَخْدَمَتْ istaxdamat	اِسْتَخْدَمَتَا istaxdamatā	اِسْتَخْدَمْنَ istaxdamna

indicative

	singular	dual	plural
1	أَسْتَخْدِمُ ʔastaxdimu	نَسْتَخْدِمُ nastaxdimu	
2m	تَسْتَخْدِمُ tastaxdimu	تَسْتَخْدِمَانِ tastaxdimāni	تَسْتَخْدِمُونَ tastaxdimūna
2f	تَسْتَخْدِمِينَ tastaxdimīna		تَسْتَخْدِمْنَ tastaxdimna
3m	يَسْتَخْدِمُ yastaxdimu	يَسْتَخْدِمَانِ yastaxdimāni	يَسْتَخْدِمُونَ yastaxdimūna
3f	تَسْتَخْدِمُ tastaxdimu	تَسْتَخْدِمَانِ tastaxdimāni	يَسْتَخْدِمْنَ yastaxdimna

subjunctive

	singular	dual	plural
1	أَسْتَخْدِمَ ʔastaxdima	نَسْتَخْدِمَ nastaxdima	
2m	تَسْتَخْدِمَ tastaxdima	تَسْتَخْدِمَا tastaxdimā	تَسْتَخْدِمُوا tastaxdimū
2f	تَسْتَخْدِمِي tastaxdimī		تَسْتَخْدِمْنَ tastaxdimna
3m	يَسْتَخْدِمَ yastaxdima	يَسْتَخْدِمَا yastaxdimā	يَسْتَخْدِمُوا yastaxdimū
3f	تَسْتَخْدِمَ tastaxdima	تَسْتَخْدِمَا tastaxdimā	يَسْتَخْدِمْنَ yastaxdimna

jussive

	singular	dual	plural
1	أَسْتَخْدِمْ ʔastaxdim	نَسْتَخْدِمْ nastaxdim	
2m	تَسْتَخْدِمْ tastaxdim	تَسْتَخْدِمَا tastaxdimā	تَسْتَخْدِمُوا tastaxdimū
2f	تَسْتَخْدِمِي tastaxdimī		تَسْتَخْدِمْنَ tastaxdimna
3m	يَسْتَخْدِمْ yastaxdim	يَسْتَخْدِمَا yastaxdimā	يَسْتَخْدِمُوا yastaxdimū
3f	تَسْتَخْدِمْ tastaxdim	تَسْتَخْدِمَا tastaxdimā	يَسْتَخْدِمْنَ yastaxdimna

imperative

	singular	dual	plural
2m	اِسْتَخْدِمْ istaxdima	اِسْتَخْدِمَا istaxdimā	اِسْتَخْدِمُوا istaxdimū
2f	اِسْتَخْدِمِي istaxdimī		اِسْتَخْدِمْنَ istaxdimna

participles

active	passive
مُسْتَخْدِم mustaxdim	مُسْتَخْدَم mustaxdam

passive

perfect	imperfect
أُسْتُخْدِمَ ustuxdima	يُسْتَخْدَمُ yustaxdamu

* If R1 is و or ي, the gerund is اِسْتِيعَال istī3āl.

hamzated measure X		و	ي	ء	other	**10s(a)**
masdar: اِسْتِئْجَار istiʔjār						**to rent**
	R^1			✓		
	R^2				✓	
	R^3				✓	

perfect

	singular	dual	plural
1	اِسْتَأْجَرْتُ istaʔjartu	اِسْتَأْجَرْنَا istaʔjarnā	
2m	اِسْتَأْجَرْتَ istaʔjarta	اِسْتَأْجَرْتُمَا istaʔjartumā	اِسْتَأْجَرْتُمْ istaʔjartum
2f	اِسْتَأْجَرْتِ istaʔjarti		اِسْتَأْجَرْتُنَّ istaʔjartunna
3m	اِسْتَأْجَرَ istaʔjara	اِسْتَأْجَرَا istaʔjarā	اِسْتَأْجَرُوا istaʔjarū
3f	اِسْتَأْجَرَتْ istaʔjarat	اِسْتَأْجَرَتَا istaʔjaratā	اِسْتَأْجَرْنَ istaʔjarna

indicative

	singular	dual	plural
1	أَسْتَأْجِرُ ʔastaʔjiru	نَسْتَأْجِرُ nastaʔjiru	
2m	تَسْتَأْجِرُ tastaʔjiru	تَسْتَأْجِرَانِ tastaʔjirāni	تَسْتَأْجِرُونَ tastaʔjirūna
2f	تَسْتَأْجِرِينَ tastaʔjirīna		تَسْتَأْجِرْنَ tastaʔjirna
3m	يَسْتَأْجِرُ yastaʔjiru	يَسْتَأْجِرَانِ yastaʔjirāni	يَسْتَأْجِرُونَ yastaʔjirūna
3f	تَسْتَأْجِرُ tastaʔjiru	تَسْتَأْجِرَانِ tastaʔjirāni	يَسْتَأْجِرْنَ yastaʔjirna

subjunctive

	singular	dual	plural
1	أَسْتَأْجِرَ ʔastaʔjira	نَسْتَأْجِرَ nastaʔjira	
2m	تَسْتَأْجِرَ tastaʔjira	تَسْتَأْجِرَا tastaʔjirā	تَسْتَأْجِرُوا tastaʔjirū
2f	تَسْتَأْجِرِي tastaʔjirī		تَسْتَأْجِرْنَ tastaʔjirna
3m	يَسْتَأْجِرَ yastaʔjira	يَسْتَأْجِرَا yastaʔjirā	يَسْتَأْجِرُوا yastaʔjirū
3f	تَسْتَأْجِرَ tastaʔjira	تَسْتَأْجِرَا tastaʔjirā	يَسْتَأْجِرْنَ yastaʔjirna

jussive

	singular	dual	plural
1	أَسْتَأْجِرْ ʔastaʔjir	نَسْتَأْجِرْ nastaʔjir	
2m	تَسْتَأْجِرْ tastaʔjir	تَسْتَأْجِرَا tastaʔjirā	تَسْتَأْجِرُوا tastaʔjirū
2f	تَسْتَأْجِرِي tastaʔjirī		تَسْتَأْجِرْنَ tastaʔjirna
3m	يَسْتَأْجِرْ yastaʔjir	يَسْتَأْجِرَا yastaʔjirā	يَسْتَأْجِرُوا yastaʔjirū
3f	تَسْتَأْجِرْ tastaʔjir	تَسْتَأْجِرَا tastaʔjirā	يَسْتَأْجِرْنَ yastaʔjirna

imperative

	singular	dual	plural
2m	اِسْتَأْجِرْ istaʔjir	اِسْتَأْجِرَا istaʔjirā	اِسْتَأْجِرُوا istaʔjirū
2f	اِسْتَأْجِرِي istaʔjirī		اِسْتَأْجِرْنَ istaʔjirna

participles

active	passive
مُسْتَأْجِر mustaʔjir	مُسْتَأْجَر mustaʔjar

passive

perfect	imperfect
أُسْتُؤْجِرَ ustuʔjira	يُسْتَأْجَرُ yustaʔjaru

hamzated measure X

masdar: اِسْتِرْآف istirʔāf

	و	ي	ء	other
R^1				✓
R^2			✓	
R^3				✓

10s(b)

to beg for mercy

perfect

	singular	dual	plural
1	اِسْتَرْأَفْتُ istarʔaftu	اِسْتَرْأَفْنَا istarʔafnā	
2m	اِسْتَرْأَفْتَ istarʔafta	اِسْتَرْأَفْتُمَا istarʔaftumā	اِسْتَرْأَفْتُمْ istarʔaftum
2f	اِسْتَرْأَفْتِ istarʔafti		اِسْتَرْأَفْتُنَّ istarʔaftunna
3m	اِسْتَرْأَفَ istarʔafa	اِسْتَرْأَفَا istarʔafā	اِسْتَرْأَفُوا istarʔafū
3f	اِسْتَرْأَفَتْ istarʔafat	اِسْتَرْأَفَتَا istarʔafatā	اِسْتَرْأَفْنَ istarʔafna

indicative

	singular	dual	plural
1	أَسْتَرْئِفُ ʔastarʔifu	نَسْتَرْئِفُ nastarʔifu	
2m	تَسْتَرْئِفُ tastarʔifu	تَسْتَرْئِفَانِ tastarʔifāni	تَسْتَرْئِفُونَ tastarʔifūna
2f	تَسْتَرْئِفِينَ tastarʔifīna		تَسْتَرْئِفْنَ tastarʔifna
3m	يَسْتَرْئِفُ yastarʔifu	يَسْتَرْئِفَانِ yastarʔifāni	يَسْتَرْئِفُونَ yastarʔifūna
3f	تَسْتَرْئِفُ tastarʔifu	تَسْتَرْئِفَانِ tastarʔifāni	يَسْتَرْئِفْنَ yastarʔifna

subjunctive

	singular	dual	plural
1	أَسْتَرْئِفَ ʔastarʔifa	نَسْتَرْئِفَ nastarʔifa	
2m	تَسْتَرْئِفَ tastarʔifa	تَسْتَرْئِفَا tastarʔifā	تَسْتَرْئِفُوا tastarʔifū
2f	تَسْتَرْئِفِي tastarʔifī		تَسْتَرْئِفْنَ tastarʔifna
3m	يَسْتَرْئِفَ yastarʔifa	يَسْتَرْئِفَا yastarʔifā	يَسْتَرْئِفُوا yastarʔifū
3f	تَسْتَرْئِفَ tastarʔifa	تَسْتَرْئِفَا tastarʔifā	يَسْتَرْئِفْنَ yastarʔifna

jussive

	singular	dual	plural
1	أَسْتَرْئِفْ ʔastarʔif	نَسْتَرْئِفْ nastarʔif	
2m	تَسْتَرْئِفْ tastarʔif	تَسْتَرْئِفَا tastarʔifā	تَسْتَرْئِفُوا tastarʔifū
2f	تَسْتَرْئِفِي tastarʔifī		تَسْتَرْئِفْنَ tastarʔifna
3m	يَسْتَرْئِفْ yastarʔif	يَسْتَرْئِفَا yastarʔifā	يَسْتَرْئِفُوا yastarʔifū
3f	تَسْتَرْئِفْ tastarʔif	تَسْتَرْئِفَا tastarʔifā	يَسْتَرْئِفْنَ yastarʔifna

imperative

	singular	dual	plural
2m	اِسْتَرْئِفْ istarʔif	اِسْتَرْئِفَا istarʔifā	اِسْتَرْئِفُوا istarʔifū
2f	اِسْتَرْئِفِي istarʔifī		اِسْتَرْئِفْنَ istarʔifna

participles

active	passive
مُسْتَرْئِف mustarʔif	مُسْتَرْأَف mustarʔaf

passive

perfect	imperfect
أُسْتُرْئِفَ usturʔifa	يُسْتَرْأَفُ yustarʔafu

hamzated measure X

masdar: اِسْتِقْرَاء istiqrāʔ

	و	ي	ء	other
R^1				✓
R^2				✓
R^3			✓	

10s(c)
to investigate

perfect

	singular	dual	plural
1	اِسْتَقْرَأْتُ istaqraʔtu	اِسْتَقْرَأْنَا istaqraʔnā	
2m	اِسْتَقْرَأْتَ istaqraʔta	اِسْتَقْرَأْتُمَا istaqraʔtumā	اِسْتَقْرَأْتُمْ istaqraʔtum
2f	اِسْتَقْرَأْتِ istaqraʔti		اِسْتَقْرَأْتُنَّ istaqraʔtunna
3m	اِسْتَقْرَأَ istaqraʔa	اِسْتَقْرَآ istaqraʔā	اِسْتَقْرَؤُوا istaqraʔū
3f	اِسْتَقْرَأَتْ istaqraʔat	اِسْتَقْرَأَتَا istaqraʔatā	اِسْتَقْرَأْنَ istaqraʔna

indicative

	singular	dual	plural
1	أَسْتَقْرِئُ ʔastaqriʔu	نَسْتَقْرِئُ nastaqriʔu	
2m	تَسْتَقْرِئُ tastaqriʔu	تَسْتَقْرِئَانِ tastaqriʔāni	تَسْتَقْرِئُونَ tastaqriʔūna
2f	تَسْتَقْرِئِينَ tastaqriʔīna		تَسْتَقْرِئْنَ tastaqriʔna
3m	يَسْتَقْرِئُ yastaqriʔu	يَسْتَقْرِئَانِ yastaqriʔāni	يَسْتَقْرِئُونَ yastaqriʔūna
3f	تَسْتَقْرِئُ tastaqriʔu	تَسْتَقْرِئَانِ tastaqriʔāni	يَسْتَقْرِئْنَ yastaqriʔna

subjunctive

	singular	dual	plural
1	أَسْتَقْرِئَ ʔastaqriʔa	نَسْتَقْرِئَ nastaqriʔa	
2m	تَسْتَقْرِئَ tastaqriʔa	تَسْتَقْرِئَا tastaqriʔā	تَسْتَقْرِئُوا tastaqriʔū
2f	تَسْتَقْرِئِي tastaqriʔī		تَسْتَقْرِئْنَ tastaqriʔna
3m	يَسْتَقْرِئَ yastaqriʔa	يَسْتَقْرِئَا yastaqriʔā	يَسْتَقْرِئُوا yastaqriʔū
3f	تَسْتَقْرِئَ tastaqriʔa	تَسْتَقْرِئَا tastaqriʔā	يَسْتَقْرِئْنَ yastaqriʔna

jussive

	singular	dual	plural
1	أَسْتَقْرِئْ ʔastaqriʔ	نَسْتَقْرِئْ nastaqriʔ	
2m	تَسْتَقْرِئْ tastaqriʔ	تَسْتَقْرِئَا tastaqriʔā	تَسْتَقْرِئُوا tastaqriʔū
2f	تَسْتَقْرِئِي tastaqriʔī		تَسْتَقْرِئْنَ tastaqriʔna
3m	يَسْتَقْرِئْ yastaqriʔ	يَسْتَقْرِئَا yastaqriʔā	يَسْتَقْرِئُوا yastaqriʔū
3f	تَسْتَقْرِئْ tastaqriʔ	تَسْتَقْرِئَا tastaqriʔā	يَسْتَقْرِئْنَ yastaqriʔna

imperative

	singular	dual	plural
2m	اِسْتَقْرِئْ istaqriʔ	اِسْتَقْرِئَا istaqriʔā	اِسْتَقْرِئُوا istaqriʔū
2f	اِسْتَقْرِئِي istaqriʔī		اِسْتَقْرِئْنَ istaqriʔna

participles

active	passive
مُسْتَقْرِئ mustaqriʔ	مُسْتَقْرَأ mustaqraʔ

passive

perfect	imperfect
اُسْتُقْرِئَ ustuqriʔa	يُسْتَقْرَأُ yustaqraʔu

geminate measure X

masdar: اِسْتِحْقَاق istiɧqāq

	و	ي	ء	*other*
R¹				✓
R²				✓
R³				✓

10g
to deserve

perfect

	singular	dual	plural
1	اِسْتَحْقَقْتُ istaɧqaqtu	اِسْتَحْقَقْنَا istaɧqaqnā	
2m	اِسْتَحْقَقْتَ istaɧqaqta	اِسْتَحْقَقْتُمَا istaɧqaqtumā	اِسْتَحْقَقْتُمْ istaɧqaqtum
2f	اِسْتَحْقَقْتِ istaɧqaqti		اِسْتَحْقَقْتُنَّ istaɧqaqtunna
3m	اِسْتَحَقَّ istaɧaqqa	اِسْتَحَقَّا istaɧaqqā	اِسْتَحَقُّوا istaɧqqū
3f	اِسْتَحَقَّتْ istaɧaqqat	اِسْتَحَقَّتَا istaɧaqqatā	اِسْتَحْقَقْنَ istaɧqaqna

indicative

	singular	dual	plural
1	أَسْتَحِقُّ ʔastaɧiqqu	نَسْتَحِقُّ nastaɧiqqu	
2m	تَسْتَحِقُّ tastaɧiqqu	تَسْتَحِقَّانِ tastaɧiqqāni	تَسْتَحِقُّونَ tastaɧiqqūna
2f	تَسْتَحِقِّينَ tastaɧiqqīna		تَسْتَحْقِقْنَ tastaɧqiqna
3m	يَسْتَحِقُّ yastaɧiqqu	يَسْتَحِقَّانِ yastaɧiqqāni	يَسْتَحِقُّونَ yastaɧiqqūna
3f	تَسْتَحِقُّ tastaɧiqqu	تَسْتَحِقَّانِ tastaɧiqqāni	يَسْتَحْقِقْنَ yastaɧqiqna

subjunctive

	singular	dual	plural
1	أَسْتَحِقَّ ʔastaɧiqqa	نَسْتَحِقَّ nastaɧiqqa	
2m	تَسْتَحِقَّ tastaɧiqqa	تَسْتَحِقَّا tastaɧiqqā	تَسْتَحِقُّوا tastaɧiqqū
2f	تَسْتَحِقِّي tastaɧiqqī		تَسْتَحْقِقْنَ tastaɧqiqna
3m	يَسْتَحِقَّ yastaɧiqqa	يَسْتَحِقَّا yastaɧiqqā	يَسْتَحِقُّوا yastaɧiqqū
3f	تَسْتَحِقَّ tastaɧiqqa	تَسْتَحِقَّا tastaɧiqqā	يَسْتَحْقِقْنَ yastaɧqiqna

jussive

	singular	dual	plural
1	أَسْتَحِقَّ ʔastaɧiqqa	نَسْتَحِقَّ nastaɧiqqa	
2m	تَسْتَحِقَّ tastaɧiqqa	تَسْتَحِقَّا tastaɧiqqā	تَسْتَحِقُّوا tastaɧiqqū
2f	تَسْتَحِقِّي tastaɧiqqī		تَسْتَحْقِقْنَ tastaɧqiqna
3m	يَسْتَحِقَّ yastaɧiqqa	يَسْتَحِقَّا yastaɧiqqā	يَسْتَحِقُّوا yastaɧiqqū
3f	تَسْتَحِقَّ tastaɧiqqa	تَسْتَحِقَّا tastaɧiqqā	يَسْتَحْقِقْنَ yastaɧqiqna

imperative

	singular	dual	plural
2m	اِسْتَحِقَّ istaɧiqqa	اِسْتَحِقَّا istaɧiqqā	اِسْتَحِقُّوا istaɧiqqū
2f	اِسْتَحِقِّي istaɧiqqī		اِسْتَحْقِقْنَ istaɧqiqna

participles

active	passive
مُسْتَحِقّ mustaɧiqq	مُسْتَحَقّ mustaɧaqq

passive

perfect	imperfect
أُسْتُحِقَّ ustuɧiqqa	يُسْتَحَقُّ yustaɧaqqu

hollow measure X

masdar: اِسْتِطَاعَة istiṭā3a[t]

	و	ي	ء	other
R¹				✓
R²	✓	✓		
R³				✓

10h

to be able to

perfect

	singular	dual	plural
1	اِسْتَطَعْتُ istaṭa3tu	اِسْتَطَعْنَا istaṭa3nā	
2m	اِسْتَطَعْتَ istaṭa3ta	اِسْتَطَعْتُمَا istaṭa3tumā	اِسْتَطَعْتُمْ istaṭa3tum
2f	اِسْتَطَعْتِ istaṭa3ti		اِسْتَطَعْتُنَّ istaṭa3tunna
3m	اِسْتَطَاعَ istaṭā3a	اِسْتَطَاعَا istaṭā3ā	اِسْتَطَاعُوا istaṭā3ū
3f	اِسْتَطَاعَتْ istaṭā3at	اِسْتَطَاعَتَا istaṭā3atā	اِسْتَطَعْنَ istaṭa3na

indicative

	singular	dual	plural
1	أَسْتَطِيعُ ʔastaṭī3u	نَسْتَطِيعُ nastaṭī3u	
2m	تَسْتَطِيعُ tastaṭī3u	تَسْتَطِيعَانِ tastaṭī3āni	تَسْتَطِيعُونَ tastaṭī3ūna
2f	تَسْتَطِيعِينَ tastaṭī3īna		تَسْتَطِعْنَ tastaṭi3na
3m	يَسْتَطِيعُ yastaṭī3u	يَسْتَطِيعَانِ yastaṭī3āni	يَسْتَطِيعُونَ yastaṭī3ūna
3f	تَسْتَطِيعُ tastaṭī3u	تَسْتَطِيعَانِ tastaṭī3āni	يَسْتَطِعْنَ yastaṭi3na

subjunctive

	singular	dual	plural
1	أَسْتَطِيعَ ʔastaṭī3a	نَسْتَطِيعَ nastaṭī3a	
2m	تَسْتَطِيعَ tastaṭī3u	تَسْتَطِيعَا tastaṭī3ā	تَسْتَطِيعُوا tastaṭī3ū
2f	تَسْتَطِيعِي tastaṭī3ī		تَسْتَطِعْنَ tastaṭi3na
3m	يَسْتَطِيعَ yastaṭī3a	يَسْتَطِيعَا yastaṭī3ā	يَسْتَطِيعُوا yastaṭī3ū
3f	تَسْتَطِيعَ tastaṭī3a	تَسْتَطِيعَا tastaṭī3ā	يَسْتَطِعْنَ yastaṭi3na

jussive

	singular	dual	plural
1	أَسْتَطِعْ ʔastaṭi3	نَسْتَطِعْ nastaṭi3	
2m	تَسْتَطِعْ tastaṭi3	تَسْتَطِيعَا tastaṭī3ā	تَسْتَطِيعُوا tastaṭī3ū
2f	تَسْتَطِيعِي tastaṭī3ī		تَسْتَطِعْنَ tastaṭi3na
3m	يَسْتَطِعْ yastaṭi3	يَسْتَطِيعَا yastaṭī3ā	يَسْتَطِيعُوا yastaṭī3ū
3f	تَسْتَطِعْ tastaṭi3	تَسْتَطِيعَا tastaṭī3ā	يَسْتَطِعْنَ yastaṭi3na

imperative

	singular	dual	plural
2m	تَسْتَطِعْ tastaṭi3	تَسْتَطِيعَا tastaṭī3ā	تَسْتَطِيعُوا tastaṭī3ū
2f	تَسْتَطِيعِي tastaṭī3ī		تَسْتَطِعْنَ tastaṭi3na

participles

active	passive
مُسْتَطِيع mustaṭī3	مُسْتَطَاع mustaṭā3

passive

perfect	imperfect
أُسْتُطِيعَ ustuṭī3a	يُسْتَطَاعُ yustaṭā3u

hamzated hollow measure X		و	ي	ء	*other*	**10h(a)**
masdar: إِسْتِضَاءَة istiḍāʔat	*R¹*				✓	to be enlightened
	R²	✓	✓			
	R³			✓		

perfect

	singular	dual	plural
1	اِسْتَضَأْتُ istaḍaʔtu	اِسْتَضَأْنَا istaḍaʔnā	
2m	اِسْتَضَأْتَ istaḍaʔta	اِسْتَضَأْتُمَا istaḍaʔtumā	اِسْتَضَأْتُمْ istaḍaʔtum
2f	اِسْتَضَأْتِ istaḍaʔti		اِسْتَضَأْتُنَّ istaḍaʔtunna
3m	اِسْتَضَاءَ istaḍāʔa	اِسْتَضَاءَا istaḍāʔā	اِسْتَضَاؤُوا* istaḍāʔū
3f	اِسْتَضَاءَتْ istaḍāʔat	اِسْتَضَاءَتَا istaḍāʔatā	اِسْتَضَأْنَ istaḍaʔna

indicative

	singular	dual	plural
1	أَسْتَضِيءُ ʔastaḍīʔu	نَسْتَضِيءُ nastaḍīʔu	
2m	تَسْتَضِيءُ tastaḍīʔu	تَسْتَضِيئَانِ tastaḍīʔāni	تَسْتَضِيئُونَ* tastaḍīʔūna
2f	تَسْتَضِيئِينَ tastaḍīʔīna		تَسْتَضِئْنَ tastaḍiʔna
3m	يَسْتَضِيءُ yastaḍīʔu	يَسْتَضِيئَانِ yastaḍīʔāni	يَسْتَضِيئُونَ* yastaḍīʔūna
3f	تَسْتَضِيءُ tastaḍīʔu	تَسْتَضِيئَانِ tastaḍīʔāni	يَسْتَضِئْنَ yastaḍiʔna

subjunctive

	singular	dual	plural
1	أَسْتَضِيءَ ʔastaḍīʔa	نَسْتَضِيءَ nastaḍīʔa	
2m	تَسْتَضِيءَ tastaḍīʔa	تَسْتَضِيئَا tastaḍīʔā	تَسْتَضِيئُوا* tastaḍīʔū
2f	تَسْتَضِيئِي tastaḍīʔī		تَسْتَضِئْنَ tastaḍiʔna
3m	يَسْتَضِيءَ yastaḍīʔa	يَسْتَضِيئَا yastaḍīʔā	يَسْتَضِيئُوا* yastaḍīʔū
3f	تَسْتَضِيءَ tastaḍīʔa	تَسْتَضِيئَا tastaḍīʔā	يَسْتَضِئْنَ yastaḍiʔna

jussive

	singular	dual	plural
1	أَسْتَضِئْ ʔastaḍiʔ	نَسْتَضِئْ nastaḍiʔ	
2m	تَسْتَضِئْ tastaḍiʔ	تَسْتَضِيئَا tastaḍīʔā	تَسْتَضِيئُوا* tastaḍīʔū
2f	تَسْتَضِيئِي tastaḍīʔī		تَسْتَضِئْنَ tastaḍiʔna
3m	يَسْتَضِئْ yastaḍiʔ	يَسْتَضِيئَا yastaḍīʔā	يَسْتَضِيئُوا* yastaḍīʔū
3f	تَسْتَضِئْ tastaḍiʔ	تَسْتَضِيئَا tastaḍīʔā	يَسْتَضِئْنَ yastaḍiʔna

imperative

	singular	dual	plural
2m	تَسْتَضِئْ tastaḍiʔ	تَسْتَضِيئَا tastaḍīʔā	تَسْتَضِيئُوا* tastaḍīʔū
2f	تَسْتَضِيئِي tastaḍīʔī		تَسْتَضِئْنَ tastaḍiʔna

participles

active	passive
مُسْتَضِيء mustaḍīʔ	مُسْتَضَاء mustaḍāʔ

passive

perfect	imperfect
أُسْتُضِيءَ ustuḍīʔa	يُسْتَضَاءُ yustaḍāʔu

*ئُونَ and ئُوا are also often spelled ؤُونَ and ؤُوا.

defective measure I

masdar: إِسْتِدْعَاء istid3āʔ

	و	ي	ء	other
R^1				✓
R^2				✓
R^3	✓	✓		

10d
to summon

perfect

	singular	dual	plural
1	اِسْتَدْعَيْتُ istad3aytu	اِسْتَدْعَيْنَا istad3aynā	
2m	اِسْتَدْعَيْتَ istad3ayta	اِسْتَدْعَيْتُمَا istad3aytumā	اِسْتَدْعَيْتُمْ istad3aytum
2f	اِسْتَدْعَيْتِ istad3ayti		اِسْتَدْعَيْتُنَّ istad3aytunna
3m	اِسْتَدْعَى* istad3ā	اِسْتَدْعَيَا istad3ayā	اِسْتَدْعُوا istad3ū
3f	اِسْتَدْعَتْ istad3at	اِسْتَدْعَتَا istad3atā	اِسْتَدْعَيْنَ istad3ayna

indicative

	singular	dual	plural
1	أَسْتَدْعِي ʔastad3ī	نَسْتَدْعِي nastad3ī	
2m	تَسْتَدْعِي tastad3ī	تَسْتَدْعِيَانِ tastad3iyāni	تَسْتَدْعُونَ tastad3ūna
2f	تَسْتَدْعِينَ tastad3īna		تَسْتَدْعِينَ tastad3īna
3m	يَسْتَدْعِي yastad3ī	يَسْتَدْعِيَانِ yastad3iyāni	يَسْتَدْعُونَ yastad3ūna
3f	تَسْتَدْعِي tastad3ī	تَسْتَدْعِيَانِ tastad3iyāni	يَسْتَدْعِينَ yastad3īna

subjunctive

	singular	dual	plural
1	أَسْتَدْعِيَ ʔastad3iya	نَسْتَدْعِيَ nastad3iya	
2m	تَسْتَدْعِيَ tastad3iya	تَسْتَدْعِيَا tastad3iyā	تَسْتَدْعُوا tastad3ū
2f	تَسْتَدْعِي tastad3ī		تَسْتَدْعِينَ tastad3īna
3m	يَسْتَدْعِيَ yastad3iya	يَسْتَدْعِيَا yastad3iyā	يَسْتَدْعُوا yastad3ūna
3f	تَسْتَدْعِيَ tastad3iya	تَسْتَدْعِيَا tastad3iyā	يَسْتَدْعِينَ yastad3īna

jussive

	singular	dual	plural
1	أَسْتَدْعِ ʔastad3i	نَسْتَدْعِ nastad3i	
2m	تَسْتَدْعِ tastad3i	تَسْتَدْعِيَا tastad3iyā	تَسْتَدْعُوا tastad3ū
2f	تَسْتَدْعِي tastad3ī		تَسْتَدْعِينَ tastad3īna
3m	يَسْتَدْعِ yastad3i	يَسْتَدْعِيَا yastad3iyā	يَسْتَدْعُوا yastad3ūna
3f	تَسْتَدْعِ tastad3i	تَسْتَدْعِيَا tastad3iyā	يَسْتَدْعِينَ yastad3īna

imperative

	singular	dual	plural
2m	اِسْتَدْعِ istad3i	اِسْتَدْعِيَا istad3iyā	اِسْتَدْعُوا istad3ū
2f	اِسْتَدْعِي istad3ī		اِسْتَدْعِينَ istad3īna

participles

active	passive
مُسْتَدْعٍ mustad3(in)	مُسْتَدْعًى mustad3(an)

passive

perfect	imperfect
أُسْتُدْعِيَ ustud3iya	يُسْتَدْعَى yustad3ā

* اِسْتَحْيَا istaħyā (*be ashamed*) is irregular in that it takes ـا instead of ـى in the 3rd person sing. perfect form.

Quadriliteral Verbs

Names	quadriliteral measure I, measure XI مجرد رباعي وزن فعلل mujarrad rubā3īy wazn fa3lala
Characteristics	• four radicals
Meanings	• formed from acronyms of common sayings • repeated radicals represent sounds and noises

Names	quadriliteral measure II, measure XII مزيد رباعي وزن تفعلل mazīd rubā3īy wazn tafa3lala
Characteristics	• first radical prefixed by ta-
Meanings	• passive or reflexive of measure I verbs • become __ • derived from nouns

Names	*quadriliteral measure III, quadriliteral measure IV, measure XIV مزيد رباعي وزن افعلل mazīd rubā3īy wazn if3alalla
Characteristics	• first radical prefixed by i- • fourth radical doubled
Meanings	• to quadriliteral verbs as measure IX verbs are to triliteral verbs

* Traditionally, Western Arabists have referred to this measure as 'quadriliteral measure IV'; however, their 'quadriliteral measure III' is obsolete in MSA (and rare in Classical Arabic). In the absence of the obsolete measure III, the designation has been shifted.

quadriliteral measure I

masdar: سَيْطَرَة sayṭara[t]

	و	ي	ء	other
R^1	✓	✓		✓
R^2	✓	✓		✓
R^3	✓	✓		✓
R^4				✓

11s

to dominate

perfect

	singular	dual	plural
1	سَيْطَرْتُ sayṭartu	سَيْطَرْنَا sayṭarnā	
2m	سَيْطَرْتَ sayṭarta	سَيْطَرْتُمَا sayṭartumā	سَيْطَرْتُم sayṭartum
2f	سَيْطَرْتِ sayṭarti		سَيْطَرْتُنَّ sayṭartunna
3m	سَيْطَرَ sayṭara	سَيْطَرَا sayṭarā	سَيْطَرُوا sayṭarū
3f	سَيْطَرَتْ sayṭarat	سَيْطَرَتَا sayṭaratā	سَيْطَرْنَ sayṭarna

indicative

	singular	dual	plural
1	أُسَيْطِرُ ʔusayṭiru	نُسَيْطِرُ nusayṭiru	
2m	تُسَيْطِرُ tusayṭiru	تُسَيْطِرَانِ tusayṭirāni	تُسَيْطِرُونَ tusayṭirūna
2f	تُسَيْطِرِينَ tusayṭirīna		تُسَيْطِرْنَ tusayṭirna
3m	يُسَيْطِرُ yusayṭiru	يُسَيْطِرَانِ yusayṭirāni	يُسَيْطِرُونَ yusayṭirūna
3f	تُسَيْطِرُ tusayṭiru	تُسَيْطِرَانِ tusayṭirāni	يُسَيْطِرْنَ yusayṭirna

subjunctive

	singular	dual	plural
1	أُسَيْطِرَ ʔusayṭira	نُسَيْطِرَ nusayṭira	
2m	تُسَيْطِرَ tusayṭira	تُسَيْطِرَا tusayṭirā	تُسَيْطِرُوا tusayṭirū
2f	تُسَيْطِرِي tusayṭirī		تُسَيْطِرْنَ tusayṭirna
3m	يُسَيْطِرَ yusayṭira	يُسَيْطِرَا yusayṭirā	يُسَيْطِرُوا yusayṭirū
3f	تُسَيْطِرَ tusayṭira	تُسَيْطِرَا tusayṭirā	يُسَيْطِرْنَ yusayṭirna

jussive

	singular	dual	plural
1	أُسَيْطِرْ ʔusayṭir	نُسَيْطِرْ nusayṭir	
2m	تُسَيْطِرْ tusayṭir	تُسَيْطِرَا tusayṭirā	تُسَيْطِرُوا tusayṭirū
2f	تُسَيْطِرِي tusayṭirī		تُسَيْطِرْنَ tusayṭirna
3m	يُسَيْطِرْ yusayṭir	يُسَيْطِرَا yusayṭirā	يُسَيْطِرُوا yusayṭirū
3f	تُسَيْطِرْ tusayṭir	تُسَيْطِرَا tusayṭirā	يُسَيْطِرْنَ yusayṭirna

imperative

	singular	dual	plural
2m	سَيْطِرْ sayṭir	سَيْطِرَا sayṭirā	سَيْطِرُوا sayṭirū
2f	سَيْطِرِي sayṭirī		سَيْطِرْنَ sayṭirna

participles

active	passive
مُسَيْطِر musayṭir	مُسَيْطَر musayṭar

passive

perfect	imperfect
سُيْطِرَ suyṭira	يُسَيْطَرُ yusayṭaru

hamz. quadriliteral measure I		و	ي	ء	other	**11s(a)**
masdar: أَقْلَمَة ʔaqlamat[t]	R^1			✓		**to acclimatize**
	R^2	✓	✓		✓	
	R^3	✓	✓		✓	
	R^4				✓	

perfect

	singular	dual	plural
1	أَقْلَمْتُ ʔaqlamtu	أَقْلَمْنَا ʔaqlamnā	
2m	أَقْلَمْتَ ʔaqlamta	أَقْلَمْتُمَا ʔaqlamtumā	أَقْلَمْتُم ʔaqlamtum
2f	أَقْلَمْتِ ʔaqlamti		أَقْلَمْتُنَّ ʔaqlamtunna
3m	أَقْلَمَ ʔaqlama	أَقْلَمَا ʔaqlamā	أَقْلَمُوا ʔaqlamū
3f	أَقْلَمَتْ ʔaqlamat	أَقْلَمَتَا ʔaqlamatā	أَقْلَمْنَ ʔaqlamna

indicative

	singular	dual	plural
1	أُؤَقْلِمُ ʔuʔaqlimu	نُؤَقْلِمُ nuʔaqlimu	
2m	تُؤَقْلِمُ tuʔaqlimu	تُؤَقْلِمَانِ tuʔaqlimāni	تُؤَقْلِمُونَ tuʔaqlimūna
2f	تُؤَقْلِمِينَ tuʔaqlimīna		تُؤَقْلِمْنَ tuʔaqlimna
3m	يُؤَقْلِمُ yuʔaqlimu	يُؤَقْلِمَانِ yuʔaqlimāni	يُؤَقْلِمُونَ yuʔaqlimūna
3f	تُؤَقْلِمُ tuʔaqlimu	تُؤَقْلِمَانِ tuʔaqlimāni	يُؤَقْلِمْنَ yuʔaqlimna

subjunctive

	singular	dual	plural
1	أُؤَقْلِمَ ʔuʔaqlima	نُؤَقْلِمَ nuʔaqlima	
2m	تُؤَقْلِمَ tuʔaqlima	تُؤَقْلِمَا tuʔaqlimā	تُؤَقْلِمُوا tuʔaqlimū
2f	تُؤَقْلِمِي tuʔaqlimī		تُؤَقْلِمْنَ tuʔaqlimna
3m	يُؤَقْلِمَ yuʔaqlima	يُؤَقْلِمَا yuʔaqlimā	يُؤَقْلِمُوا yuʔaqlimū
3f	تُؤَقْلِمَ tuʔaqlima	تُؤَقْلِمَا tuʔaqlimā	يُؤَقْلِمْنَ yuʔaqlimna

jussive

	singular	dual	plural
1	أُؤَقْلِمْ ʔuʔaqlim	نُؤَقْلِمْ nuʔaqlim	
2m	تُؤَقْلِمْ tuʔaqlim	تُؤَقْلِمَا tuʔaqlimā	تُؤَقْلِمُوا tuʔaqlimū
2f	تُؤَقْلِمِي tuʔaqlimī		تُؤَقْلِمْنَ tuʔaqlimna
3m	يُؤَقْلِمْ yuʔaqlim	يُؤَقْلِمَا yuʔaqlimā	يُؤَقْلِمُوا yuʔaqlimū
3f	تُؤَقْلِمْ tuʔaqlim	تُؤَقْلِمَا tuʔaqlimā	يُؤَقْلِمْنَ yuʔaqlimna

imperative

	singular	dual	plural
2m	أَقْلِمْ ʔaqlim	أَقْلِمَا ʔaqlimā	أَقْلِمُوا ʔaqlimū
2f	أَقْلِمِي ʔaqlimī		أَقْلِمْنَ ʔaqlimna

participles

active	passive
مُؤَقْلِم muʔaqlim	مُؤَقْلَم muʔaqlam

passive

perfect	imperfect
أُقْلِمَ ʔuqlima	يُؤَقْلَمُ yuʔaqlalu

hamz. quadriliteral measure I

masdar: طَمْأَنَة ṭamʔana[t]

	و	ي	ء	other
R^1	✓	✓		✓
R^2	✓	✓		✓
R^3			✓	
R^4				✓

11s(b)

to reassure

perfect

	singular	dual	plural
1	طَمْأَنْتُ ṭamʔantu	طَمْأَنَّا ṭamʔannā	
2m	طَمْأَنْتَ ṭamʔanta	طَمْأَنْتُمَا ṭamʔantumā	طَمْأَنْتُم ṭamʔantum
2f	طَمْأَنْتِ ṭamʔanti		طَمْأَنْتُنَّ ṭamʔantunna
3m	طَمْأَنَ ṭamʔana	طَمْأَنَا ṭamʔanā	طَمْأَنُوا ṭamʔanū
3f	طَمْأَنَتْ ṭamʔanat	طَمْأَنَتَا ṭamʔanatā	طَمْأَنَّ ṭamʔanna

indicative

	singular	dual	plural
1	أُطَمْئِنُ ʔuṭamʔinu	نُطَمْئِنُ nuṭamʔinu	
2m	تُطَمْئِنُ tuṭamʔinu	تُطَمْئِنَانِ tuṭamʔināni	تُطَمْئِنُونَ tuṭamʔinūna
2f	تُطَمْئِنِينَ tuṭamʔinīna		تُطَمْئِنَّ tuṭamʔinna
3m	يُطَمْئِنُ yuṭamʔinu	يُطَمْئِنَانِ yuṭamʔināni	يُطَمْئِنُونَ yuṭamʔinūna
3f	تُطَمْئِنُ tuṭamʔinu	تُطَمْئِنَانِ tuṭamʔināni	يُطَمْئِنَّ yuṭamʔinna

subjunctive

	singular	dual	plural
1	أُطَمْئِنَ ʔuṭamʔina	نُطَمْئِنَ nuṭamʔina	
2m	تُطَمْئِنَ tuṭamʔina	تُطَمْئِنَا tuṭamʔinā	تُطَمْئِنُوا tuṭamʔinū
2f	تُطَمْئِنِي tuṭamʔinī		تُطَمْئِنَّ tuṭamʔinna
3m	يُطَمْئِنَ yuṭamʔina	يُطَمْئِنَا yuṭamʔinā	يُطَمْئِنُوا yuṭamʔinū
3f	تُطَمْئِنَ tuṭamʔina	تُطَمْئِنَا tuṭamʔinā	يُطَمْئِنَّ yuṭamʔinna

jussive

	singular	dual	plural
1	أُطَمْئِنْ ʔuṭamʔin	نُطَمْئِنْ nuṭamʔin	
2m	تُطَمْئِنْ tuṭamʔin	تُطَمْئِنَا tuṭamʔinā	تُطَمْئِنُوا tuṭamʔinū
2f	تُطَمْئِنِي tuṭamʔinī		تُطَمْئِنَّ tuṭamʔinna
3m	يُطَمْئِنْ yuṭamʔin	يُطَمْئِنَا yuṭamʔinā	يُطَمْئِنُوا yuṭamʔinū
3f	تُطَمْئِنْ tuṭamʔin	تُطَمْئِنَا tuṭamʔinā	يُطَمْئِنَّ yuṭamʔinna

imperative

	singular	dual	plural
2m	طَمْئِنْ ṭamʔin	طَمْئِنَا ṭamʔinā	طَمْئِنُوا ṭamʔinū
2f	طَمْئِنِي ṭamʔinī		طَمْئِنَّ ṭamʔinna

participles

active	passive
مُطَمْئِن muṭamʔin	مُطَمْأَن muṭamʔan

passive

perfect	imperfect
طُمْئِنَ ṭumʔina	يُطَمْأَنُ yuṭamʔanu

quadriliteral measure II **masdar:** تَدَهْوُر tadahwur		و	ي	ء	other	**12s** **to deteriorate**
	R¹	✓	✓		✓	
	R²	✓	✓		✓	
	R³	✓	✓		✓	
	R⁴				✓	

perfect

	singular	dual	plural
1	تَدَهْوَرْتُ tadahwartu	تَدَهْوَرْنَا tadahwarnā	
2m	تَدَهْوَرْتَ tadahwarta	تَدَهْوَرْتُمَا tadahwartumā	تَدَهْوَرْتُم tadahwartum
2f	تَدَهْوَرْتِ tadahwarti		تَدَهْوَرْتُنَّ tadahwartunna
3m	تَدَهْوَرَ tadahwara	تَدَهْوَرَا tadahwarā	تَدَهْوَرُوا tadahwarū
3f	تَدَهْوَرَتْ tadahwarat	تَدَهْوَرَتَا tadahwaratā	تَدَهْوَرْنَ tadahwarna

indicative

	singular	dual	plural
1	أَتَدَهْوَرُ ʔatadahwaru	نَتَدَهْوَرُ natadahwaru	
2m	تَتَدَهْوَرُ tatadahwaru	تَتَدَهْوَرَانِ tatadahwarāni	تَتَدَهْوَرُونَ tatadahwarūna
2f	تَتَدَهْوَرِينَ tatadahwarīna		تَتَدَهْوَرْنَ tatadahwarna
3m	يَتَدَهْوَرُ yatadahwaru	يَتَدَهْوَرَانِ yatadahwarāni	يَتَدَهْوَرُونَ yatadahwarūna
3f	تَتَدَهْوَرُ tatadahwaru	تَتَدَهْوَرَانِ tatadahwarāni	يَتَدَهْوَرْنَ yatadahwarna

subjunctive

	singular	dual	plural
1	أَتَدَهْوَرَ ʔatadahwara	نَتَدَهْوَرَ natadahwara	
2m	تَتَدَهْوَرَ tatadahwara	تَتَدَهْوَرَا tatadahwarā	تَتَدَهْوَرُوا tatadahwarū
2f	تَتَدَهْوَرِي tatadahwarī		تَتَدَهْوَرْنَ tatadahwarna
3m	يَتَدَهْوَرَ yatadahwara	يَتَدَهْوَرَا yatadahwarā	يَتَدَهْوَرُوا yatadahwarū
3f	تَتَدَهْوَرَ tatadahwara	تَتَدَهْوَرَا tatadahwarā	يَتَدَهْوَرْنَ yatadahwarna

jussive

	singular	dual	plural
1	أَتَدَهْوَرْ ʔatadahwar	نَتَدَهْوَرْ natadahwar	
2m	تَتَدَهْوَرْ tatadahwar	تَتَدَهْوَرَا tatadahwarā	تَتَدَهْوَرُوا tatadahwarū
2f	تَتَدَهْوَرِي tatadahwarī		تَتَدَهْوَرْنَ tatadahwarna
3m	يَتَدَهْوَرْ yatadahwar	يَتَدَهْوَرَا yatadahwarā	يَتَدَهْوَرُوا yatadahwarū
3f	تَتَدَهْوَرْ tatadahwar	تَتَدَهْوَرَا tatadahwarā	يَتَدَهْوَرْنَ yatadahwarna

imperative

	singular	dual	plural
2m	تَدَهْوَرْ tadahwar	تَدَهْوَرَا tadahwarā	تَدَهْوَرُوا tadahwarū
2f	تَدَهْوَرِي tadahwarī		تَدَهْوَرْنَ tadahwarna

participles

active
مُتَدَهْوَر mutadahwar

hamz. quadriliteral measure II		و	ي	ء	*other*	**12s(a)**
masdar: تَأَقْلُم taʔaqlum	R^1			✓		to acclimatize oneself
	R^2	✓	✓		✓	
	R^3	✓	✓		✓	
	R^4				✓	

perfect

	singular	dual	plural
1	تَأَقْلَمْتُ taʔaqlamtu	تَأَقْلَمْنَا taʔaqlamnā	
2m	تَأَقْلَمْتَ taʔaqlamta	تَأَقْلَمْتُمَا taʔaqlamtumā	تَأَقْلَمْتُم taʔaqlamtum
2f	تَأَقْلَمْتِ taʔaqlamti		تَأَقْلَمْتُنَّ taʔaqlamtunna
3m	تَأَقْلَمَ taʔaqlama	تَأَقْلَمَا taʔaqlamā	تَأَقْلَمُوا taʔaqlamū
3f	تَأَقْلَمَتْ taʔaqlamat	تَأَقْلَمَتَا taʔaqlamatā	تَأَقْلَمْنَ taʔaqlamna

indicative

	singular	dual	plural
1	أَتَأَقْلَمُ ʔataʔaqlamu	نَتَأَقْلَمُ nataʔaqlamu	
2m	تَتَأَقْلَمُ tataʔaqlamu	تَتَأَقْلَمَانِ tataʔaqlamāni	تَتَأَقْلَمُونَ tataʔaqlamūna
2f	تَتَأَقْلَمِينَ tataʔaqlamīna		تَتَأَقْلَمْنَ tataʔaqlamna
3m	يَتَأَقْلَمُ yataʔaqlamu	يَتَأَقْلَمَانِ yataʔaqlamāni	يَتَأَقْلَمُونَ yataʔaqlamūna
3f	تَتَأَقْلَمُ tataʔaqlamu	تَتَأَقْلَمَانِ tataʔaqlamāni	يَتَأَقْلَمْنَ yataʔaqlamna

subjunctive

	singular	dual	plural
1	أَتَأَقْلَمَ ʔataʔaqlama	نَتَأَقْلَمَ nataʔaqlama	
2m	تَتَأَقْلَمَ tataʔaqlama	تَتَأَقْلَمَا tataʔaqlamā	تَتَأَقْلَمُوا tataʔaqlamū
2f	تَتَأَقْلَمِي tataʔaqlamī		تَتَأَقْلَمْنَ tataʔaqlamna
3m	يَتَأَقْلَمَ yataʔaqlama	يَتَأَقْلَمَا yataʔaqlamā	يَتَأَقْلَمُوا yataʔaqlamū
3f	تَتَأَقْلَمَ tataʔaqlama	تَتَأَقْلَمَا tataʔaqlamā	يَتَأَقْلَمْنَ yataʔaqlamna

jussive

	singular	dual	plural
1	أَتَأَقْلَمْ ʔataʔaqlam	نَتَأَقْلَمْ nataʔaqlam	
2m	تَتَأَقْلَمْ tataʔaqlam	تَتَأَقْلَمَا tataʔaqlamā	تَتَأَقْلَمُوا tataʔaqlamū
2f	تَتَأَقْلَمِي tataʔaqlamī		تَتَأَقْلَمْنَ tataʔaqlamna
3m	يَتَأَقْلَمْ yataʔaqlam	يَتَأَقْلَمَا yataʔaqlamā	يَتَأَقْلَمُوا yataʔaqlamū
3f	تَتَأَقْلَمْ tataʔaqlam	تَتَأَقْلَمَا tataʔaqlamā	يَتَأَقْلَمْنَ yataʔaqlamna

imperative

	singular	dual	plural
2m	تَأَقْلَمْ taʔaqlam	تَأَقْلَمَا taʔaqlamā	تَأَقْلَمُوا taʔaqlamū
2f	تَأَقْلَمِي taʔaqlamī		تَأَقْلَمْنَ taʔaqlamna

participles

active
مُتَأَقْلَم mutaʔaqlam

quadriliteral measure III

masdar: اِقْشِعْرَار iqši3rār

	و	ي	ء	*other*
R^1	✓	✓		✓
R^2	✓	✓		✓
R^3	✓	✓		✓
R^4				✓

13s
to shiver

perfect

	singular	dual	plural
1	اِقْشَعْرَرْتُ iqša3rartu	اِقْشَعْرَرْنَا iqša3rarnā	
2m	اِقْشَعْرَرْتَ iqša3rarta	اِقْشَعْرَرْتُمَا iqša3rartumā	اِقْشَعْرَرْتُمْ iqša3rartum
2f	اِقْشَعْرَرْتِ iqaša3rarti		اِقْشَعْرَرْتُنَّ iqša3rartunna
3m	اِقْشَعَرَّ iqša3arra	اِقْشَعَرَّا iqša3arrā	اِقْشَعَرُّوا iqša3arrū
3f	اِقْشَعَرَّتْ iqša3arrat	اِقْشَعَرَّتَا iqša3arratā	اِقْشَعْرَرْنَ iqša3rarna

indicative

	singular	dual	plural
1	أَقْشَعِرُّ ʔaqša3irru	نَقْشَعِرُّ naqša3irru	
2m	تَقْشَعِرُّ taqša3irru	تَقْشَعِرَّانِ taqša3irrāni	تَقْشَعِرُّونَ taqša3irrūna
2f	تَقْشَعِرِّينَ taqša3irrīna		تَقْشَعْرِرْنَ taqša3rirna
3m	تَقْشَعِرُّ taqša3irru	يَقْشَعِرَّانِ yaqša3irrāni	يَقْشَعِرُّونَ yaqša3irrūna
3f	يَقْشَعِرُّ yaqša3irru	تَقْشَعِرَّانِ taqša3irrāni	يَقْشَعْرِرْنَ yaqša3rirna

subjunctive

	singular	dual	plural
1	أَقْشَعِرَّ ʔaqša3irra	نَقْشَعِرَّ naqša3irra	
2m	تَقْشَعِرَّ taqša3irra	تَقْشَعِرَّا taqša3irrā	تَقْشَعِرُّوا taqša3irrū
2f	تَقْشَعِرِّي taqša3irrī		تَقْشَعْرِرْنَ taqša3rirna
3m	تَقْشَعِرَّ taqša3irra	يَقْشَعِرَّا yaqša3irrā	يَقْشَعِرُّوا yaqša3irrū
3f	يَقْشَعِرَّ yaqša3irra	تَقْشَعِرَّا taqša3irrā	يَقْشَعْرِرْنَ yaqša3rirna

jussive

	singular	dual	plural
1	أَقْشَعْرِرْ ʔaqša3rir	نَقْشَعْرِرْ naqša3rir	
2m	تَقْشَعْرِرْ taqša3rir	تَقْشَعِرَّا taqša3irrā	تَقْشَعِرُّوا taqša3irrū
2f	تَقْشَعِرِّي taqša3irrī		تَقْشَعْرِرْنَ taqša3rirna
3m	تَقْشَعْرِرْ taqša3rir	يَقْشَعِرَّا yaqša3irrā	يَقْشَعِرُّوا yaqša3irrū
3f	يَقْشَعْرِرْ yaqša3rir	تَقْشَعِرَّا taqša3irrā	يَقْشَعْرِرْنَ yaqša3rirna

imperative

	singular	dual	plural
2m	اِقْشَعْرِرْ iqša3rir	اِقْشَعِرَّا iqša3irrā	اِقْشَعِرُّوا iqša3irrū
2f	اِقْشَعِرِّي iqša3irrī		اِقْشَعْرِرْنَ iqša3rirna

participles

active
مُقْشَعِرّ muqša3irr

hamz. quadriliteral meas. III

masdar: اِطْمِئْنَان iṭmiʔnān

	و	ي	ء	other
R^1	✓	✓		✓
R^2	✓	✓		✓
R^3			✓	
R^4				✓

13s(a)

to be calm

perfect

	singular	dual	plural
1	اِطْمَأْنَنْتُ iṭmaʔnantu	اِطْمَأْنَنَّا iṭmaʔnannā	
2m	اِطْمَأْنَنْتَ iṭmaʔnanta	اِطْمَأْنَنْتُمَا iṭmaʔnantumā	اِطْمَأْنَنْتُمْ iṭmaʔnantum
2f	اِطْمَأْنَنْتِ iṭamaʔnanti		اِطْمَأْنَنْتُنَّ iṭmaʔnantunna
3m	اِطْمَأَنَّ iṭmaʔanna	اِطْمَأَنَّا iṭmaʔannā	اِطْمَأَنُّوا iṭmaʔannū
3f	اِطْمَأَنَّتْ iṭmaʔannat	اِطْمَأَنَّتَا iṭmaʔannatā	اِطْمَأْنَنَّ iṭmaʔnanna

indicative

	singular	dual	plural
1	أَطْمَئِنُّ ʔaṭmaʔinnu	نَطْمَئِنُّ naṭmaʔinnu	
2m	تَطْمَئِنُّ taṭmaʔinnu	تَطْمَئِنَّانِ taṭmaʔinnāni	تَطْمَئِنُّونَ taṭmaʔinnūna
2f	تَطْمَئِنِّينَ taṭmaʔinnīna		تَطْمَأْنِنَّ taṭmaʔninna
3m	تَطْمَئِنُّ taṭmaʔinnu	يَطْمَئِنَّانِ yaṭmaʔinnāni	يَطْمَئِنُّونَ yaṭmaʔinnūna
3f	يَطْمَئِنُّ yaṭmaʔinnu	تَطْمَئِنَّانِ taṭmaʔinnāni	يَطْمَأْنِنَّ yaṭmaʔninna

subjunctive

	singular	dual	plural
1	أَطْمَئِنَّ ʔaṭmaʔinna	نَطْمَئِنَّ naṭmaʔinna	
2m	تَطْمَئِنَّ taṭmaʔinna	تَطْمَئِنَّا taṭmaʔinnā	تَطْمَئِنُّوا taṭmaʔinnū
2f	تَطْمَئِنِّي taṭmaʔinnī		تَطْمَأْنِنَّ taṭmaʔninna
3m	تَطْمَئِنَّ taṭmaʔinna	يَطْمَئِنَّا yaṭmaʔinnā	يَطْمَئِنُّوا yaṭmaʔinnū
3f	يَطْمَئِنَّ yaṭmaʔinna	تَطْمَئِنَّا taṭmaʔinnā	يَطْمَأْنِنَّ yaṭmaʔninna

jussive

	singular	dual	plural
1	أَطْمَأْنِنْ ʔaṭmaʔnin	نَطْمَأْنِنْ naṭmaʔnin	
2m	تَطْمَأْنِنْ taṭmaʔnin	تَطْمَئِنَّا taṭmaʔinnā	تَطْمَئِنُّوا taṭmaʔinnū
2f	تَطْمَئِنِّي taṭmaʔinnī		تَطْمَأْنِنَّ taṭmaʔninna
3m	تَطْمَأْنِنْ taṭmaʔnin	يَطْمَئِنَّا yaṭmaʔinnā	يَطْمَئِنُّوا yaṭmaʔinnū
3f	يَطْمَأْنِنْ yaṭmaʔnin	تَطْمَئِنَّا taṭmaʔinnā	يَطْمَأْنِنَّ yaṭmaʔninna

imperative

	singular	dual	plural
2m	اِطْمَأْنِنْ iṭmaʔnin	اِطْمَئِنَّا iṭmaʔinnā	اِطْمَئِنُّوا iṭmaʔinnū
2f	اِطْمَئِنِّي iṭmaʔinnī		اِطْمَأْنِنَّ iṭmaʔninna

participles

active
مُطْمَئِنّ muṭmaʔinn

Index

Measure I

1s1			masdar
بحث	*baħata*	search	بحث *baħt*
برع	*bara3a*	be proficient	براعة *barā3a*^{t}
بعث	*ba3ata*	send	بعث *ba3t*
بلع	*bala3a*	swallow	بلع *bal3*
بهر	*bahara*	overwhelm	بهر *bahr*
تعس	*ta3asa*	become miserable	تعاسة *ta3āsa*^{t}
جحد	*jaħada*	renounce	جحد *jaħd* جحود *juħūd*
جرح	*jaraħa*	injure	جرح *jarħ*
جرع	*jara3a*	swallow	جرع *jar3*
جعل	*ja3ala*	make	جعل *ja3l*
جمع	*jama3a*	collect	جمع *jam3*
جهد	*jahada*	endeavor	جهد *jahd*
جهر	*jahara*	be revealed	جهر *jahr* جهار *jihār*
خدع	*xada3a*	deceive	خدعة *xud3a*^{t}
خضع	*xaḍa3a*	submit	خضوع *xuḍū3*
خلع	*xala3a*	take off	خلع *xal3*
خنع	*xana3a*	be meek	خنوع *xunū3*
دبغ	*dabaɣa*	tan	دبغ *dabɣ*
دعس	*da3asa*	tread	دعس *da3s*
دعم	*da3ama*	support	دعم *da3m*
دفع	*dafa3a*	push	دفع *daf3*
دمع	*dama3a*	water	دمع *dam3*
ذبح	*đabaħa*	slaughter	ذبح *đabħ*
ذبل	*đabala*	wilt	ذبول *đubūl*
ذهب	*đahaba*	go	ذهاب *đahāb*
رجح	*rajaħa*	outweigh	رجوح *rujūħ* رجحان *rujħān*
رحل	*raħala*	travel	رحيل *raħīl*
رضع	*raḍa3a*	suckle	رضاعة *raḍā3a*^{t}
رعب	*ra3aba*	terrify	رعب *ru3b*
رعد	*ra3ada*	clap	رعد *ra3d*
رفع	*rafa3a*	raise	رفع *raf3*
ركع	*raka3a*	kneel	ركوع *rukū3*
رهن	*rahana*	pawn	رهن *rahn*
زحف	*zaħafa*	crawl	زحف *zaħf*
زخر	*zaxara*	abound	زخر *zaxr*
زرع	*zara3a*	plant	زرع *zar3*
زعل	*za3ila*	become upset	زعل *za3al*
زهر	*zahara*	be radiant	زهور *zuhūr*
زهق	*zahaqa*	become bored	زهق *zahq* زهوق *zuhūq*
سبح	*sabaħa*	swim	سباحة *sibāħa*^{t}
سحب	*saħaba*	pull	سحب *saħb*
سحج	*saħaja*	scrape	سحج *saħj*
سحر	*saħara*	enchant	سحر *siħr*
سحق	*saħaqa*	crush	سحق *saħq*
سفع	*safa3a*	scorch	سفع *saf3*
سمح	*samaħa*	allow	سماح *samāħ*
شحذ	*šaħađa*	sharpen	شحذ *šaħđ*
شحن	*šaħana*	ship	شحن *šaħn*
شرح	*šaraħa*	explain	شرح *šarħ*
شرع	*šara3a*	begin	شروع *šurū3*
شغل	*šaɣala*	fill	شغل *šuɣl*
شمل	*šamala*	include	شمل *šam(a)l* شمول *šumūl*
صرع	*ṣara3a*	knock down	صرع *ṣar3*
صفع	*ṣafa3a*	slap	صفع *ṣaf3*
صنع	*ṣana3a*	manufacture	صنع *ṣan3* or *ṣun3*
ضغط	*ḍaɣaṭa*	press	ضغط *ḍaɣṭ*
ضلع	*ḍala3a*	side	ضلع *ḍal3*
طبخ	*ṭabaxa*	cook	طبخ *ṭabx*
طبع	*ṭaba3a*	print	طبع *ṭab3*
طحن	*ṭahana*	grind	طحن *ṭaħn*
طرح	*ṭaraħa*	subtract	طرح *ṭarħ*
طعن	*ṭa3ana*	stab	طعن *ṭa3n*
طمح	*ṭamaħa*	aspire	طموح *ṭumūħ*
ظهر	*ẓahara*	appear	ظهور *ẓuhūr*
عجب	*3ajiba*	be amazed	عجب *3ajab*
فتح	*fataħa*	open	فتح *fatħ*
فحص	*faħaṣa*	examine	فحص *faħṣ*
فرغ	*faraɣa*	be empty	فراغ *farāɣ*
فرق	*fariqa*	be afraid	فرق *faraq*

فزع *fazi3a*	be afraid	فزع *faza3*
فسخ *fasaxa*	void, annul	فسخ *fasx*
فضح *faḍaħa*	disgrace	فضح *faḍħ*
فعل *fa3ala*	do	فعل *fa3l* or *fi3l*
فلح *falaħa*	split	فلح *falħ*
قرع *qara3a*	knock	قرع *qar3*
قطع *qaṭa3a*	cut	قطع *qaṭ3*
قلع *qala3a*	take off	قلع *qal3*
قمع *qama3a*	suppress	قمع *qam3*
قهر *qahara*	conquer	قهر *qahr*
كبح *kabaħa*	restrain	كبح *kabħ*
كدح *kadaħa*	toil	كدح *kadħ*
كسح *kasaħa*	sweep	كسح *kasħ*
كمل *kamala*	be completed	كمال *kamāl* or كمول *kumūl*
لدغ *ladaɣa*	sting	لدغ *ladɣ*
لسع *lasa3a*	sting	لسع *las3*
لعن *la3ana*	curse	لعن *la3n*
لفح *lafaħa*	burn	لفح *lafħ*
لمح *lamaħa*	glance	لمح *lamħ*
لمع *lama3a*	shine	لمع *lam3* or لمعان *lama3ān*
لهث *lahaŧa*	pant	لهاث *luhāŧ* لهث *lahŧ*
مدح *madaħa*	commend	مدح *madħ*
مزح *mazaħa*	joke	مزاح *muzāħ* مزح *mazħ*
مسح *masaħa*	wipe	مسح *masħ*
مضغ *maḍaɣa*	chew	مضغ *maḍɣ*
ملخ *malaxa*	dislocate	ملخ *malx*
منح *manaħa*	provide	منح *manħ*
منع *mana3a*	forbid	منع *man3*
نبح *nabaħa*	bark	نباح *nubāħ*
نجح *najaħa*	succeed	نجاح *najāħ*
نحب *naħaba*	weep	نحب *naħb* نحيب *naħīb*
نحس *naħasa*	jinx	نحس *naħas*
نزح *nazaħa*	migrate	نزوح *nuzūħ*
نزع *naza3a*	remove	نزع *naz3*
نسخ *nasaxa*	copy	نسخ *nasx*
نصح *naṣaħa*	advise	نصح *naṣħ* or *nuṣħ* نصيحة *naṣīħa*^{t}
نعت *na3ata*	characterize	نعت *na3t*
نعس *na3asa*	become sleepy	نعاس *nu3ās* نعس *na3s*
نفع *nafa3a*	be useful	نفع *naf3*
نهب *nahaba*	plunder	نهب *nahb*
نهج *nahaja*	pursue	نهج *nahj*
نهض *nahaḍa*	get up	نهوض *nuhūḍ* نهض *nahḍ*
نهق *nahaqa*	bray	نهيق *nahīq*
هرع *hara3a*	hurry	هرع *hara3*

1s1(a)

ثأر *ŧaʔara*	avenge	ثأر *ŧaʔr*
دأب *daʔaba*	persist	دأب *daʔb*
رأس *raʔasa*	head	رئاسة *riʔāsa*^{t}
زأر *zaʔara*	roar	زئير *zaʔīr* زأر *zaʔr*
سأل *saʔala*	ask	سؤال *suʔāl*
لأم *laʔama*	bandage	لأم *laʔm*
مأن *maʔana*	provide supplies	مأن *maʔn*

1s1(b)

بدأ *badaʔa*	begin	بدء *badʔ*
برأ *baraʔa*	create	برء *barʔ*
خسأ *xasaʔa*	drive out	خسء *xasʔ* خسوء *xusūʔ*
درأ *daraʔa*	ward off	درء *darʔ* دروء *durūʔ*
طرأ *ṭaraʔa*	happen	طرء *ṭarʔ*
فجأ *fajaʔa*	surprise	فجاءة *fujāʔa*^{t} فجأة *fajʔa*^{t}
قرأ *qaraʔa*	read	قراءة *qirāʔa*^{t}
لجأ *lajaʔa*	resort	لجوء *lujūʔ*
ملأ *malaʔa*	fill	ملء *malʔ*
نتأ *nataʔa*	protrude	نتوء *nutūʔ*
نشأ *našaʔa*	grow up	نشأة *našʔa*^{t} نشوء *nušūʔ*
هدأ *hadaʔa*	calm down	هدوء *hudūʔ*
هزأ *hazaʔa*	mock	هزء *huzʔ*

1s2

بذل *bađala*	exert	بذل *bađl*
جدل *jadala*	twist	جدل *jadl*
جذب *jađaba*	attract	جذب *jađb*
جلب *jalaba*	fetch	جلب *jalb*
جلس *jalasa*	sit	جلوس *julūs*
حبس *ħabasa*	imprison	حبس *ħabs*
حتم *ħatama*	make indispensable	حتم *ħatm*
حجز *ħajaza*	reserve	حجز *ħajz*
حذف *ħađafa*	omit	حذف *ħađf*

حرث	ħarata	plow	حرث ħart
حرق	ħaraqa	burn	حرق ħarq
حرم	ħarama	deprive	حرمان ħirmān
حزم	ħazama	bind	حزم ħazm
حسم	ħasama	sever	حسم ħasm
حشر	ħašara	wedge	حشر ħašr
حصد	ħaṣada	harvest	حصاد ħaṣād
حصر	ħaṣara	limit	حصر ħaṣr
حفر	ħafara	dig	حفر ħafr
حفل	ħafala	gather	حفل ħafl
حقد	ħaqada	be spiteful	حقد ħaqd
حقن	ħaqana	inject	حقن ħaqn
حلف	ħalafa	swear	حلف ħalf
حلق	ħalaqa	shave	حلاقة ħilāqa^t حلق ħalq
حمل	ħamala	lift	حمل ħaml
خبز	xabaza	bake	خبز xabz
خبط	xabaṭa	knock	خبط xabṭ
ختم	xatama	stamp	ختم xatm
ختم	xatama	conclude	ختام xitām
ختن	xatana	circumcise	ختان xitān
خدم	xadama	serve	خدمة xidma^t
خرق	xaraqa	pierce	خرق xarq
خرم	xarama	pierce	خرم xarm
خصب	xaṣaba	be fertile	خصب xiṣb
خطر	xaṭara	occur	خطور xuṭūr
خطف	xaṭafa	kidnap	خطف xaṭf
خفض	xafaḍa	lower	خفض xafḍ
خفق	xafaqa	beat	خفق xafq
خفق	xafaqa	beat	خفقان xafaqān
خلط	xalaṭa	mix	خلط xalṭ
دفن	dafana	bury	دفن dafn
ربط	rabaṭa	tie	ربط rabṭ
رجع	raja3a	return	رجوع rujū3
رفس	rafasa	kick	رفس rafs
رفض	rafaḍa	reject	رفض rafḍ
زفر	zafara	exhale	زفير zafīr
سبق	sabaqa	precede	سبق sabq
ستر	satara	veil	ستر satr
سرق	saraqa	steal	سرقة sariqa^t
سفك	safaka	shed blood	سفك safk
شتم	šatama	abuse	شتم šatm
شخر	šaxara	snore	شخير šaxīr
صبر	ṣabara	tolerate	صبر ṣabr
صدر	ṣadara	be published	صدور ṣudūr صدر ṣadr

صدم	ṣadama	hit	صدم ṣadm
صرف	ṣarafa	spend	صرف ṣarf
صفر	ṣafara	whistle	صفير ṣafīr
صفق	ṣafaqa	slam (shut)	صفق ṣafq
صلب	ṣalaba	crucify	صلب ṣalb
ضبط	ḍabaṭa	adjust	ضبط ḍabṭ
ضرب	ḍaraba	hit	ضرب ḍarb
ضرط	ḍaraṭa	fart loudly	ضراط ḍurāṭ ضرط ḍarṭ
طرف	ṭarafa	blink	طرف ṭarf
ظلم	ẓalama	wrong	ظلم ẓulm
عبس	3abasa	frown	عبس 3abs عبوس 3ubūs
عجز	3ajaza	be incapable	عجز 3ajz
عجن	3ajana	knead	عجن 3ajn
عدل	3adala	relinquish	عدول 3udūl
عذر	3ađara	excuse	عذر 3uđr معذرة ma3đira^t
عرض	3araḍa	show	عرض 3arḍ
عرف	3arafa	know	معرفة ma3rifa^t
عزف	3azafa	play	عزف 3azf
عزف	3azafa	refrain	عزوف 3uzūf
عزل	3azala	remove	عزل 3azl
عزم	3azama	decide	عزم 3azm
عصر	3aṣara	squeeze	عصر 3aṣr
عصف	3aṣafa	storm	عصف 3aṣf
عصم	3aṣama	protect	عصم 3aṣm
عطس	3aṭasa	sneeze	عطس 3aṭs
عقد	3aqada	hold	عقد 3aqd
عقل	3aqala	comprehend	عقل 3aql
عكس	3akasa	reflect	عكس 3aks
عمد	3amada	support	عمد 3amd
عمر	3amara	live long	عمر 3umr
غرز	ɣaraza	prick	غرز ɣarz
غرس	ɣarasa	plant	غرس ɣars
غزل	ɣazala	spin	غزل ɣazl
غسل	ɣasala	wash	غسل ɣasl
غطس	ɣaṭasa	dive	غطس ɣaṭs
غفر	ɣafara	forgive	مغفرة maɣfira^t غفران ɣufrān
غلب	ɣalaba	defeat	غلب ɣalb
غمز	ɣamaza	wink	غمز ɣamz
غمس	ɣamasa	plunge	غمس ɣams
فتل	fatala	twist	فتل fatl
فتن	fatana	charm	فتن fatn فتون futūn
فرد	farada	flatten	فرد fard

فرز *faraza*	sort	فرز *farz*
فرض *faraḍa*	impose	فرض *farḍ*
فسد *fasada*	decay	فساد *fasād*
فصل *faṣala*	separate	فصل *faṣl*
فقد *faqada*	lose	فقدان *fiqdān* or فقد *fuqdān* *faqd*
فقس *faqasa*	hatch	فقس *faqs*
قبض *qabaḍa*	arrest	قبض *qabḍ*
قذف *qaḏafa*	throw	قذف *qaḏf*
قرض *qaraḍa*	clip	قرض *qarḍ*
قسم *qasama*	divide	قسم *qasm*
قشر *qašara*	peel	قشر *qašr*
قصد *qaṣada*	intend	قصد *qaṣd*
قصف *qaṣafa*	bomb	قصف *qaṣf*
قطف *qaṭafa*	pick	قطف *qaṭf*
قفز *qafaza*	jump	قفز *qafz*
قلب *qalaba*	invert	قلب *qalb*
قلص *qalaṣa*	shrink	قلوص *qulūṣ*
كبس *kabasa*	squeeze	كبس *kabs*
كدم *kadama*	bruise	كدم *kadm*
كذب *kaḏaba*	lie	كذب *kiḏb*
كسب *kasaba*	earn	كسب *kasb*
كسر *kasara*	break	كسر *kasr*
كسف *kasafa*	eclipse	كسوف *kusūf*
كشط *kašaṭa*	scrape (off)	كشط *kašṭ*
كشف *kašafa*	discover	كشف *kašf*
كفر *kafara*	be an infidel	كفر *kufr* كفران *kufrān*
لطم *laṭama*	slap	لطم *laṭm*
لفت *lafata*	turn	لفت *laft*
لفظ *lafaẓa*	pronounce	لفظ *lafẓ*
لمس *lamasa*	touch	لمس *lams*
مزق *mazaqa*	tear	مزق *mazq*
مسك *masaka*	hold	مسك *mask*
ملك *malaka*	have	ملك *mulk*
نبذ *nabaḏa*	discard	نبذ *nabḏ*
نبر *nabara*	emphasize	نبر *nabr*
نبض *nabaḍa*	beat	نبض *nabḍ*
نبع *naba3a*	well up	نبع *nab3* نبوع *nubū3*
نتج *nataja*	result	نتاج *nitāj*
نحب *naħaba*	weep	نحب *naħb* نحيب *naħīb*
نحت *naħata*	sculpt	نحت *naħt*
نزح *nazaħa*	migrate	نزوح *nuzūħ*
نزف *nazafa*	bleed	نزف *nazf*
نزل *nazala*	descend	نزول *nuzūl*
نسب *nasaba*	refer	نسبة *nisba^{t}* نسب *nasab*
نسف *nasafa*	blow up	نسف *nasf*
نظم *naẓama*	arrange	نظم *naẓm* نظام *niẓām*
نهش *nahaša*	bite	نهش *nahš*
هبط *habaṭa*	descend	هبوط *hubūṭ*
هتف *hatafa*	chant	هتاف *hutāf*
هدر *hadara*	roar	هدر *hadr* هدير *hadīr*
هدف *hadafa*	aim	هدف *hadf*
هدم *hadama*	demolish	هدم *hadm*
هزل *hazala*	become skinny	هزل *hazl*
هزم *hazama*	defeat	هزم *hazm*
هضم *haḍama*	digest	هضم *haḍm*
هلك *halaka*	be ruined	هلاك *halāk*
همز *hamaza*	hamzate	همز *hamz*
همس *hamasa*	whisper	همس *hams*

1s2(a)

أبر *ʔabara*	prick	أبر *ʔabr*
أسر *ʔasara*	capture	أسر *ʔasr*

1s3

بتر *batara*	amputate	بتر *batr*
بذر *baḏara*	sow	بذر *baḏr*
بذل *baḏala*	exert	بذل *baḏl*
برد *barada*	file (down)	برد *bard*
برز *baraza*	stand out	بروز *burūz*
برق *baraqa*	flash	برق *barq*
برك *baraka*	kneel down	بروك *burūk*
برم *barama*	spin	برم *barm*
بزغ *bazaɣa*	dawn	بزوغ *buzūɣ*
بسط *basaṭa*	extend	بسط *basṭ*
بشر *bašara*	grate	بشر *bašar*
بصق *baṣaqa*	spit	بصق *baṣq*
بصم *baṣama*	imprint	بصم *baṣm*
بلغ *balaɣa*	reach	بلوغ *bulūɣ*
ترك *taraka*	leave	ترك *tark*
ثبت *tabata*	be proven	ثبوت *tabūt*
ثبت *tabata*	be fixed	ثبات *tabāt*
ثقب *taqaba*	pierce	ثقب *taqb*
جبر *jabara*	force	جبر *jabr*
جرف *jarafa*	sweep away	جرف *jarf*
جزر *jazara*	butcher	جزر *jazr*

جلب	*jalaba*	fetch	جلب *jalb*
جلد	*jalada*	whip	جلد *jald*
جمد	*jamada*	freeze	جمود *jumūd*
جمل	*jamala*	summarize	جمل *jaml*
جهر	*jahara*	be loud	جهارة *jahāra*^{t}
حجب	*ɧajaba*	veil	حجب *ɧajb*
حجز	*ɧajaza*	reserve	حجز *ɧajz*
حدث	*ɧadaŧa*	happen	حدوث *ɧudūŧ*
حرث	*ɧaraŧa*	plow	حرث *ɧarŧ*
حرس	*ɧarasa*	guard	حراسة *ɧirāsa*^{t}
حزم	*ɧazama*	be resolute	حزم *ɧazm*
حسب	*ɧasaba*	calculate	حساب *ɧisāb* حسب *ɧasb*
حسد	*ɧasada*	envy	حسد *ɧasad*
حشد	*ɧašada*	gather	حشد *ɧašd*
حشر	*ɧašara*	wedge	حشر *ɧašr*
حصد	*ɧaşada*	harvest	حصاد *ɧaşād*
حصر	*ɧaşara*	limit	حصر *ɧaşr*
حصل	*ɧaşala*	happen	حصول *ɧuşūl*
حضر	*ɧaḑara*	come	حضور *ɧuḑūr*
حضن	*ɧaḑana*	hug	حضن *ɧiḑn*
حظر	*ɧaz̧ara*	ban	حظر *ɧaz̧r*
حقن	*ɧaqana*	inject	حقن *ɧaqn*
حكم	*ɧakama*	rule	حكم *ɧukm*
حلب	*ɧalaba*	milk	حلب *ɧalb*
حلم	*ɧalama*	dream	حلم *ɧulm*
حلم	*ɧalama*	be patient	حلم *ɧilm*
خبر	*xabara*	test	خبرة *xibra*^{t}
خدم	*xadama*	serve	خدمة *xidma*^{t}
خذل	*xađala*	disappoint	خذلان *xiđlān*
خرج	*xaraja*	exit	خروج *xurūj*
خرق	*xaraqa*	pierce	خرق *xarq*
خزن	*xazana*	store	خزن *xazn*
خطب	*xaţaba*	address	خطبة *xuţba*^{t}
خطب	*xaţaba*	propose	خطبة *xiţba*^{t}
خطر	*xaţara*	occur	خطور *xuţūr*
خفق	*xafaqa*	beat	خفق *xafq*
خفق	*xafaqa*	beat	خفقان *xafaqān*
خلص	*xalaşa*	arrive	خلوص *xulūş*
خلص	*xalaşa*	become pure	خلاص *xalāş*
خلف	*xalafa*	be the successor	خلافة *xilāfa*^{t}
خلق	*xalaqa*	create	خلق *xalq*
خمد	*xamada*	go out	خمود *xumūd*
خنق	*xanaqa*	strangle	خنق *xanq*
دخل	*daxala*	enter	دخول *duxūl*
دخن	*daxana*	smoke	دخن *daxan*
درز	*daraza*	stitch	درز *darz*
درس	*darasa*	study	درس *dars*
دمج	*damaja*	integrate	دموج *dumūj*
دمغ	*damaɣa*	stamp	دمغ *damɣ*
دهن	*dahana*	paint	دهن *dahn*
ذكر	*đakara*	remember	تذكار *tađkār* ذكر *đikr*
ذكر	*đakara*	report	ذكر *đikr*
ربط	*rabaţa*	tie	ربط *rabţ*
رتق	*rataqa*	darn	رتق *ratq*
رجف	*rajafa*	convulse	رجف *rajf* رجفان *rajafān*
رجم	*rajama*	stone	رجم *rajm*
رذل	*rađala*	reject	رذل *rađl*
رزق	*razaqa*	bless	رزق *razq*
رسب	*rasaba*	fail	رسوب *rusūb*
رسم	*rasama*	draw	رسم *rasm*
رشد	*rašada*	be grown up	رشد *rušd*
رشق	*rašuqa*	be agile	رشاقة *rašāqa*^{t}
رشق	*rašaqa*	pelt	رشق *rašq*
رصد	*raşada*	observe	رصد *raşd*
رصف	*raşafa*	pave	رصف *raşf*
رعد	*ra3ada*	clap	رعد *ra3d*
رفس	*rafasa*	kick	رفس *rafs*
رفض	*rafaḑa*	reject	رفض *rafḑ*
رفق	*rafaqa*	be nice	رفق *rafq*
رقب	*raqaba*	observe	رقابة *raqāba*^{t}
رقص	*raqaşa*	dance	رقص *raqş*
ركد	*rakada*	be stagnant	ركود *rukūd*
ركض	*rakaḑa*	jog	ركض *rakḑ*
ركل	*rakala*	kick	ركل *rakl*
ركم	*rakama*	accumulate	ركم *rakm*
ركن	*rakana*	park	ركون *rukūn*
رمق	*ramaqa*	regard	رمق *ramq*
زعم	*za3ama*	claim	زعم *za3m*
سبق	*sabaqa*	precede	سبق *sabq*
ستر	*satara*	veil	ستر *satr*
سجد	*sajada*	prostrate	سجود *sujūd*
سجن	*sajana*	imprison	سجن *sajn*
سخن	*saxana*	become hot	سخونة *suxūna*^{t} سخانة *saxāna*^{t}
سرد	*sarada*	enumerate	سرد *sard*
سعل	*sa3ala*	cough	سعال *su3āl*
سفك	*safaka*	shed blood	سفك *safk*
سقط	*saqaţa*	fall	سقوط *suqūţ*

سكب	*sakaba*	spill	سكب *sakb*
سكت	*sakata*	become quiet	سكوت *sukūt*
سكن	*sakana*	live	سكن *sakan*
سكن	*sakana*	become calm	سكون *sukūn*
سلب	*salaba*	deprive	سلب *salb*
سلخ	*salaxa*	skin	سلخ *salx*
سلق	*salaqa*	boil	سلق *salq*
سلك	*salaka*	behave	سلوك *sulūk*
سند	*sanada*	support	سنود *sunūd*
شتم	*šatama*	abuse	شتم *šatm*
شجب	*šajaba*	denounce	شجب *šajb*
شرد	*šarada*	stray	شرود *šurūd*
شطب	*šaṭaba*	cross out	شطب *šaṭb*
شطر	*šaṭara*	halve	شطر *šaṭr*
شطف	*šaṭafa*	rinse	شطف *šaṭf*
شعر	*ša3ara*	feel	شعور *šu3ūr*
شغر	*šaɣara*	become vacant	شغور *šuɣūr*
شكر	*šakara*	thank	شكر *šukr*
شكل	*šakala*	mark with diacritics	شكل *šakl*
شمل	*šamala*	include	شمل *šam(a)l* شمول *šumūl*
شنق	*šanaqa*	hang	شنق *šanq*
صبغ	*ṣabaɣa*	dye	صبغ *ṣabɣ*
صدر	*ṣadara*	be published	صدور *ṣudūr* صدر *ṣadr*
صدق	*ṣadaqa*	be truthful	صدق *ṣidq*
صرخ	*ṣaraxa*	shout	صراخ *ṣurāx*
صلح	*ṣaluḥa*	be suitable	صلاحية *ṣalāḥīya*[t] صلاح *ṣalāḥ*
صمت	*ṣamata*	be quiet	صمت *ṣamt*
صمد	*ṣamada*	be steadfast	صمود *ṣumūd*
ضبط	*ḍabaṭa*	adjust	ضبط *ḍabṭ*
طبخ	*ṭabaxa*	cook	طبخ *ṭabx*
طرد	*ṭarada*	expel	طرد *ṭard*
طرق	*ṭaraqa*	knock	طرق *ṭarq*
طعن	*ṭa3ana*	stab	طعن *ṭa3n*
طلب	*ṭalaba*	request	طلب *ṭalab*
طلع	*ṭala3a*	rise	طلوع *ṭulū3*
عبد	*3abada*	worship	عبادة *3ibāda*[t]
عبر	*3abara*	cross	عبور *3ubūr*
عثر	*3atara*	find	عثور *3utūr*
عجن	*3ajana*	knead	عجن *3ajn*
عرك	*3araka*	injure badly	عرك *3ark*
عطس	*3aṭasa*	sneeze	عطس *3aṭs*

علك	*3alaka*	chew	علك *3alk*
علن	*3alana*	become known	علانية *3alānīya*[t]
عمر	*3amara*	live long	عمر *3umr*
غدر	*ɣadara*	deceive	غدر *ɣadr*
غرب	*ɣaraba*	leave	غرب *ɣarb*
غرب	*ɣaraba*	set	غروب *ɣurūb*
غفل	*ɣafala*	neglect	غفلة *ɣafla*[t]
غمر	*ɣamara*	flood	غمر *ɣamr*
فتك	*fataka*	decimate	فتك *fatk*
فجر	*fajara*	work as a prostitute	فجور *fujūr*
فرش	*faraša*	spread (out)	فرش *farš*
فرط	*faraṭa*	be excessive	فرط *farṭ*
فرق	*faraqa*	differentiate	فرق *farq*
فرم	*farama*	mince	فرم *farm*
فسد	*fasada*	decay	فساد *fasād*
فضل	*faḍala*	be left over	فضل *faḍl*
فطر	*faṭara*	eat breakfast	فطور *fuṭūr*
قتل	*qatala*	kill	قتل *qatl*
قتم	*qatama*	darken	قتامة *qatāma*[t]
قرص	*qaraṣa*	sting	قرص *qarṣ*
قشر	*qašara*	peel	قشر *qašr*
قصر	*qaṣara*	limit	قصر *qaṣr*
قطر	*qaṭara*	drip	قطر *qaṭr* قطران *qaṭarān*
قعد	*qa3ada*	sit	قعود *qu3ūd*
كتب	*kataba*	write	كتابة *kitāba*[t]
كدم	*kadama*	bruise	كدم *kadm*
كسد	*kasada*	become stagnant	كساد *kasād*
كشف	*kašafa*	discover	كشف *kašf*
كفل	*kafala*	vouch	كفالة *kafāla*[t]
كمن	*kamana*	be hidden	كمون *kumūn*
كنس	*kanasa*	sweep	كنس *kans*
لذع	*laḏa3a*	burn	لذع *laḏ3*
لطف	*laṭafa*	be kind	لطف *luṭf* لطافة *laṭāfa*[t]
لكم	*lakama*	punch	لكم *lakm*
لمس	*lamasa*	touch	لمس *lams*
مثل	*matala*	appear	مثول *mutūl*
مخط	*maxaṭa*	blow one's nose	مخط *maxṭ*
مرق	*maraqa*	shoot by	مروق *murūq*
مرن	*marana*	be flexible	مرونة *murūna*[t]
مزج	*mazaja*	mix	مزج *mazj*
مسك	*masaka*	hold	مسك *mask*

مضغ	*maḍaɣa*	chew	مضغ *maḍɣ*
مكث	*makaŧa*	remain	مكوث *mukūŧ* مكث *makŧ*
ملح	*malaɧa*	salt	ملاحة *malāɧa*^{t} ملوحة *mulūɧa*^{t}
ملس	*malusa*	be smooth	ملاسة *malāsa*^{t}
ملك	*malaka*	have	ملك *mulk*
منع	*mana3a*	become immune	مناعة *manā3a*^{t}
نبت	*nabata*	grow	نبت *nabt*
نثر	*naŧara*	scatter	نثر *naŧr*
نجم	*najama*	stem	نجوم *nujūm*
نحت	*naɧata*	sculpt	نحت *naɧt*
ندب	*nadaba*	mourn	ندب *nadb*
ندر	*nadara*	be rare	ندر *nadr* ندور *nudūr*
نسب	*nasaba*	refer	نسبة *nisba*^{t} نسب *nasab*
نسج	*nasaja*	weave	نسج *nasj*
نشد	*našada*	pursue	نشد *našd*
نشر	*našara*	spread	نشر *našr*
نشل	*našala*	pickpocket	نشل *našl*
نصب	*naṣaba*	cheat	نصب *naṣb*
نصر	*naṣara*	aid	نصر *naṣr* نصرة *nuṣra*^{t}
نطق	*naṭaqa*	pronounce	نطق *nuṭq*
نظر	*naẓara*	look	نظر *naẓar*
نعس	*na3asa*	become sleepy	نعاس *nu3ās* نعس *na3s*
نعم	*na3ama*	enjoy	نعمة *na3ma*^{t}
نعم	*na3uma*	be soft	نعومة *nu3ūma*^{t}
نفخ	*nafaxa*	inflate	نفخ *nafx*
نفذ	*nafađa*	penetrate	نفاذ *nafāđ*
نفض	*nafaḍa*	dust (off)	نفض *nafḍ*
نقد	*naqada*	criticize	نقد *naqd*
نقش	*naqaša*	engrave	نقش *naqš*
نقص	*naqaṣa*	decrease	نقص *naqṣ* نقصان *nuqṣān*
نقض	*naqaḍa*	rescind	نقض *naqḍ*
نقل	*naqala*	transport	نقل *naql*
نهب	*nahaba*	plunder	نهب *nahb*
هبط	*habaṭa*	descend	هبوط *hubūṭ*
هجر	*hajara*	abandon	هجر *hajr*
هجم	*hajama*	attack	هجوم *hujūm*
هرب	*haraba*	flee	هروب *hurūb* هرب *harab*
هرس	*harasa*	squash	هرس *hars*
همز	*hamaza*	hamzate	همز *hamz*

1s3(a)

أثر	*ʔaŧara*	cite	أثر *ʔaŧr* أثارة *ʔaŧāra*^{t}
أجر	*ʔajara*	reward	أجر *ʔajr*
أخذ	*ʔaxađa*	take	أخذ *ʔaxđ*
أكل	*ʔakala*	eat	أكل *ʔakl*
أمر	*ʔamara*	order sb to (do)	أمر *ʔamr*
أمل	*ʔamala*	hope	أمل *ʔamal*

1s4

بشع	*baši3a*	be ugly	بشاعة *bašā3a*^{t}
تبع	*tabi3a*	pursue	تبع *taba3*
تعب	*ta3iba*	become tired	تعب *ta3ab*
تفه	*tafiha*	be trivial	تفاهة *tafāha*^{t}
تلف	*talifa*	be destroyed	تلف *talaf*
جلد	*jalida*	be frozen	جلد *jalad*
جهل	*jahila*	not know	جهل *jahl* جهالة *jahāla*^{t}
حبل	*ɧabila*	become pregnant	حبل *ɧabal*
حذر	*ɧađira*	beware	حذر *ɧiđr* حذر *ɧađar*
حرج	*ɧarija*	be narrow	حرج *ɧaraj*
حرص	*ɧariṣa*	desire	حرص *ɧirṣ*
حزن	*ɧazina*	become sad	حزن *ɧuzn*
حسب	*ɧasiba*	consider	حسبان *ɧisbān*
حفظ	*ɧafiẓa*	memorize	حفظ *ɧifẓ*
حمد	*ɧamida*	glorify	حمد *ɧamd*
حمس	*ɧamisa*	be zealous	حماس *ɧamās*
خجل	*xajila*	be shy	خجل *xajal*
خدر	*xadira*	be numb	خدر *xadar*
خرس	*xarisa*	be quiet	خرس *xaras*
خسر	*xasira*	lose	خسر *xusr*
خصب	*xaṣiba*	be fertile	خصب *xiṣb*
دعر	*da3ira*	be indecent	دعر *da3ar*
دهش	*dahiša*	be amazed	دهش *dahaš*
ذهل	*đahila*	be amazed	ذهول *đuhūl*
رحم	*raɧima*	have mercy	رحمة *raɧma*^{t}
رضع	*raḍi3a*	suckle	رضاعة *raḍā3a*^{t}
رغب	*raɣiba*	desire	رغبة *raɣba*^{t}
ركب	*rakiba*	ride	ركوب *rukūb*
سخر	*saxira*	mock	سخرية *suxrīya*^{t}
سخط	*saxiṭa*	resent	سخط *saxaṭ* or *suxṭ*
سرب	*sariba*	leak	سرب *sarab*
سعد	*sa3ida*	be happy	سعادة *sa3āda*^{t}

سكر *sakira*	get drunk	سكر *sukr*
سلم *salima*	be safe and sound	سلامة *salāma^t*
سمع *sami3a*	hear	سماع *samā3* سمع *sam3*
سمن *samina*	become fat	سمن *simn* سمانة *samāna^t*
سهد *sahida*	have insomnia	سهاد *suhād* سهد *sahad*
سهر *sahira*	stay up all night	سهر *sahar*
شبع *šabi3a*	become full	شبع *šab3*
شرب *šariba*	drink	شرب *šurb*
شهد *šahida*	witness	شهود *šuhūd*
شهد *šahida*	testify	شهادة *šahāda^t*
شهق *šahiqa*	inhale	شهيق *šahīq*
صعد *ṣa3ida*	rise	صعود *ṣu3ūd*
ضجر *ḍajira*	be fed up	ضجر *ḍajar*
ضحك *ḍaḫika*	laugh	ضحك *ḍaḫk*
ضمن *ḍamina*	guarantee	ضمان *ḍamān*
طمع *ṭami3a*	covet	طمع *ṭama3*
ظفر *ẓafira*	win	ظفر *ẓafar*
عبث *3abita*	play around	عبث *3abat*
عجل *3ajila*	hurry (up)	عجلة *3ajala^t* عجل *3ajal*
عدم *3adima*	lack	عدم *3adam*
عرق *3ariqa*	sweat	عرق *3araq*
عشق *3ašiqa*	love	عشق *3išq*
عطش *3aṭiša*	become thirsty	عطش *3aṭaš*
عفن *3afina*	rot	عفن *3afan*
علق *3aliqa*	become stuck	علق *3alaq*
علق *3aliqa*	concern	علاقة *3alāqa^t*
علم *3alima*	know	علم *3ilm*
عمل *3amila*	work	عمل *3amal*
عهد *3ahida*	be familiar	عهد *3ahd*
غرق *ɣariqa*	drown	غرق *ɣaraq*
غضب *ɣaḍiba*	become angry	غضب *ɣaḍab*
غلط *ɣaliṭa*	be wrong	غلط *ɣalaṭ*
فرح *fariḫa*	be glad	فرح *faraḫ*
فشل *fašila*	fail	فشل *fašal*
فهم *fahima*	understand	فهم *fahm*
قبل *qabila*	accept	قبول *qabūl*
قدر *qadira*	be able to	قدر *qadar*
قدم *qadima*	arrive	قدوم *qudūm*
قرف *qarifa*	loathe	قرف *qaraf*

قلق *qaliqa*	worry	قلق *qalaq*
قنع *qani3a*	be satisfied	قناعة *qanā3a^t*
كبر *kabira*	grow old	كبر *kibar*
كره *kariha*	hate	كره *kurh* or *karh*
كسل *kasila*	become lazy	كسل *kasal*
لبث *labita*	linger	لبث *labt*
لبس *labisa*	wear	لبس *lubs*
لحس *laḫisa*	lick	لحس *laḫs*
لحق *laḫiqa*	follow	لحاق *laḫāq*
لزق *laziqa*	adhere	لزوق *luzūq*
لزم *lazima*	be necessary	لزوم *luzūm*
لصق *laṣiqa*	stick	لصق *laṣq*
لعب *la3iba*	play	لعب *la3(i)b* or *li3b*
مخض *maxiḍa*	be in labor	مخاض *maxāḍ*
مرح *mariḫa*	be cheerful	مرح *maraḫ*
مرض *mariḍa*	become ill	مرض *maraḍ*
ندم *nadima*	regret	ندم *nadam*
نزل *nazila*	stay	نزلة *nazla^t*
نشب *našiba*	break out	نشوب *nušūb*
نشط *našiṭa*	become active	نشاط *našāṭ*
نشف *našifa*	dry out	نشف *našaf*
نضج *naḍija*	ripen	نضج *nuḍj*
نفد *nafida*	run out	نفاد *nafād*
نهق *nahiqa*	bray	نهيق *nahīq*
وجع *waji3a*	hurt	وجع *waja3*
وسخ *wasixa*	become dirty	وسخ *wasax*
ولع *wali3a*	catch fire	ولع *wala3* ولوع *walū3*
يقظ *yaqiẓa*	be alert	يقظ *yaqaẓ*

1s4(a)

أثم *ʔaṯima*	sin	إثم *ʔiṯm*
أجل *ʔajila*	hesitate	أجل *ʔajal*
أذن *ʔaḏina*	allow	إذن *ʔiḏn*
أرق *ʔariqa*	suffer from insomnia	أرق *ʔaraq*
أزف *ʔazifa*	approach	أزف *ʔazaf*
أسف *ʔasifa*	be sorry	أسف *ʔasaf*
ألف *ʔalifa*	become accustomed	ألف *ʔalf*
أمن *ʔamina*	feel safe	أمن *ʔamn* أمان *ʔamān*
أنف *ʔanifa*	disdain	أنفة *ʔanafa^t*

1s4(b)

بئس	baʔisa	become miserable	بؤس buʔs
سئم	saʔima	be fed up	سأم saʔm سآمة saʔāma^{t}
كئب	kaʔiba	become depressed	كآبة kaʔāba^{t}
يئس	yaʔisa	give up hope	يأس yaʔs

1s4(c)

برئ	bariʔa	be innocent	براءة barāʔa^{t}
خطئ	xaṭiʔa	be mistaken	خطأ xaṭaʔ
دفئ	dafiʔa	become warm	دفاء difāʔ
صدئ	ṣadiʔa	rust	صدأ ṣadaʔ
هنئ	haniʔa	be delighted	هناء hanāʔ هنأ hanaʔ

1s5

حسب	ɦasiba	consider	حسبان ɦisbān
ربح	rabiɦa	gain	ربح ribɦ
عطل	3aṭila	be unemployed	عطل 3aṭal

1s6

بخل	baxula	be tightfisted	بخل buxl
بدن	baduna	become fat	بدانة badāna^{t}
برد	baruda	become cold	برود burūd
بسط	basuṭa	be simple	بساطة basāṭa^{t}
بصر	baṣura	perceive	بصر baṣr
بعد	ba3uda	be far	بعد bu3d
ثبت	tabuta	be proven	ثبوت tabūt
ثبت	tabuta	be fixed	ثبات tabāt
ثقل	taqula	become heavy	ثقالة taqāla^{t} ثقل tiql
جدر	jadura	be worthy	جدارة jadāra^{t}
جرؤ	jaruʔa	have the courage	جرأة jurʔa^{t}
جمد	jamuda	freeze	جمود jumūd
جمل	jamula	become beautiful	جمال jamāl
حرم	ɦaruma	be forbidden	حرمة ɦurma^{t}
حسن	ɦasuna	become beautiful	حسن ɦusn
حمز	ɦamuza	be strong	حمازة ɦamāza^{t}
حمض	ɦamuḍa	be sour	حموضة ɦumūḍa^{t}
خبث	xabuta	be malicious	خبث xubt خباثة xabāta^{t}
ذبل	đabula	wilt	ذبول đubūl
سهل	sahula	become easy	سهولة suhūla^{t}
صرم	ṣaruma	be strict	صرامة ṣarāma^{t}
صعب	ṣa3uba	be difficult	صعوبة ṣu3ūba^{t}
صلب	ṣaluba	become stiff	صلابة ṣalāba^{t}
صلح	ṣaluɦa	be suitable	صلاحية ṣalāɦīya^{t} صلاح ṣalāɦ
ضعف	ḍa3ufa	become weak	ضعف da3f or du3f
طهر	ṭahura	be clean	طهارة ṭahāra^{t}
عدل	3adula	be fair	عدالة 3adāla^{t}
عرض	3aruḍa	be wide	عرض 3arḍ
عنف	3anufa	become violent	عنف 3unf
غرب	ɣaruba	be strange	غرابة ɣarāba^{t}
غرب	ɣaruba	set	غروب ɣurūb
غمض	ɣamuḍa	become dark	غموض ɣumūḍ
فحش	faɦuša	become obscene	فحش fuɦš
قبح	qabuɦa	be ugly	قبح qubɦ
قدس	qadusa	be holy	قدس quds or qudus
قدم	qaduma	be old	قدم qidam
قرب	qaruba	approach	قرب qurb
قصر	qaṣura	become short	قصر qaṣr
كبر	kabura	grow	كبر kibar
كثر	katura	abound	كثرة katra^{t}
كثف	katufa	thicken	كثافة katāfa^{t}
كمل	kamula	be completed	كمال kamāl كمول kumūl
متن	matuna	be sturdy	متانة matāna^{t}
نحف	naɦufa	lose weight	نحافة naɦāfa^{t}
وثق	watuqa	be firm	وثاقة watāqa^{t}
وسم	wasuma	be handsome	وسامة wasāma^{t}
وقح	waquɦa	be insolent	وقاحة waqāɦa^{t}

1s6(a)

أمن	ʔamuna	be faithful	أمانة ʔamāna^{t}

1s6(b)

بؤس	baʔusa	be brave	بأس baʔs
ضؤل	ḍaʔula	be scanty	ضآلة ḍaʔāla^{t}

1s6(c)

بطؤ	baṭuʔa	be slow	بطء buṭʔ

1g1

ظل *ẓalla*	continue	ظل *ẓall*
عض *3aḍḍa*	bite	عض *3aḍḍ*
قر *qarra*	settle down	قرار *qarār*
مر *marra*	become bitter	مرارة *marāra*^{t}
مس *massa*	touch	مس *mass* مساس *misās*
مص *maṣṣa*	suck	مص *maṣṣ*
مل *malla*	become bored	ملل *malal*
ود *wadda*	want	ود *wadd* or وداد *wudd* or *widd* *wadād*

1g2

تم *tamma*	be complete	تمام *tamām*
جد *jadda*	be serious	جد *jidd*
جف *jaffa*	dry	جفاف *jafāf*
جل *jalla*	be majestic	جلال *jalāl*
حد *ħadda*	mourn	حداد *ħidād*
حر *ħarra*	be hot	حر *ħarr* حرارة *ħarāra*^{t}
حق *ħaqqa*	be true	حق *ħaqq*
حل *ħalla*	befall	حلول *ħulūl*
حل *ħalla*	occupy	حل *ħill*
حن *ħanna*	sympathize	حنان *ħanān* حنة *ħanna*^{t}
حن *ħanna*	long	حنين *ħanīn*
دب *dabba*	creep	دبيب *dabīb*
ذل *đalla*	be submissive	ذل *đull*
رف *raffa*	twitch	رفيف *rafīf*
رن *ranna*	ring	رنين *ranīn*
سد *sadda*	be appropriate	سدود *sudūd*
شب *šabba*	break out	شبوب *šubūb*
شد *šadda*	pull taut	شد *šadd*
شد *šadda*	be intense	شدة *šidda*^{t}
صح *ṣaħħa*	be correct	صحة *ṣiħħa*^{t}
ضج *ḍajja*	be noisy	ضج *ḍajj* ضجيج *ḍajīj*
ضل *ḍalla*	stray	ضلال *ḍalāl*
طن *ṭanna*	hum	طنين *ṭanīn*
عز *3azza*	become strong	عز *3izz* عزة *3izza*^{t}
غط *ɣaṭṭa*	snore	غطيط *ɣaṭīṭ*
فر *farra*	run away	فرار *firār*
قر *qarra*	be chilly	قر *qarr*
قل *qalla*	be less	قلة *qilla*^{t} قل *qill*
نق *naqqa*	croak	نقيق *naqīq*
نم *namma*	reveal	نم *namm*
هر *harra*	growl	هرير *harīr*

1g2(a)

أن *ʔanna*	moan	أنين *ʔanīn*

1g3

بت *batta*	decide	بت *batt*
بث *baṯṯa*	spread	بث *baṯṯ*
بل *balla*	moisten	بلل *balal*
جث *jaṯṯa*	uproot	جث *jaṯṯ*
جر *jarra*	pull	جر *jarr*
جز *jazza*	cut	جز *jazz*
جن *janna*	become dark	جنون *junūn*
حث *ħaṯṯa*	urge sb to (do)	حث *ħaṯṯ*
حج *ħajja*	make a pilgrimage	حج *ħajj*
حد *ħadda*	limit	حد *ħadd*
حد *ħadda*	mourn	حداد *ħidād*
حر *ħarra*	be hot	حر *ħarr* حرارة *ħarāra*^{t}
حط *ħaṭṭa*	land	حطوط *ħuṭūṭ*
حط *ħaṭṭa*	put	حط *ħaṭṭ*
حف *ħaffa*	surround	حف *ħaff*
حك *ħakka*	rub	حك *ħakk*
حل *ħalla*	solve	حل *ħall*
خص *xaṣṣa*	be characteristic	خصوص *xuṣūṣ*
خط *xaṭṭa*	write	خط *xaṭṭ*
دق *daqqa*	knock	دق *daqq*
دل *dalla*	show	دلالة *dalāla*^{t}
رج *rajja*	jar	رج *rajj*
رد *radda*	reply	رد *radd*
رش *rašša*	spray	رش *rašš*
رض *raḍḍa*	bruise	رض *raḍḍ*
زج *zajja*	throw	زج *zajj*
سب *sabba*	insult	سب *sabb*
سد *sadda*	block	سد *sadd*
سر *sarra*	please	سرور *surūr*
سك *sakka*	mint	سك *sakk*
سن *sanna*	sharpen	سن *sann*
شد *šadda*	pull taut	شد *šadd*

شق	*šaqqa*	split	شق *šaqq*
شك	*šakka*	doubt	شك *šakk*
شل	*šalla*	paralyze	شلل *šalal*
شم	*šamma*	smell	شم *šamm*
شن	*šanna*	launch	شن *šann*
صب	*ṣabba*	pour	صب *ṣabb*
صد	*ṣadda*	repel	صد *ṣadd*
ضخ	*ḍaxxa*	pump	ضخ *ḍaxx*
ضر	*ḍarra*	harm	ضر *ḍarr*
ضم	*ḍamma*	attach	ضم *ḍamm*
ظن	*ẓanna*	think	ظن *ẓann*
عد	*3adda*	count	عد *3add*
عم	*3amma*	become prevalent	عموم *3umūm*
غر	*ɣarra*	mislead	غرور *ɣurūr*
غش	*ɣašša*	cheat	غش *ɣašš* or *ɣišš*
غص	*ɣaṣṣa*	choke	غصص *ɣaṣaṣ*
غض	*ɣaḍḍa*	avert	غض *ɣaḍḍ*
فض	*faḍḍa*	drill	فض *faḍḍ*
فك	*fakka*	untie	فك *fakk*
فل	*falla*	dent	فل *full*
قص	*qaṣṣa*	tell	قصص *qaṣaṣ*
قص	*qaṣṣa*	cut	قص *qaṣṣ*
كح	*kaḥḥa*	cough	كحة *kuḥḥa^t*
كف	*kaffa*	abstain	كف *kaff*
كن	*kanna*	hide	كنون *kunūn*
لف	*laffa*	wrap	لف *laff*
لم	*lamma*	collect	لم *lamm*
مد	*madda*	stretch	مد *madd*
مر	*marra*	pass	مر *marr* مرور *murūr*
مر	*marra*	become bitter	مرارة *marāra^t*
مص	*maṣṣa*	suck	مص *maṣṣ*
من	*manna*	bestow	من *mann*
نص	*naṣṣa*	stipulate	نص *naṣṣ*
نط	*naṭṭa*	spring	نط *naṭṭ*
هب	*habba*	blow	هب *habb*
هز	*hazza*	shake	هز *hazz*
هم	*hamma*	worry	هم *hamm*

1g3(a)

أز	*ʔazza*	buzz	أزيز *ʔazīz*

1a1

ودع	*wada3a*	leave	ودع *wad3*
وضع	*waḍa3a*	put	وضع *waḍ3*
وقع	*waqa3a*	fall	وقوع *wuqū3*
وهب	*wahaba*	grant	وهب *wahb*

1a1(a)

وثأ	*waŧaʔa*	sprain	وثء *waŧʔ*

1a2

وثب	*waŧaba*	hop	وثب *waŧb*
وثق	*waŧiqa*	trust	ثقة *ŧiqa^t*
وجب	*wajaba*	be necessary for sb	وجوب *wujūb*
وجد	*wajada*	find	وجود *wujūd*
وجم	*wajama*	be silent	وجوم *wujūm*
وخز	*waxaza*	prick	وخز *waxz*
ورد	*warada*	arrive	ورود *wurūd*
وزن	*wazana*	weigh	وزن *wazn*
وسم	*wasama*	mark	وسم *wasm*
وصف	*waṣafa*	describe	وصف *waṣf*
وصف	*waṣafa*	prescribe	وصفة *waṣfa^t*
وصل	*waṣala*	arrive	وصول *wuṣūl*
وصل	*waṣala*	connect	وصل *waṣl* صلة *ṣila^t*
وضح	*waḍaḥa*	become clear	وضوح *wuḍūḥ*
وعد	*wa3ada*	promise	وعد *wa3d*
وعظ	*wa3aẓa*	preach	وعظ *wa3ẓ* عظة *3iẓa^t*
وفد	*wafada*	come	وفود *wufūd*
وقف	*waqafa*	stop	وقوف *wuqūf* وقف *waqf*
ولد	*walada*	bear	ولادة *wilāda^t*
ومض	*wamaḍa*	flash	وميض *wamīḍ*

1a3

وسع	*wasi3a*	be wide	سعة *sa3a^t*
وسع	*wasi3a*	be possible	وسع *wus3*

1a3(a)

وطئ	*waṭiʔa*	tread	وطء *waṭʔ*

1a4

ورث	*wariŧa*	inherit	ورث *wirŧ* إرث *ʔirŧ*
وفق	*wafiqa*	be suitable	وفق *wafq*

1h1

حار	*ḥāra*	be confused	حيرة *ḥayra^t*
خاف	*xāfa*	be afraid	خوف *xawf*

زال *zāla*	cease	زيل *zayl*
غار *ɣāra*	be jealous	غيرة *ɣayra*^{t}
كاد *kāda*	be about to (do)	كيد *kayd*
نام *nāma*	sleep	نوم *nawm*
نال *nāla*	win	نيل *nayl* منال *manāl*
هاب *hāba*	fear	هيبة *hayba*^{t} مهابة *mahāba*^{t}

1h1(a)

شاء *šāʔa*	want	مشيئة *mašīʔa*^{t}

1h2

بات *bāta*	spend the night	مبيت *mabīt*
باض *bāḍa*	lay an egg	بيض *bayḍ*
باع *bā3a*	sell	بيع *bay3*
بان *bāna*	become evident	بيان *bayān*
تاه *tāha*	get lost	توه *tawh*
حاض *ħāḍa*	menstruate	حيض *ħayḍ*
حان *ħāna*	approach	حين *ħayn* or
خاب *xāba*	fail	خيبة *xayba*^{t}
دان *dāna*	lend	دين *dayn*
دان *dāna*	profess	دين *dīn* ديانة *diyāna*^{t}
زاد *zāda*	increase	زيادة *ziyāda*^{t}
زاف *zāfa*	be fake	زيف *zayf*
سار *sāra*	march	سير *sayr*
شاع *šā3a*	become public	شيوع *šuyū3*
سال *sāla*	flow	سيلان *sayalān*
شان *šāna*	disgrace	شين *šayn*
صاح *ṣāħa*	shout	صياح *ṣiyāħ*
صاد *ṣāda*	hunt	صيد *ṣayd*
صار *ṣāra*	become	صيرورة *ṣayrūra*^{t} صير *ṣayr*
ضاع *ḍā3a*	get lost	ضياع *ḍayā3*
ضاق *ḍāqa*	become narrow	ضيق *ḍīq*
طاب *ṭāba*	delight	طيبة *ṭība*^{t}
طار *ṭāra*	fly	طيران *ṭayarān*
طاش *ṭāša*	become heedless	طيشان *ṭayašān*
عاش *3āša*	live	عيش *3ayš*
غاب *ɣāba*	be absent	غياب *ɣiyāb*
غام *ɣāma*	become cloudy	غيم *ɣaym*

فاض *fāḍa*	flood	فيضان *fayaḍān*
قاس *qāsa*	measure	قياس *qiyās*
كاد *kāda*	deceive	كيد *kayd* مكيدة *makīda*^{t}
لاق *lāqa*	fit	ليق *layq*
مال *māla*	lean	ميل *mayl*
ناك *nāka*	fuck	نيك *nayk*

1h2(a)

جاء *jāʔa*	come	مجيء *majīʔ*
ناء *nāʔa*	be raw	نيء *nayʔ* نيوء *nuyūʔ*

1h3

باح *bāħa*	disclose	بوح *bawħ*
باس *bāsa*	kiss	بوس *baws*
بال *bāla*	urinate	بول *bawl*
تاب *tāba*	repent	توبة *tawba*^{t}
ثار *ŧāra*	revolt	ثورة *ŧawra*^{t}
جاب *jāba*	explore	جوب *jawb*
جار *jāra*	oppress	جور *jawr*
جاز *jāza*	be allowed	جواز *jawāz*
جاع *jā3a*	become hungry	جوع *jū3*
جال *jāla*	roam around	جول *jawl* تجوال *tajwāl*
حاك *ħāka*	knit	حياكة *ħiyāka*^{t}
حال *ħāla*	prevent	حيلولة *ħaylūla*^{t}
خار *xāra*	moo	خوار *xuwār*
خاض *xāḍa*	wade	خوض *xawḍ*
خان *xāna*	betray	خيانة *xiyāna*^{t}
دار *dāra*	revolve	دوران *dawarān* دور *dawr*
داس *dāsa*	tread	دوس *daws*
دام *dāma*	continue	دوام *dawām* دوم *dawm*
ذاب *đāba*	melt	ذوبان *đawabān* ذوب *đawb*
ذاق *đāqa*	taste	ذوق *đawq*
راج *rāja*	be in circulation	رواج *rawāj*
راح *rāħa*	go	رواح *rawāħ*
راد *rāda*	explore	رود *rawd*
راع *rā3a*	delight	روع *raw3*
راق *rāqa*	please	روق *rawq*
رام *rāma*	crave	روم *rawm*
زار *zāra*	visit	زيارة *ziyāra*^{t}
زال *zāla*	disappear	زوال *zawāl*

ساح sāħa	tour	سياحة siyāħa^t
ساد sāda	become master	سيادة siyāda^t
ساس sāsa	rule	سياسة siyāsa^t
ساق sāqa	drive	سياقة siyāqa^t سوق sawq
صاغ şāɣa	shape	صياغة şiyāɣa^t
صام şāma	fast	صوم şawm صيام şiyām
صان şāna	maintain	صيانة şiyāna^t
طال ţāla	become long	طول ţūl
عاد 3āda	return	عودة 3awda^t عود 3awd
عاذ 3āđa	take refuge	عياذ 3iyāđ
عاق 3āqa	hinder	عوق 3awq
عال 3āla	provide	عول 3awl
عام 3āma	swim	عوم 3awm
غار ɣāra	penetrate	غور ɣawr
غاص ɣāşa	dive	غوص ɣawş
فات fāta	pass	فوات fawāt
فار fāra	boil	فوران fawarān فور fawr
فاز fāza	win	فوز fawz
فاق fāqa	surpass	فوق fawq
قات qāta	feed	قوت qūt
قاد qāda	lead	قيادة qiyāda^t
قال qāla	say	قول qawl
قام qāma	stand up	قيام qiyām
كان kāna	be	كون kawn
لاذ lāđa	seek refuge	لوذ lawđ
لام lāma	blame	لوم lawm
مات māta	die	موت mawt
ناب nāba	represent	نيابة niyāba^t
ناص nāşa	avoid	مناص manāş
ناف nāfa	exceed	نوف nawf
هال hāla	frighten	هول hawl
هان hāna	be easy	هون hawn

1h3(a)

آب ʔāba	return	إياب ʔiyāb
آن ʔāna	approach	أون ʔūn

1h3(b)

ساء sāʔa	become bad	سوء sūʔ or sawʔ
ماء māʔa	meow	مواء muwāʔ موء mawʔ
ناء nāʔa	be weighed down	نوء nawʔ

1d1

دهى dahā	befall	دهي dahy
رعى ra3ā	guard	رعي ra3y رعاية ri3āya^t
سعى sa3ā	striev	سعي sa3y
نهى nahā	forbid	نهي nahy

1d1(a)

أبى ʔabā	refuse	إباء ʔibāʔ

1d1(b)

رأى raʔā	see	رؤية ruʔya^t

1d2

برى barā	sharpen	بري bary
بغى baɣā	wrong	بغي baɣy
بغى baɣā	whore	بغاء biɣāʔ
بغى baɣā	long for	بغاء buɣāʔ
بكى bakā	cry	بكاء bukāʔ
بنى banā	build	بناء banāʔ
ثنى ŧanā	bend	ثني ŧany
جرى jarā	run	جري jary
جزى jazā	punish	جزاء jazāʔ
جنى janā	inflict	جناية jināya^t
حكى ħakā	tell	حكاية ħikāya^t
حمى ħamā	protect	حماية ħimāya^t
حوى ħawā	contain	حواية ħawāya^t
درى darā	know	دراية dirāya^t
ذوى đawā	fade	ذو đawy
رمى ramā	throw	رمي ramy رماية rimāya^t
روى rawā	narrate	رواية riwāya^t
زنى zanā	fornicate	زنى zin(an) زناء zināʔ
سرى sarā	hold true	سريان sarayān
سقى saqā	water	سقي saqy
شفى šafā	cure	شفاء šifāʔ
شوى šawā	roast	شي šayy
طلى ţalā	paint	طلي ţaly
طوى ţawā	fold (up)	طي ţayy
عصى 3aşā	disobey	معصية ma3şiya^t عصيان 3işyān
عنى 3anā	mean	عني 3any
عنى 3anā	concern	عناية 3ināya^t
عوى 3awā	howl	عواء 3uwāʔ

غلى ɣalā	boil	غلي ɣaly غليان ɣalayān
غوى ɣawā	seduce	غواية ɣawāya^{t}
فدى fadā	sacrifice	فداء fidāʔ
قضى qaḍā	spend	قضاء qaḍāʔ
قلى qalā	fry	قلي qalī^{y}
كفى kafā	be enough	كفاية kifāya^{t}
كوى kawā	iron	كي kayy
لوى lawā	twist	لوي luwī^{y}
مشى mašā	walk	مشي mašy
مضى maḍā	pass	مضي muḍī^{y}
نفى nafā	deny	نفي nafy
نوى nawā	plan	نية nīya^{t}
هدى hadā	guide	هدى hud(an)
هوى hawā	fall down	هوي huwī^{y}

1d2(a)

أتى ʔatā	come	إتيان ʔityān
أوى ʔawā	take shelter	إيواء ʔīwāʔ

1d2(b)

وعى wa3ā	perceive	وعي wa3y
وفى wafā	keep	وفاء wafāʔ
وقى waqā	protect	وقي waqy وقاية wiqāya^{t}

1d3

بدا badā	seem	بدو budū^{w}
تلا talā	recite	تلاوة talāwa^{t}
تلا talā	follow	تلو tulū^{w}
جلا jalā	polish	جلي jaly
حشا ɦašā	stuff	حشو ɦašw
حلا ɦalā	be sweet	حلاوة ɦalāwa^{t}
حنا ɦanā	bend	حنو ɦanw
خطا xaṭā	step	خطو xaṭw
دعا da3ā	invite	دعاء du3āʔ
ربا rabā	exceed	ربو rubū^{w}
رثا raṯā	lament	رثو raṯw
رجا rajā	ask	رجاء rajāʔ
رغا raɣā	foam	رغو raɣw
سخا saxā	be generous	سخاء saxāʔ
سطا saṭā	burglarize	سطو saṭw
سما samā	be high	سمو sumū^{w}
سنا sanā	shine	سناء sanāʔ
شكا šakā	complain	شكوى šakwā شكاية šikāya^{t}
صحا ṣaɦā	wake up	صحو ṣaɦw
صفا ṣafā	become pure	صفو ṣafw صفاء ṣafāʔ
عدا 3adā	gallop	عدو 3adw
عفا 3afā	pardon	عفو 3afw
علا 3alā	rise	علو 3ulū^{w}
غدا ɣadā	become	غدو ɣudū^{w}
غزا ɣazā	invade	غزو ɣazw
غفا ɣafā	nap	غفو ɣafw
غلا ɣalā	be expensive	غلاء ɣalāʔ
قسا qasā	be cruel	قسوة qaswa^{t}
قفا qafā	follow	قفو qafw
كسا iktasā	cover	كسو kasw
محا maɦā	erase	محو maɦw
نجا najā	survive	نجاة najā^{t}
نما namā	develop	نماء namāʔ نمو numū^{w}
هفا hafā	err	هفو hafw

1d4

بقي baqiya	stay	بقاء baqāʔ
بلي baliya	wear out	بلى bil(an)
حظي ɦaẓiya	enjoy	حظوة ɦiẓwa^{t}
حمي ɦamiya	become hot	حمو ɦamw
حيي ɦayiya	be shy	حياء ɦayāʔ
خشي xašiya	be afraid	خشية xašya^{t}
خفي xafiya	be hidden	خفاء xafāʔ
خلا xalā	be free	خلاء xalāʔ
دمي damiya	bleed	دمى dam(an)
دهي dahiya	be resourceful	دهاء dahāʔ
رضي raḍiya	be satisfied	رضى riḍ(an) رضاء riḍāʔ
شظي šaẓiya	splinter	شظى šaẓ(an)
طغي ṭaɣiya	tyrannize	طغي ṭaɣy طغيان ṭuɣyān
عري 3ariya	undress	عري 3ury
عشي 3ašiya	have poor eyesight	عشا 3ašā
عمي 3amiya	go blind	عمى 3am(an)
غشي ɣašiya	cover	غشاوة ɣašāwa^{t}
فني faniya	perish	فناء fanāʔ
قوي qawiya	become strong	قوة quwwa^{t}
لقي laqiya	meet	لقاء liqāʔ
نسي nasiya	forget	نسيان nisyān نسي nasy
هوي hawiya	love	هوى haw(an)

1d4(a)		
أسي *ʔasiya*	grieve	أسى *ʔas(an)*

1d4(b)		
حي *ħayya*	live	حياة *ħayāᵗ*

1d5		
ولي *waliya*	follow	ولاية *wilāyaᵗ*

Measures II-X

2s	
بحر *baħħara*	sail
بخر *baxxara*	vaporize
بدد *baddada*	scatter
بدل *baddala*	change
بذر *bađđara*	waste
برد *barrada*	cool
برر *barrara*	justify
برك *barraka*	bless
بسط *bassaṭa*	simplify
بشر *baššara*	preach
بقع *baqqa3a*	stain
بكر *bakkara*	be early
بلط *ballaṭa*	tile
بلغ *ballaɣa*	report
بلل *ballala*	moisten
بنج *bannaja*	anesthesize
بوز *bawwaza*	pout
بيض *bayyaḍa*	whiten
بين *bayyana*	show
تبل *tabbala*	spice
توج *tawwaja*	crown
ثبت *tabbata*	fix
ثقف *taqqafa*	educate
ثلث *tallata*	triple
ثمن *tammana*	value
جبس *jabbasa*	set in plaster
جدد *jaddada*	renew
جدف *jaddafa*	row
جذف *jađđafa*	row
جرب *jarraba*	try
جرد *jarrada*	peel
جسد *jassada*	embody
جصص *jaṣṣaṣa*	plaster
جعد *ja33ada*	wrinkle
جفف *jaffafa*	dry
جلد *jallada*	freeze
جمد *jammada*	freeze
جمع *jamma3a*	gather
جمل *jammala*	beautify
جند *jannada*	recruit
جنس *jannasa*	naturalize
جنن *jannana*	madden
جهز *jahhaza*	prepare
جود *jawwada*	improve
جوع *jawwa3a*	keep hungry
جوف *jawwafa*	hollow out
جيش *jayyaša*	mobilize
حبل *ħabbala*	impregnate
حتم *ħattama*	make indispensable
حجب *ħajjaba*	veil
حدث *ħaddata*	speak
حدد *ħaddada*	specify
حدق *ħaddaqa*	stare
حذر *ħađđara*	warn
حرر *ħarrara*	liberate
حرض *ħarraḍa*	incite
حرف *ħarrafa*	pervert
حرق *ħarraqa*	burn
حرك *ħarraka*	move
حرم *ħarrama*	ban
حزن *ħazzana*	sadden
حسن *ħassana*	improve
حصل *ħaṣṣala*	collect
حصن *ħaṣṣana*	immunize
حضر *ħaḍḍara*	prepare
حطم *ħaṭṭama*	smash
حقق *ħaqqaqa*	achieve
حكم *ħakkama*	make sb a ruler
حلف *ħallafa*	swear in
حلق *ħallaqa*	circle

حلل	*ħallala*	analyze
حلى	*ħallā*	sweeten
حمد	*ħammada*	praise highly
حمر	*ħammara*	roast
حمص	*ħammaşa*	toast
حمل	*ħammala*	load
حنط	*ħannaţa*	embalm
حنك	*ħannaka*	sophisticate
حنن	*ħannana*	move
حول	*ħawwala*	transform
حير	*ħayyara*	confuse
خبر	*xabbara*	tell
خجل	*xajjala*	embarrass
خدر	*xaddara*	drug
خرب	*xarraba*	destroy
خرط	*xarraţa*	chop
خزن	*xazzana*	store
خصب	*xaşşaba*	fertilize
خصص	*xaşşaşa*	devote
خطط	*xaţţaţa*	plan
خفض	*xaffađa*	lower
خفف	*xaffafa*	lighten
خلص	*xallaşa*	save
خلف	*xallafa*	leave behind
خمس	*xammasa*	multiply by five
خمن	*xammana*	guess
خوف	*xawwafa*	frighten
خيب	*xayyaba*	cause to fail
خيط	*xayyaţa*	sew
خيل	*xayyala*	cause to believe
خيم	*xayyama*	camp
دبب	*dabbaba*	grind
دبر	*dabbara*	arrange
دبس	*dabbasa*	staple
دخن	*daxxana*	smoke
درب	*darraba*	train
درج	*darraja*	gradate
درس	*darrasa*	teach
درع	*darra3a*	armor
دعم	*da33ama*	support
دقق	*daqqaqa*	examine
دلع	*dalla3a*	spoil
دلك	*dallaka*	massage
دلل	*dallala*	prove
دمر	*dammara*	destroy
دور	*dawwara*	turn

دول	*dawwala*	internationalize
دون	*dawwana*	record
ذكر	*đakkara*	remind
ذلل	*đallala*	overcome
ذوب	*đawwaba*	melt
ربت	*rabbata*	pat
ربع	*rabba3a*	square
رتب	*rattaba*	arrange
رجح	*rajjaħa*	prefer
رجع	*rajja3a*	return
رحب	*raħħaba*	welcome
رحل	*raħħala*	make leave
رخص	*raxxaşa*	permit
ردد	*raddada*	repeat
رسخ	*rassaxa*	reinforce
رسم	*rassama*	delimit
رشح	*raššaħa*	nominate
رطب	*raţţaba*	moisturize
رفع	*raffa3a*	raise
رفه	*raffaha*	entertain
رقط	*raqqaţa*	spot
رقم	*raqqama*	punctuate
ركب	*rakkaba*	make ride
ركز	*rakkaza*	focus
رمم	*rammama*	restore
روج	*rawwaja*	launch
روح	*rawwaħa*	fan
روع	*rawwa3a*	terrify
زعل	*za33ala*	upset
زمر	*zammara*	blow
زوج	*zawwaja*	marry off
زود	*zawwada*	equip
زور	*zawwara*	falsify
زول	*zawwala*	remove
زيف	*zayyafa*	counterfeit
زين	*zayyana*	decorate
سبب	*sabbaba*	cause
سبق	*sabbaqa*	do ahead of time
سجل	*sajjala*	register
سخر	*saxxara*	utilize
سخن	*saxxana*	heat (up)
سدد	*saddada*	pay
سدس	*saddasa*	multiply by six
سرح	*sarraħa*	style
سرع	*sarra3a*	accelerate
سطح	*saţţaħa*	flatten

سطر	*saţţara*	line
سعر	*sa33ara*	price
سكن	*sakkana*	calm
سلح	*sallaħa*	arm
سلف	*sallafa*	advance
سلك	*sallaka*	unclog
سلم	*sallama*	greet
سمر	*sammara*	nail
سمم	*sammama*	poison
سهل	*sahhala*	make easy
سود	*sawwada*	blacken
سيس	*sayyasa*	politicize
سوق	*sawwaqa*	market
سير	*sayyara*	start
سيل	*sayyala*	liquefy
شبه	*šabbaha*	liken
شتت	*šattata*	scatter
شجب	*šajjaba*	denounce
شجع	*šajja3a*	encourage
شحم	*šaħħama*	grease
شخص	*šaxxaşa*	identify
شدد	*šaddada*	emphasize
شرح	*šarraħa*	slice
شرد	*šarrada*	displace
شرع	*šarra3a*	legislate
شرف	*šarrafa*	honor
شغل	*šaɣɣala*	employ
شقق	*šaqqaqa*	split
شكل	*šakkala*	form
شمع	*šamma3a*	wax
شوش	*šawwaša*	confuse
شوق	*šawwaqa*	interest
شوه	*šawwaha*	disfigure
شيع	*šayya3a*	escort
صحح	*şaħħaħa*	correct
صحى	*şaħħā*	wake up
صدر	*şaddara*	export
صدق	*şaddaqa*	believe
صرح	*şarraħa*	
صرف	*şarrafa*	exchange
صعد	*şa33ada*	escalate
صغر	*şaɣɣara*	make smaller
صفف	*şaffafa*	line up
صفق	*şaffaqa*	applaud
صلب	*şallaba*	harden
صلح	*şallaħa*	repair

صمم	*şammama*	design
صنف	*şannafa*	classify
صوب	*şawwaba*	aim
صوت	*şawwata*	vote
صور	*şawwara*	photograph
صير	*şayyara*	cause to be
ضحى	*ḑaħħā*	sacrifice
ضخم	*ḑaxxama*	inflate
ضرر	*ḑarrara*	harm
ضرم	*ḑarrama*	light
ضعف	*ḑa33afa*	double
ضلل	*ḑallala*	lead astray
ضمد	*ḑammada*	bandage
ضمن	*ḑammana*	include
ضيع	*ḑayya3a*	waste
ضيف	*ḑayyafa*	entertain
ضيق	*ḑayyaqa*	make narrower
طبع	*ţabba3a*	normalize
طبق	*ţabbaqa*	apply
طبل	*ţabbala*	drum
طرز	*ţarraza*	embroider
طعم	*ţa33ama*	vaccinate
طلق	*ţallaqa*	divorce
طهر	*ţahhara*	cleanse
طور	*ţawwara*	develop
طوع	*ţawwa3a*	subdue
طوف	*ţawwafa*	roam around
طول	*ţawwala*	lengthen
طيب	*ţayyaba*	make pleasant
ظلل	*z̧allala*	shade
عبد	*3abbada*	pave
عبر	*3abbara*	express
عتم	*3attama*	darken
عجل	*3ajjala*	hurry
عدد	*3addada*	enumerate
عدل	*3addala*	modify
عدن	*3addana*	mine
عذب	*3ađđaba*	torture
عرب	*3arraba*	Arabicize
عرض	*3arraḑa*	subject
عرف	*3arrafa*	introduce
عزز	*3azzaza*	reinforce
عشش	*3aššaša*	nest
عطر	*3aţţara*	perfume
عطل	*3aţţala*	break down
عظم	*3az̧z̧ama*	glorify

عفن	*3affana*	rot
عقب	*3aqqaba*	follow
عقد	*3aqqada*	complicate
عقم	*3aqqama*	sterilize
علب	*3allaba*	package
علق	*3allaqa*	attach
علل	*3allala*	justify
علم	*3allama*	teach
عمد	*3ammada*	baptize
عمر	*3ammara*	grant a long life
عمق	*3ammaqa*	deepen
عمم	*3ammama*	make public
عنف	*3annafa*	scold
عود	*3awwada*	accustom
عوذ	*3awwađa*	protect
عوض	*3awwaḍa*	compensate
عوق	*3awwaqa*	hinder
عوم	*3awwama*	set afloat
عيط	*3ayyaṭa*	yell
عين	*3ayyana*	appoint
غبر	*ɣabbara*	make dusty
غرز	*ɣarraza*	get stuck
غرق	*ɣarraqa*	drown
غرم	*ɣarrama*	fine
غفل	*ɣaffala*	make mindless
غلف	*ɣallafa*	cover
غمض	*ɣammaḍa*	obscure
غير	*ɣayyara*	change
فتش	*fattaša*	inspect
فتل	*fattala*	twist
فجر	*fajjara*	explode
فخخ	*faxxaxa*	booby- trap
فرح	*farraħa*	please
فرش	*farraša*	brush
فرغ	*farraɣa*	empty
فرق	*farraqa*	divide
فزع	*fazza3a*	scare
فسر	*fassara*	clarify
فصل	*faṣṣala*	divide
فضل	*faḍḍala*	prefer
فعل	*fa33ala*	activate
فكر	*fakkara*	think
فكك	*fakkaka*	disassemble
فهم	*fahhama*	make understand
فوت	*fawwata*	miss
فوض	*fawwaḍa*	authorize

فوق	*fawwaqa*	aim
قبل	*qabbala*	kiss
قتل	*qattala*	slaughter
قدر	*qaddara*	estimate
قدس	*qaddasa*	deem holy
قدم	*qaddama*	introduce
قرب	*qarraba*	bring close
قرر	*qarrara*	decide
قسم	*qassama*	divide
قصر	*qaṣṣara*	shorten
قطر	*qaṭṭara*	distill
قطع	*qaṭṭa3a*	cut up
قلب	*qallaba*	invert
قلد	*qallada*	imitate
قلص	*qallaṣa*	contract
قلل	*qallala*	reduce
قلم	*qallama*	clip
قنع	*qanna3a*	mask
قوس	*qawwasa*	bend
قوم	*qawwama*	arrange
قيم	*qayyama*	value
قيد	*qayyada*	bind
كبب	*kabbaba*	form a ball out of
كبر	*kabbara*	enlarge
كتب	*kattaba*	make write
كتل	*kattala*	amass
كثف	*kattafa*	make thick
كدس	*kaddasa*	accumulate
كرر	*karrara*	repeat
كرر	*karrara*	refine
كرس	*karrasa*	dedicate
كرم	*karrama*	bestow of honors
كسر	*kassara*	shatter
كعب	*ka33aba*	cube
كفل	*kaffala*	appoint sb as guarantor
كلف	*kallafa*	cost
كلم	*kallama*	speak
كمل	*kammala*	complete
كوم	*kawwama*	pile up
كون	*kawwana*	form
كيف	*kayyafa*	regulate
لبد	*labbada*	cover with clouds
لبس	*labbasa*	dress
لثم	*lattama*	cover
لحن	*laħħana*	compose

لخص *laxxaṣa*	summarize
لطخ *laṭṭaxa*	stain
لفق *laffaqa*	fabricate
لقب *laqqaba*	address
لقح *laqqaħa*	vaccinate
لقن *laqqana*	teach
لمح *lammaħa*	hint
لمع *lamma3a*	polish
لوث *lawwaŧa*	pollute
لوح *lawwaħa*	wave
لون *lawwana*	color
لين *layyana*	soften
متن *mattana*	fortify
مثل *maŧŧala*	represent
محص *maħħaṣa*	examine closely
مدد *maddada*	extend
مرر *marrara*	pass
مرض *marraḍa*	nurse
مرن *marrana*	train
مزق *mazzaqa*	tear up
مسد *massada*	stroke
مشط *maššaṭa*	comb
مغط *maɣɣaṭa*	stretch
مكن *makkana*	enable
منع *manna3a*	immunize
مهد *mahhada*	prepare
موج *mawwaja*	wave
مول *mawwala*	fund
مون *mawwana*	supply
ميز *mayyaza*	differentiate
نبه *nabbaha*	warn
نجد *najjada*	upholster
نجم *najjama*	practice astrology
ندد *naddada*	criticize
نزل *nazzala*	download
نسق *nassaqa*	coordinate
نشط *naššaṭa*	energize
نشف *naššafa*	dry
نصب *naṣṣaba*	nominate
نصر *naṣṣara*	convert to Christianity
نصف *naṣṣafa*	halve
نظف *naẓẓafa*	clean
نظم *naẓẓama*	arrange
نعم *na33ama*	soften
نغص *naɣɣaṣa*	upset

نفذ *naffađa*	implement
نفر *naffara*	alienate
نقب *naqqaba*	drill
نقح *naqqaħa*	revise
نقص *naqqaṣa*	reduce
نقط *naqqaṭa*	dot
نكر *nakkara*	disguise
نور *nawwara*	illuminate
نوع *nawwa3a*	diversify
نوم *nawwama*	put to bed
نون *nawwana*	add nunation
نوه *nawwaha*	point out
هدد *haddada*	threaten
هدم *haddama*	demolish
هذب *hađđaba*	educate
هرب *harraba*	smuggle
هرج *harraja*	behave in a silly way
هشم *haššama*	destroy
همش *hammaša*	marginalize
هول *hawwala*	intimidate
هون *hawwana*	make easy
هين *hayyana*	verbally abuse
هيج *hayyaja*	agitate
وبخ *wabbaxa*	scold
وثق *waŧŧaqa*	document
وجه *wajjaha*	guide
وحد *waħħada*	unite
ودع *wadda3a*	say goodbye
ورث *warraŧa*	leave (in one's will)
ورد *warrada*	blossom
ورط *warraṭa*	involve
وزع *wazza3a*	distribute
وسخ *wassaxa*	make dirty
وسع *wassa3a*	widen
وشم *waššama*	tattoo
وصل *waṣṣala*	deliver
وضب *waḍḍaba*	arrange
وضح *waḍḍaħa*	clarify
وطد *waṭṭada*	stabilize
وظف *waẓẓafa*	employ
وفر *waffara*	save
وفق *waffaqa*	reconcile
وقت *waqqata*	schedule
وقر *waqqara*	revere

وقع	*waqqa3a*	sign
وقف	*waqqafa*	arrest
ولد	*wallada*	generate
يسر	*yassara*	make easy

2s(a)

أبد	*ʔabbada*	perpetuate
أثث	*ʔaŧŧaŧa*	furnish
أثر	*ʔaŧŧara*	affect
أجج	*ʔajajja*	light
أجر	*ʔajjara*	rent out
أجل	*ʔajjala*	postpone
أخر	*ʔaxxara*	postpone
أدب	*ʔaddaba*	educate
أذن	*ʔađđana*	call to prayer
أرخ	*ʔarraxa*	date
أرق	*ʔarraqa*	not let sleep
أسس	*ʔassasa*	establish
أشر	*ʔaššara*	stamp
أكد	*ʔakkada*	confirm
ألف	*ʔallafa*	write
ألم	*ʔallama*	hurt
أمم	*ʔammama*	nationalize
أمن	*ʔammana*	reassure
أنب	*ʔannaba*	scold
أنث	*ʔannaŧa*	make feminine
أهب	*ʔahhaba*	make ready
أهل	*ʔahhala*	qualify
أوه	*ʔawwaha*	sigh
أيد	*ʔayyada*	support

2s(b)

رأس	*raʔʔasa*	make president

2s(c)

برأ	*barraʔa*	acquit
بطأ	*baṭṭaʔa*	slow down
جزأ	*jazzaʔa*	divide
حنأ	*ħannaʔa*	dye with henna
خبأ	*xabbaʔa*	hide
دفأ	*daffaʔa*	make warm
عبأ	*3abbaʔa*	load
هدأ	*haddaʔa*	calm
هنأ	*hannaʔa*	congratulate
هيأ	*hayyaʔa*	prepare

2d

ثنى	*ŧannā*	double
جلى	*jallā*	reveal
حيا	*ħayyā*	greet
خلى	*xallā*	vacate
دلى	*dallā*	dangle
ربى	*rabbā*	raise
رقى	*raqqā*	advance
روى	*rawwā*	irrigate
سلى	*sallā*	entertain
سمى	*sammā*	call
سوى	*sawwā*	settle
صفى	*ṣaffā*	purify
صلى	*ṣallā*	pray
عرى	*3arrā*	undress
غذى	*ɣađđā*	feed
غرى	*ɣarrā*	glue
غطى	*ɣaṭṭā*	cover
غنى	*ɣannā*	sing
قسى	*qassā*	harden
قوى	*qawwā*	strengthen
لبى	*labbā*	comply
لوى	*lawwā*	bend
نجى	*najjā*	rescue
نقى	*naqqā*	purify
نمى	*nammā*	develop
هجى	*hajjā*	spell
هوى	*hawwā*	ventilate
وصى	*waṣṣā*	advise
وعى	*wa33ā*	make aware
ولى	*wallā*	pass

2d(a)

أدى	*ʔaddā*	cause
أوى	*ʔawwā*	shelter

3s

باحث	*bāħaŧa*	discuss
بادر	*bādara*	hurry
بادل	*bādala*	exchange
بارز	*bāraza*	duel
بارك	*bāraka*	bless
باشر	*bāšara*	undertake
بالغ	*bālaɣa*	exaggerate
تابع	*tāba3a*	track
تاجر	*tājara*	deal

تاخم	*tāxama*	be adjacent
ثابر	*tābara*	persist
جادل	*jādala*	quarrel
جامع	*jāma3a*	have sexual intercourse
جامل	*jāmala*	compliment
جاهد	*jāhada*	strive
جاهر	*jāhara*	reveal
جاوب	*jāwaba*	answer
جاور	*jāwara*	neighbor
جاوز	*jāwaza*	exceed
حادث	*ḫādata*	converse
حاذر	*ḫāđara*	beware
حارب	*ḫāraba*	fight
حاسب	*ḫāsaba*	settle an account
حاصر	*ḫāşara*	besiege
حاضر	*ḫāḑara*	lecture
حافظ	*ḫāfaẓa*	maintain
حاكم	*ḫākama*	prosecute
حالف	*ḫālafa*	enter into an alliance
حاور	*ḫāwara*	have a conversation
حاول	*ḫāwala*	try
حايد	*ḫāyada*	stay away
خابر	*xābara*	call
خادع	*xāda3a*	deceive
خاصر	*xāşara*	put one's arm around sb's waist
خاطب	*xāţaba*	address
خاطر	*xāţara*	risk
خالف	*xālafa*	violate
داعب	*dā3aba*	tease
دافع	*dāfa3a*	defend
داهم	*dāhama*	raid
ذاكر	*đākara*	study
راجع	*rāja3a*	review
رادف	*rādafa*	be synonymous
راسل	*rāsala*	exchange letters
رافق	*rāfaqa*	accompany
راقب	*rāqaba*	observe
راهق	*rāhaqa*	reach puberty
راهن	*rāhana*	bet
راوح	*rāwaḫa*	fluctuate
راوغ	*rāwaɣa*	dodge
زارع	*zāra3a*	farm

زامل	*zāmala*	be an associate
زاول	*zāwala*	practice
زايد	*zāyada*	outbid
سابق	*sābaqa*	race
سارع	*sāra3a*	hurry
ساعد	*sā3ada*	help
سافر	*sāfara*	travel
سامح	*sāmaḫa*	forgive
ساند	*sānada*	support
ساهم	*sāhama*	participate
ساوم	*sāwama*	haggle
ساير	*sāyara*	comply
شابه	*šābaha*	resemble
شاجر	*šājara*	fight
شارك	*šāraka*	participate
شاغب	*šāɣaba*	riot
شاهد	*šāhada*	watch
شاور	*šāwara*	consult
صاحب	*şāḫaba*	befriend
صادر	*şādara*	confiscate
صادف	*şādafa*	meet by chance
صادق	*şādaqa*	befriend
صادم	*şādama*	collide
صارع	*şāra3a*	struggle
صافح	*şāfaḫa*	shake hands
صالح	*şālaḫa*	make peace
ضاحك	*ḑāḫaka*	laugh
ضارب	*ḑāraba*	speculate
ضارع	*ḑāra3a*	be similar
ضاعف	*ḑā3afa*	double
ضايق	*ḑāyaqa*	disturb
طابق	*ţābaqa*	agree
طارد	*ţārada*	chase
طالب	*ţālaba*	demand
طالع	*ţāla3a*	read
ظاهر	*ẓāhara*	support
عاتب	*3ātaba*	blame
عادل	*3ādala*	equal
عارض	*3āraḑa*	oppose
عارك	*3āraka*	fight
عاصر	*3āşara*	be contemporaneous
عاقب	*3āqaba*	punish
عاكس	*3ākasa*	contradict
عالج	*3ālaja*	treat
عامل	*3āmala*	treat

عاند	*3ānada*	become stubborn
عانق	*3ānaqa*	hug
عاهد	*3āhada*	enter into a contract
عاون	*3āwana*	help
عايد	*3āyada*	wish a happy holiday
غادر	*ɣādara*	leave
غافل	*ɣāfala*	surprise
غامر	*ɣāmara*	risk
غاير	*ɣāyara*	be dissimilar
فاخر	*fāxara*	boast
فارق	*fāraqa*	quit
فاصل	*fāṣala*	separate
فاقم	*fāqama*	aggravate
فاوض	*fāwaḍa*	negotiate
قابل	*qābala*	meet
قاتل	*qātala*	battle
قارب	*qāraba*	approach
قارن	*qārana*	compare
قاسم	*qāsama*	share
قاطع	*qāṭa3a*	dissociate oneself
قامر	*qāmara*	gamble
قاول	*qāwala*	make a deal
قاوم	*qāwama*	resist
كاتب	*kātaba*	correspond
كافح	*kāfaḫa*	struggle
كالم	*kālama*	speak
لاحظ	*lāḫaẓa*	notice
لاحق	*lāḫaqa*	pursue
لاطف	*lāṭafa*	stroke
لاكم	*lākama*	box
ماثل	*māṯala*	resemble
مارس	*mārasa*	practice
مازج	*māzaja*	be a mixture
مانع	*māna3a*	object
نازع	*nāza3a*	struggle
ناسب	*nāsaba*	fit
ناشد	*nāšada*	plead
ناضل	*nāḍala*	struggle
نافس	*nāfasa*	compete
نافق	*nāfaqa*	be a hypocrite
ناقش	*nāqaša*	discuss
ناقض	*nāqaḍa*	contradict
ناهض	*nāhaḍa*	oppose
ناوب	*nāwaba*	alternate
ناور	*nāwara*	maneuver
ناول	*nāwala*	submit
هاتر	*hātara*	abuse
هاتف	*hātafa*	telephone
هاجر	*hājara*	migrate
هاجم	*hājama*	attack
واجه	*wājaha*	face
وازن	*wāzana*	balance
واصف	*wāṣafa*	specify
واصل	*wāṣala*	continue
واظب	*wāẓaba*	persist
واعد	*wā3ada*	arrange to meet
وافق	*wāfaqa*	agree
واكب	*wākaba*	accompany
ياسر	*yāsara*	indulge

3s(a)

آخذ	*ʔāxađa*	blame
آزر	*ʔāzara*	help
آلم	*ʔālama*	hurt
آمر	*ʔāmara*	consult

3s(b)

ساءل	*sāʔala*	call to account
لاءم	*lāʔama*	fit

3s(c)

فاجأ	*fājaʔa*	surprise
كافأ	*kāfaʔa*	reward
مالأ	*mālaʔa*	help
ناوأ	*nāwaʔa*	oppose

3g

حاج	*ḫājja*	debate
حاد	*ḫādda*	diverge
قاص	*qāṣṣa*	retaliate

3d

بارى	*bārā*	compete
بالى	*bālā*	care
باهى	*bāhā*	boast
حاكى	*ḫākā*	imitate
حامى	*ḫāmā*	defend
راعى	*rā3ā*	observe
ساوى	*sāwā*	equal
عادى	*3ādā*	show animosity

عافى	*3āfā*	heal
عانى	*3ānā*	suffer
قاسى	*qāsā*	suffer
قاضى	*qāḍā*	prosecute
كارى	*kārā*	rent out
لاقى	*lāqā*	meet
ناجى	*nājā*	whisper
نادى	*nādā*	call out
وازى	*wāzā*	parallel

3d(a)

آتى	*ʔātā*	give

4s

أبحر	*ʔabħara*	sail
أبدع	*ʔabda3a*	create
أبرد	*ʔabrada*	hail
أبرز	*ʔabraza*	highlight
أبطل	*ʔabṭala*	cancel
أبعد	*ʔab3ada*	remove
أبغض	*ʔabɣaḍa*	detest
أبلج	*ʔablaja*	shine
أبلغ	*ʔablaɣa*	inform
أبهج	*ʔabhaja*	make happy
أبهم	*ʔabhama*	obscure
أتعب	*ʔat3aba*	tire
أتقن	*ʔatqana*	be proficient
أتلف	*ʔatlafa*	destroy
أثبت	*ʔaṯbata*	prove
أثقل	*ʔaṯqala*	make heavier
أثلج	*ʔaṯlaja*	snow
أثمر	*ʔaṯmara*	bear fruit
أجبر	*ʔajbara*	force
أجرم	*ʔajrama*	commit a crime
أجمع	*ʔajma3a*	reach a consensus
أجمل	*ʔajmala*	generalize
أجهض	*ʔajhaḍa*	miscarry
أحبط	*ʔaħbaṭa*	frustrate
أحجم	*ʔaħjama*	abstain
أحدث	*ʔaħdaṯa*	cause
أحرج	*ʔaħraja*	embarrass
أحرز	*ʔaħraza*	attain
أحرق	*ʔaħraqa*	burn
أحرم	*ʔaħrama*	enter a state of ritual consecration for hajj
أحزن	*ʔaħzana*	sadden
أحسن	*ʔaħsana*	be good
أحضر	*ʔaħḍara*	bring
أخبر	*ʔaxbara*	tell
أخجل	*ʔaxjala*	embarrass
أخرج	*ʔaxraja*	take out
أخرس	*ʔaxrasa*	make quiet
أخفق	*ʔaxfaqa*	fail
أخلص	*ʔaxlaṣa*	be loyal
أخمد	*ʔaxmada*	extinguish
أدخل	*ʔadxala*	admit
أدرك	*ʔadraka*	realize
أدمج	*ʔadmaja*	integrate
أدمن	*ʔadmana*	be addicted
أدمى	*ʔadmā*	make bleed
أدهش	*ʔadhaša*	surprise
أذعر	*ʔaḏ3ara*	alarm
أذنب	*ʔaḏnaba*	be guilty
أذهل	*ʔaḏhala*	amaze
أربح	*ʔarbaħa*	let gain
أربك	*ʔarbaka*	confuse
أرجع	*ʔarja3a*	return
أرسل	*ʔarsala*	send
أرشد	*ʔaršada*	guide
أرضع	*ʔarḍa3a*	nurse
أرعب	*ʔar3aba*	terrify
أرغم	*ʔarɣama*	make
أرفق	*ʔarfaqa*	attach
أرهب	*ʔarhaba*	terrorize
أرهق	*ʔarhaqa*	exhaust
أزعج	*ʔaz3aja*	disturb
أزمع	*ʔazma3a*	be determined
أزمن	*ʔazmana*	last a long time
أزهر	*ʔazhara*	bloom
أسرع	*ʔasra3a*	hurry
أسرف	*ʔasrafa*	waste
أسعد	*ʔas3ada*	make happy
أسعف	*ʔas3afa*	relieve
أسفر	*ʔasfara*	disclose
أسقط	*ʔasqaṭa*	drop
أسكت	*ʔaskata*	silence
أسكر	*ʔaskara*	make drunk
أسكن	*ʔaskana*	house
أسلم	*ʔaslama*	surrender
أسهر	*ʔashara*	keep awake
أسهل	*ʔushila*	have diarrhea

أسهم	ʔashama	participate
أشبه	ašbaha	resemble
أشرف	ʔašrafa	supervise
أشرق	ʔašraqa	rise
أشعر	ʔaš3ara	notify
أشعل	ʔaš3ala	set on fire
أشغل	ʔašɣala	occupy
أشفق	ʔašfaqa	sympathize
أشمس	ʔašmasa	be sunny
أشهر	ʔašhara	announce
أصبح	ʔaṣbaħa	become
أصدر	ʔaṣdara	publish
أصلح	ʔaṣlaħa	repair
أصمت	ʔaṣmata	silence
أضحك	ʔaḍħaka	make laugh
أضرب	ʔaḍraba	abandon
أضرم	ʔaḍrama	light
أضعف	ʔaḍ3afa	weaken
أطرب	ʔaṭraba	sing
أطعم	ʔaṭ3ama	feed
أطلع	ʔaṭla3a	tell
أطلق	ʔaṭlaqa	release
أظلم	ʔaẓlama	get dark
أظهر	ʔaẓhara	show
أعتق	ʔa3taqa	free
أعتم	ʔa3tama	get dark
أعجب	ʔa3jaba	please
أعجز	ʔa3jaza	weaken
أعجم	ʔa3jama	dot
أعدم	ʔa3dama	execute
أعذر	ʔa3đara	have an excuse
أعرب	ʔa3raba	express
أعضل	ʔa3ḍala	become puzzling
أعظم	ʔa3ẓama	regard as remarkable
أعقب	ʔa3qaba	come after
أعلم	ʔa3lama	notify
أعلن	ʔa3lana	announce
أعمر	ʔa3mara	construct
أغرق	ʔaɣraqa	drown
أغرم	ʔuɣrima	fine
أغضب	ʔaɣḍaba	anger
أغفل	ʔaɣfala	neglect
أغلق	ʔaɣlaqa	close
أغمض	ʔaɣmaḍa	close one's eyes
أفتن	ʔaftana	fascinate
أفرج	ʔafraja	release
أفرح	ʔafraħa	please
أفرد	ʔafrada	isolate
أفرط	ʔafraṭa	overdo
أفرغ	ʔafraɣa	empty
أفرق	ʔafraqa	frighten
أفزع	ʔafza3a	scare
أفسح	ʔafsaħa	clear the way
أفسد	ʔafsada	spoil
أفطر	ʔafṭara	break one's fast
أفعم	ʔaf3ama	fill up
أفلت	ʔaflata	escape
أفلح	ʔaflaħa	prosper
أفلس	ʔaflasa	go bankrupt
أقبل	ʔaqbala	approach
أقدم	ʔaqdama	undertake
أقرض	ʔaqraḍa	lend
أقرف	ʔaqrafa	disgust
أقسم	ʔaqsama	swear
أقطع	ʔaqṭa3a	assign
أقعد	ʔaq3ada	seat
أقفل	ʔaqfala	lock
أقلع	ʔaqla3a	leave
أقلق	ʔaqlaqa	worry
أقنع	ʔaqna3a	persuade
أقال	ʔaqāla	dismiss
أكثر	ʔakŧara	(do) frequently
أكرم	ʔakrama	welcome warmly
أكره	ʔakraha	force
أكمل	ʔakmala	complete
ألجأ	ʔaljaʔa	shelter
ألجم	ʔaljama	rein in
ألحق	ʔalħaqa	attach
ألزم	ʔalzama	force
ألصق	ʔalṣaqa	attach
ألفت	ʔalfata	attract
ألقح	ʔalqaħa	pollinate
ألمح	ʔalmaħa	glance
ألهب	ʔalhaba	kindle
ألهم	ʔalhama	inspire
أمتع	ʔamta3a	let sb enjoy
أمرض	ʔamraḍa	sicken
أمسك	ʔamsaka	hold
أمطر	ʔamṭara	rain
أمكن	ʔamkana	be possible
أنتج	ʔantaja	produce

أنتن	*ʔantana*	stink
أنجب	*ʔanjaba*	beget
أنجز	*ʔanjaza*	achieve
أنذر	*ʔanđara*	warn
أنزل	*ʔanzala*	cause to descend
أنصت	*ʔanṣata*	listen
أنصف	*ʔanṣafa*	treat justly
أنعش	*ʔan3aša*	revive
أنعم	*ʔan3ama*	bestow
أنفق	*ʔanfaqa*	spend
أنقذ	*ʔanqađa*	rescue
أنقص	*ʔanqaṣa*	reduce
أنقع	*ʔanqa3a*	soak
أنكر	*ʔankara*	deny
أهلك	*ʔahlaka*	destroy
أهمل	*ʔahmala*	neglect
أوفد	*ʔawfada*	send
أوقع	*ʔawqa3a*	drop

4s(a)

آثر	*ʔātara*	prefer
آجر	*ʔājara*	rent out
آسف	*ʔāsafa*	distress
آمن	*ʔāmana*	believe

4s(b)

أكأب	*ʔakʔaba*	depress

4s(c)

أبطأ	*ʔabṭaʔa*	slow down
أخطأ	*ʔaxṭaʔa*	make a mistake
أرجأ	*ʔarjaʔa*	postpone
أطفأ	*ʔaṭfaʔa*	put out
أقرأ	*ʔaqraʔa*	have read
أملأ	*ʔamlaʔa*	fill
أنبأ	*ʔanbaʔa*	inform
أنشأ	*ʔanšaʔa*	build

4g

أتم	*ʔatamma*	finish
أجد	*ʔajadda*	be determined
أجل	*ʔajalla*	admire
أجن	*ʔajanna*	madden
أحب	*ʔaḫabba*	love
أحس	*ʔaḫassa*	feel
أحك	*ʔaḫakka*	itch
أحل	*ʔaḫalla*	replace
أذل	*ʔađalla*	humiliate
أسر	*ʔasarra*	please
أشع	*ʔaša33a*	emit
أشل	*ʔašalla*	cripple
أصر	*ʔaṣarra*	insist
أصم	*ʔaṣamma*	go deaf
أضر	*ʔaḍarra*	harm
أطل	*ʔṭalla*	overlook
أظل	*ʔaẓalla*	shade
أعد	*ʔa3adda*	prepare
أعز	*ʔa3azza*	value
أقر	*ʔaqarra*	ratify
أكن	*ʔakanna*	hide
ألح	*ʔalaḫḫa*	urge
أمد	*ʔamadda*	help
أمر	*ʔamarra*	make pass
أمل	*ʔamalla*	bore
أهم	*ʔahamma*	be important

4a1

أوجب	*ʔawjaba*	obligate
أوجد	*ʔawjada*	create
أوجز	*ʔawjaza*	abridge
أوجع	*ʔawja3a*	hurt
أودع	*ʔawda3a*	deposit
أورد	*ʔawrada*	cite
أوشك	*ʔawšaka*	be about to (do)
أوصد	*ʔawṣada*	close
أوصل	*ʔawṣala*	deliver
أوضح	*ʔawḍaḫa*	clarify
أوقف	*ʔawqafa*	stop

4a1(a)

أومأ	*ʔawmaʔa*	point

4a2

أيقظ	*ʔayqaẓa*	wake up

4h

أباح	*ʔabāḫa*	disclose
أباد	*ʔabāda*	exterminate
أباض	*ʔabāḍa*	ovulate
أبان	*ʔabāna*	explain
أتاح	*ʔatāḫa*	provide
أثار	*ʔatāra*	excite

أجاب	*ʔajāba*	answer
أجاد	*ʔajāda*	master
أجاز	*ʔajāza*	allow
أحاط	*ʔaħāṭa*	surround
أحال	*ʔaħāla*	refer
أخاف	*ʔaxāfa*	frighten
أدار	*ʔadāra*	direct
أدان	*ʔadāna*	condemn
أذاب	*ʔađāba*	dissolve
أذاع	*ʔađā3a*	broadcast
أراح	*ʔarāħa*	relieve
أراد	*ʔarāda*	want
أراق	*ʔarāqa*	spill
أراب	*ʔarāba*	make feel suspicious
أزال	*ʔazāla*	remove
أزاح	*ʔazāħa*	pull back
أشار	*ʔašāra*	indicate
أشاد	*ʔašāda*	praise
أشاع	*ʔašā3a*	spread
أصاب	*ʔaṣāba*	hit
أضاع	*ʔaḍā3a*	lose
أضاف	*ʔaḍāfa*	add
أطاع	*ʔaṭā3a*	obey
أطاق	*ʔaṭāqa*	be able to stand
أطال	*ʔaṭāla*	lengthen
أعاد	*ʔa3āda*	return
أعار	*ʔa3āra*	lend
أعاق	*ʔa3āqa*	hinder
أعال	*ʔa3āla*	provide
أعان	*ʔa3āna*	relieve
أغاث	*ʔaɣāta*	help
أغار	*ʔaɣāra*	raid
أغاظ	*ʔaɣāẓa*	anger
أفاد	*ʔafāda*	benefit
أقات	*ʔaqāta*	nourish
أقام	*ʔaqāma*	reside
أمات	*ʔamāta*	kill
أنار	*ʔanāra*	illuminate
أهان	*ʔahāna*	insult
أهاب	*ʔahāba*	frighten
أهاج	*ʔahāja*	agitate

4h(a)

أساء	*ʔasāʔa*	harm
أضاء	*ʔaḍāʔa*	illuminate

4d

أبدى	*ʔabdā*	show
أبقى	*ʔabqā*	leave (behind)
أبكى	*ʔabkā*	make cry
أثنى	*ʔatnā*	praise
أجدى	*ʔajdā*	be useful
أجرى	*ʔajrā*	perform
أجلى	*ʔajlā*	evacuate
أحصى	*ʔaħṣā*	count
أحمى	*ʔaħmā*	heat
أحيا	*ʔaħyā*	revive
أخفى	*ʔaxfā*	hide
أدلى	*ʔadlā*	express
أرخى	*ʔarxā*	loosen
أرضى	*ʔarḍā*	satisfy
أزكى	*ʔazkā*	increase
أسمى	*ʔasmā*	call
أشجى	*ʔašjā*	move
أصحى	*ʔaṣħā*	wake up
أصدى	*ʔaṣdā*	echo
أضحى	*ʔaḍħā*	become
أعدى	*ʔa3dā*	infect
أعطى	*ʔa3ṭā*	give
أعفى	*ʔa3fā*	release
أعمى	*ʔa3mā*	blind
أغرى	*ʔaɣrā*	tempt
أغلى	*ʔaɣlā*	boil
أفتى	*ʔaftā*	issue a fatwa
أفشى	*ʔafšā*	spread
أقصى	*ʔaqṣā*	remove
ألغى	*ʔalɣā*	cancel
ألقى	*ʔalqā*	throw
ألهى	*ʔalhā*	amuse
أمسى	*ʔamsā*	become
أمضى	*ʔamḍā*	sign
أملى	*ʔamlā*	dictate
أنسى	*ʔansā*	make
أنمى	*ʔanmā*	increase
أنهى	*ʔanhā*	finish
أهدى	*ʔahdā*	give
أغمي	*ʔuɣmiya*	faint

4d(a)

آتى	*ʔātā*	give
آذى	*ʔāđā*	hurt
آوى	*ʔāwā*	shelter

4d(b)

أوحى *ʔawɦā*	give an impression of
أوصى *ʔawṣā*	recommend
أولى *ʔawlā*	entrust

4d(c)

أرى *ʔarā*	show

5s

تبخر *tabaxxara*	evaporate
تبرع *tabarra3a*	donate
تبرم *tabarrama*	get bored
تبلل *taballala*	become wet
تبين *tabayyana*	become clear
تتوج *tatawwaja*	be crowned
تجدد *tajaddada*	be renewed
تجسس *tajassasa*	spy
تجعد *taja33uda*	become wrinkled
تجمد *tajammada*	freeze
تجمع *tajamma3a*	gather
تجنب *tajannaba*	avoid
تجنس *tajannasa*	be naturalized
تجهز *tajahhaza*	get ready
تجهم *tajahhama*	frown
تجول *tajawwala*	stroll
تحدث *taɦaddaṯa*	speak
تحدد *taɦaddada*	be determined
تحرج *taɦarraja*	refrain
تحرر *taɦarrara*	be freed
تحرش *taɦarraša*	harass
تحرق *taɦarraqa*	burn
تحرك *taɦarraka*	move
تحسن *taɦassana*	improve
تحصن *taɦaṣṣana*	become immune
تحضر *taɦaḍḍara*	get ready
تحطم *taɦaṭṭama*	break
تحفظ *taɦaffaẓa*	be reserved
تحقق *taɦaqqaqa*	prove to be true
تحكم *taɦakkama*	be in control
تحمس *taɦammasa*	be enthusiastic
تحمل *taɦammala*	endure
تحنط *taɦannaṭa*	be embalmed
تحول *taɦawwala*	change
تحير *taɦayyara*	be confused
تخرج *taxarraja*	graduate
تخصص *taxaṣṣaṣa*	specialize
تخلص *taxallaṣa*	be free
تخلف *taxallafa*	fall behind
تخلل *taxallala*	penetrate
تخمر *taxammara*	ferment
تخوف *taxawwafa*	be afraid
تخيل *taxayyala*	imagine
تدخل *tadaxxala*	interfere
تدرب *tadarraba*	practice
تدرج *tadarraja*	be gradated
تدفق *tadaffaqa*	flow
تدين *tadayyana*	profess
تذكر *tađakkara*	remember
تذمر *tađammara*	complain
تذوق *tađawwaqa*	taste
تذيل *tađayyala*	tail
ترتب *tarattaba*	derive
تردد *taraddada*	hesitate
ترشح *taraššaɦa*	be nominated
ترفق *taraffaqa*	be friendly
تركز *tarakkaza*	be focused
ترهب *tarahhaba*	threaten
تزعم *taza33ama*	lead
تزلج *tazallaja*	ski
تزوج *tazawwaja*	get married
تسبب *tasabbaba*	cause
تسجل *tasajjala*	sign up
تسرب *tasarraba*	leak
تسرع *tasarra3a*	be hasty
تسلح *tasallaɦa*	arm oneself
تسلق *tasallaqa*	climb
تسلل *tasallala*	sneak away
تسلم *tasallama*	receive
تسمم *tasammama*	be poisoned
تسهل *tasahhala*	become easy
تسوس *tasawwasa*	decay
تسوق *tasawwaqa*	go shopping
تسول *tasawwala*	beg
تشتت *tašattata*	scatter
تشدد *tašaddada*	be harsh
تشرد *tašarrada*	be displaced
تشرف *tašarrafa*	be honored
تشعب *taša33aba*	branch out
تشكل *tašakkala*	be formed
تشمس *tašammasa*	bask in the sun
تشوش *tašawwaša*	become confused

تصرف	*taṣarrafa*	act
تصفح	*taṣaffaħa*	skim (through)
تصلب	*taṣallaba*	harden
تصور	*taṣawwara*	imagine
تصوف	*taṣawwuf*	mysticism
تضخم	*taḍaxxama*	become inflated
تضرر	*taḍarrara*	be hurt
تضمخ	*taḍammaxa*	perfume
تضمن	*taḍammana*	include
تطرف	*taṭarrafa*	be extreme
تطرق	*taṭarraqa*	touch on
تطفل	*taṭaffala*	intrude
تطلب	*taṭallaba*	require
تطلع	*taṭalla3a*	look forward
تطور	*taṭawwara*	develop
تطوع	*taṭawwa3a*	volunteer
تظلل	*taẓallala*	be shaded
تعجب	*ta3ajjaba*	be surprised
تعدد	*ta3addada*	be numerous
تعذر	*ta3ađđara*	be impossible
تعرض	*ta3arraḍa*	be subjected
تعرف	*ta3arrafa*	become acquainted
تعرق	*ta3arraqa*	sweat
تعصب	*ta3aṣṣaba*	become intolerant
تعطش	*ta3aṭṭaša*	thirst
تعطل	*ta3aṭṭala*	break down
تعفن	*ta3affana*	rot
تعقب	*ta3aqqaba*	pursue
تعقد	*ta3aqqada*	become complicated
تعلق	*ta3allaqa*	be connected
تعلم	*ta3allama*	learn
تعمد	*ta3ammada*	(do) deliberately
تعمق	*ta3ammaqa*	delve deeply
تعنت	*ta3annata*	become stubborn
تعهد	*ta3ahhada*	undertake
تعود	*ta3awwada*	get used
تعين	*ta3ayyana*	be appointed
تغلب	*taɣallaba*	overcome
تغيب	*taɣayyaba*	be absent
تغير	*taɣayyara*	change
تفتح	*tafattaħa*	open up
تفجر	*tafajjara*	explode
تفحص	*tafaħħaṣa*	inquire
تفرج	*tafarraja*	watch
تفرد	*tafarrada*	withdraw
تفرع	*tafarra3a*	branch out
تفرغ	*tafarraɣa*	have free time
تفرق	*tafarraqa*	scatter
تفضل	*tafaḍḍala*	be so kind as to
تفقد	*tafaqqada*	go to see
تفكر	*tafakkara*	reflect
تفكك	*tafakkaka*	disintegrate
تفهم	*tafahhama*	come to understand
تفوق	*tafawwaqa*	outdo
تقبل	*taqabbala*	receive
تقدر	*taqaddara*	be estimated
تقدم	*taqaddama*	progress
تقرر	*taqarrara*	be decided
تقطر	*taqaṭṭara*	drip
تقطع	*taqaṭṭa3a*	be cut
تقلب	*taqallaba*	fluctuate
تقلص	*taqallaṣa*	contract
تقوس	*taqawwasa*	be bent
تقيد	*taqayyada*	be bound
تكبر	*takabbara*	be arrogant
تكتل	*takattala*	gather in a group
تكثف	*takaŧŧafa*	thicken
تكدس	*takaddasa*	accumulate
تكرر	*takarrara*	be repeated
تكلم	*takallama*	speak
تكوم	*takawwama*	pile up
تكون	*takawwana*	consist
تكيف	*takayyafa*	be regulated
تلبد	*talabbada*	become overcast
تلطخ	*talaṭṭaxa*	become stained
تلفظ	*talaffaẓa*	pronounce
تلهب	*talahhaba*	blaze
تلهف	*talahhafa*	yearn
تلوث	*talawwaŧa*	become polluted
تمتع	*tamatta3a*	enjoy
تمثل	*tamaŧŧala*	take the form
تمدد	*tamaddada*	stretch
تمرد	*tamarrada*	disobey
تمرس	*tamarrasa*	practice
تمرن	*tamarrana*	practice
تمزق	*tamazzaqa*	tear
تمسك	*tamassaka*	persist
تمطط	*tamaṭṭaṭa*	stretch
تمغط	*tamaɣɣaṭa*	stretch

تمكن	*tamakkana*	be able to (do)
تمهل	*tamahhala*	be leisurely
تموج	*tamawwaja*	ripple
تميز	*tamayyaza*	be distinguished
تنبه	*tanabbaha*	notice
تنزه	*tanazzaha*	stroll
تنشق	*tanaššaqa*	inhale
تنصت	*tanaṣṣata*	eavesdrop
تنظف	*tanaẓẓafa*	be cleaned
تنفس	*tanaffasa*	breathe
تنقل	*tanaqqala*	be transported
تنكر	*tanakkara*	be disguised
تنهد	*tanahhada*	sigh
تنوع	*tanawwaʕa*	become diverse
تهرب	*taharraba*	evade
تهشم	*tahaššama*	be destroyed
تهكم	*tahakkama*	make fun
تهور	*tahawwara*	be rash
توتر	*tawattara*	become tense
توجب	*tawajjaba*	be necessary
توجع	*tawajjaʕa*	agonize
توجه	*tawajjaha*	head
توحد	*tawaħħada*	unite
توحش	*tawaħħaša*	become savage
تورط	*tawarraṭa*	become involved
تورم	*tawarrama*	swell up
توزع	*tawazzaʕa*	be distributed
توسط	*tawassaṭa*	mediate
توسع	*tawassaʕa*	widen
توسل	*tawassala*	beg
توشم	*tawaššama*	get a tattoo
توصل	*tawaṣṣala*	reach
توضح	*tawaḍḍaħa*	become clear
توفر	*tawaffara*	be fulfilled
توقع	*tawaqqaʕa*	expect
توقف	*tawaqqafa*	quit
توهج	*tawahhaja*	glow
تيسر	*tayassara*	become easy
تيقن	*tayaqqana*	be certain

5s(a)

تأثر	*taʔaθθara*	be influenced
تأجج	*taʔajjaja*	burn
تأخر	*taʔaxxara*	be late
تأسس	*taʔassasa*	be established
تأسف	*taʔassafa*	regret
تأكد	*taʔakkada*	be certain
تألف	*taʔallafa*	consist
تألق	*taʔallaqa*	shine
تألم	*taʔallama*	be in pain
تأمل	*taʔammala*	contemplate
تأهب	*taʔahhaba*	be ready
تأهل	*taʔahhala*	be qualified
تأوه	*taʔawwaha*	sigh

5s(b)

ترأس	*taraʔʔasa*	head

5s(c)

تجزأ	*tajazzaʔa*	divide
تقيأ	*taqayyaʔa*	vomit
تنبأ	*tanabbaʔa*	predict
تهزأ	*tahazzaʔa*	make fun

5d

تبقى	*tabaqqā*	remain
تبنى	*tabannā*	adopt
تثنى	*taθannā*	double
تجلى	*tajallā*	become obvious
تحدى	*taħaddā*	challenge
تحرى	*taħarrā*	examine
تخطى	*taxaṭṭā*	cross
تخلى	*taxallā*	give up
تدنى	*tadannā*	sink
تربى	*tarabbā*	be raised
تسلى	*tasallā*	have a good time
تسنى	*tasannā*	be feasible
تشكى	*tašakkā*	complain
تصدى	*taṣaddā*	confront
تعدى	*taʕaddā*	exceed
تعشى	*taʕaššā*	eat dinner
تغدى	*taɣaddā*	eat lunch
تغذى	*taɣađđā*	be fed
تغنى	*taɣannā*	sing
تفشى	*tafaššā*	become pandemic
تقوى	*taqawwā*	become strong
تلقى	*talaqqā*	receive
تلوى	*talawwā*	bend
تمشى	*tamaššā*	stroll
تمطى	*tamaṭṭā*	stretch
تمنى	*tamannā*	hope
تهجى	*tahajjā*	spell
توفى	*tawaffā*	pass away

تولى	*tawalla*	take over

5d(a)

تأنى	*taʔannā*	take one's time

6s

تباحث	*tabāħata*	discuss together
تبادل	*tabādala*	exchange
تتابع	*tatāba3a*	follow in succession
تجاهل	*tajāhala*	ignore
تجاوب	*tajāwaba*	agree
تجاوز	*tajāwaza*	pass
تحالف	*taħālafa*	form an alliance
تخاصم	*taxāṣama*	quarrel
تخاطب	*taxāṭaba*	have a conversation
تداخل	*tadāxala*	intertwine
تدارك	*tadāraka*	rectify
تداول	*tadāwala*	circulate
ترابط	*tarābaṭa*	be interrelated
تراجع	*tarāja3a*	retreat
تراسل	*tarāsala*	exchange
تراكم	*tarākama*	accumulate
تراوح	*tarāwaħa*	range
تزامن	*tazāmana*	coincide
تزاوج	*tazāwaja*	intermarry
تزايد	*tazāyada*	increase
تسابق	*tasābaqa*	race
تسارع	*tasāra3a*	hurry
تساقط	*tasāqaṭa*	collapse
تسامح	*tasāmaħa*	be tolerant
تساهل	*tasāhala*	be tolerant
تساوم	*tasāwama*	argue (with each other) over a price
تشابه	*tašābaha*	be similar to each other
تشاجر	*tašājara*	fight with each other
تشارك	*tašāraka*	participate together
تشاور	*tašāwara*	consult
تصاحب	*taṣāħaba*	become friends
تصادف	*taṣādafa*	happen
تصادق	*taṣādaqa*	become friends
تصادم	*taṣādama*	collide
تصاعد	*taṣā3ada*	climb
تصافح	*taṣāfaħa*	shake hands
تصالح	*taṣālaħa*	make peace
تضاحك	*taḍāħaka*	laugh together
تضارب	*taḍāraba*	fight each other
تضاعف	*taḍā3afa*	be doubled
تضامن	*taḍāmana*	combine forces
تضايق	*taḍāyaqa*	be disturbed
تظاهر	*taẓāhara*	demonstrate
تعادل	*ta3ādala*	tie
تعارض	*ta3āraḍa*	be incompatible
تعارف	*ta3ārafa*	get to know each other
تعارك	*ta3āraka*	fight with each other
تعاطف	*ta3āṭafa*	sympathize
تعاقب	*ta3āqaba*	be consecutive
تعاقد	*ta3āqada*	make a contract
تعامل	*ta3āmala*	deal
تعانق	*ta3ānaqa*	hug each other
تعاون	*ta3āwana*	cooperate
تعايش	*ta3āyaša*	coexist
تغافل	*taɣāfala*	neglect
تغاير	*taɣāyara*	vary
تفاعل	*tafā3ala*	interact
تفاقم	*tafāqama*	become aggravated
تفاهم	*tafāhama*	understand each other
تفاوت	*tafāwata*	conflict
تفاوض	*tafāwaḍa*	negotiate
تقابل	*taqābala*	get together
تقاتل	*taqātala*	battle
تقارب	*taqāraba*	approach each other
تقاطع	*taqāṭa3a*	intersect
تقاعد	*taqā3ada*	retire
تقاعس	*taqā3asa*	refrain
تقامر	*taqāmara*	gamble with each other
تكاتب	*takātaba*	write to each other
تكاثر	*takāṯara*	reproduce
تكامل	*takāmala*	be finished
تلاعب	*talā3aba*	play
تماثل	*tamāṯala*	match

تمارض	*tamāraḍa*	feign illness
تنازل	*tanāzala*	relinquish
تناسب	*tanāsaba*	be compatible
تناسق	*tanāsaqa*	be coordinated
تناسل	*tanāsala*	reproduce
تنافس	*tanāfasa*	compete
تناقش	*tanāqaša*	debate
تناقض	*tanāqaḍa*	clash
تناوب	*tanāwaba*	take turns
تناول	*tanāwala*	deal with
تهامس	*tahāmasa*	whisper to each other
تواتر	*tawātara*	recur
تواجد	*tawājada*	exist
توازن	*tawāzana*	balance
تواصل	*tawāṣala*	continue
تواضع	*tawāḍa3a*	behave modestly
توافر	*tawāfara*	be fulfilled
توافق	*tawāfaqa*	conform
توالد	*tawālada*	reproduce

6s(a)

تآلف	*taʔālafa*	harmonize
تآمر	*taʔāmara*	conspire

6s(b)

تثاءب	*taŧāʔaba*	yawn
تساءل	*tasāʔala*	wonder
تشاءم	*tašāʔama*	be pessimistic
تضاءل	*taḍāʔala*	diminish
تفاءل	*tafāʔala*	be optimistic
تلاءم	*talāʔama*	comply

6g

تضاد	*taḍādda*	contradict each other

6d

تبارى	*tabārā*	compete
تتالى	*tatālā*	be successive
تداعى	*tadā3ā*	evoke each other
تداوى	*tadāwā*	be treated
تساوى	*tasāwā*	be even
تعاطى	*ta3āṭā*	practice
تعافى	*ta3āfā*	recover
تعالى	*ta3ālā*	be high
تفادى	*tafādā*	avoid
تقاضى	*taqāḍā*	charge
تناهى	*tanāhā*	come to an end
توازى	*tawāzā*	be parallel
توالى	*tawālā*	follow in succession

6d(a)

تآخى	*taʔāxā*	fraternize

7s

انبثق	*inbaŧaqa*	spring
انحدر	*inɦadara*	slope
انحرف	*inɦarafa*	become perverted
انخفض	*inxafaḍa*	decrease
اندرج	*indaraja*	be included
اندفع	*indafa3a*	rush
اندلع	*indala3a*	break out
اندمج	*indamaja*	integrate
اندهش	*indahaša*	be amazed
انزعج	*inza3aja*	be annoyed
انزلق	*inzalaqa*	slide
انسجم	*insajama*	get along
انسحب	*insaɦaba*	withdraw
انشغل	*inšaɣala*	be busy
انصرف	*inṣarafa*	depart
انصرم	*inṣarama*	pass
انضبط	*inḍabaṭa*	be disciplined
انطبع	*inṭaba3a*	be printed
انطبق	*inṭabaqa*	be applicable
انطلق	*inṭalaqa*	depart
انعتق	*in3ataqa*	free oneself
انعدم	*in3adama*	be non- existent
انعزل	*in3azala*	become isolated
انعطف	*in3aṭafa*	turn
انعقد	*in3aqada*	be held
انعكس	*in3akasa*	be reflected
انغرس	*inɣarasa*	be planted
انفتح	*infataɦa*	open up
انفجر	*infajara*	explode
انفرد	*infarada*	withdraw
انفصل	*infaṣala*	separate
انفضح	*infaḍaɦa*	be disgraced
انفعل	*infa3ala*	become upset
انقرض	*inqaraḍa*	become extinct
انقسم	*inqasama*	be divided

انقطع	*inqaṭa3a*	be severed
انقلب	*inqalaba*	overturn
انكسر	*inkasara*	break
انكشف	*inkašafa*	be uncovered
انهمر	*inhamara*	pour down

7s(a)

انطفأ	*inṭafaʔa*	go out
انكفأ	*inkafaʔa*	retreat

7g

انسد	*insadda*	be obstructed
انشق	*inšaqqa*	split off
انضم	*inḍamma*	join
انفض	*infaḍḍa*	scatter
انقض	*inqaḍḍa*	pounce
انكب	*inkabba*	dedicate oneself

7h

انحاز	*inḥāza*	be biased in favor
انطاد	*inṭāda*	go up in the air
انقاد	*inqāda*	obey
انهار	*inhāra*	collapse

7d

انبغى	*inbaɣā*	should
انحنى	*inḥanā*	bend
انطوى	*inṭawā*	contain
انقضى	*inqaḍā*	expire

8s

ابتسر	*ibtasara*	begin prematurely
ابتسم	*ibtasama*	smile
ابتعد	*ibta3ada*	stay away
ابتكر	*ibtakara*	devise
ابتلع	*ibtala3a*	swallow
ابتهج	*ibtahaja*	be happy
اجترف	*ijtarafa*	shovel
اجتمع	*ijtama3a*	assemble
اجتهد	*ijtahada*	work hard
احتبس	*iḥtabasa*	retain
احتجز	*iḥtajaza*	arrest
احتدم	*iḥtadama*	erupt
احتذر	*iḥtađara*	beware
احترس	*iḥtarasa*	be vigilant
احترف	*iḥtarafa*	be professional
احترق	*iḥtaraqa*	burn
احترم	*iḥtarama*	respect
احتسب	*iḥtasaba*	calculate
احتشم	*iḥtašama*	become modest
احتضن	*iḥtaḍana*	hug
احتفظ	*iḥtafaẓa*	preserve
احتفل	*iḥtafala*	celebrate
احتقر	*iḥtaqara*	despise
احتقن	*iḥtaqana*	be congested
احتكر	*iḥtikara*	monopolize
احتمل	*iḥtamala*	be possible
اختبر	*ixtabara*	experiment
اختتم	*ixtatama*	end
اخترع	*ixtara3a*	invent
اخترق	*ixtaraqa*	penetrate
اختصر	*ixtaṣara*	shorten
اختطف	*ixtaṭafa*	kidnap
اختلج	*ixtalaja*	convulse
اختلس	*ixtalasa*	embezzle
اختلط	*ixtalaṭa*	mix
اختلف	*ixtalafa*	differ
اختنق	*ixtanaqa*	choke
ارتبط	*irtabaṭa*	be connected
ارتبك	*irtabaka*	be confused
ارتجف	*irtajafa*	tremble
ارتزق	*irtazaqa*	live
ارتعب	*irta3aba*	be terrified
ارتعش	*irta3aša*	shiver
ارتفع	*irtafa3a*	rise
ارتقب	*irtaqaba*	anticipate
ارتكب	*irtakaba*	commit
ارتكز	*irtakaza*	be focused
استبق	*istabaqa*	be premature
استلف	*istalafa*	borrow
استلم	*istalama*	receive
استمع	*istama3a*	listen
استند	*istanada*	depend
اشتبك	*ištabaka*	clash
اشتبه	*ištabaha*	suspect
اشترط	*ištaraṭa*	stipulate
اشترك	*ištaraka*	participate
اشتعل	*išta3ala*	catch on fire
اشتغل	*ištaɣala*	work
اشتمل	*ištamala*	contain
اشتهر	*ištahara*	be famous
اصطنع	*iṣṭana3a*	produce

اضطلع	*iɖʈala3a*	take upon oneself
اضطهد	*iɖʈahada*	persecute
اعتبر	*i3tabara*	consider
اعتدل	*i3tadala*	become moderate
اعتذر	*i3tađara*	apologize
اعترض	*i3taraɖa*	object
اعترف	*i3tarafa*	confess
اعتزل	*i3tazala*	isolate oneself
اعتزم	*i3tazama*	be determined
اعتصم	*i3taʂama*	adhere
اعتقد	*i3taqada*	believe
اعتقل	*i3taqala*	arrest
اعتمد	*i3tamada*	lean
اعتنق	*i3tanaqa*	take up
اغترب	*iɣtaraba*	emigrate
اغتصب	*iɣtaʂaba*	rape
افتتح	*iftataɧa*	open
افتتن	*iftatana*	be charmed
افتخر	*iftaxara*	boast
افترس	*iftarasa*	devour
افترض	*iftaraɖa*	suppose
افترق	*iftaraqa*	separate
افتعل	*ifta3ala*	concoct
افتقد	*iftaqada*	miss
افتقر	*iftaqara*	be in need
افتكر	*iftakara*	remember
اقتبس	*iqtabasa*	quote
اقتبل	*iqtabala*	receive
اقتحم	*iqtaɧama*	intrude
اقترب	*iqtaraba*	approach
اقترح	*iqtaraɧa*	suggest
اقترض	*iqtaraɖa*	borrow
اقترع	*iqtara3a*	vote
اقترف	*iqtarafa*	commit
اقتصد	*iqtaʂada*	save
اقتصر	*iqtaʂara*	be restricted
اقتضب	*iqtaɖaba*	summarize
اقتطع	*iqtaʈa3a*	remove
اقتطف	*iqtaʈafa*	select
اقتلع	*iqtala3a*	uproot
اقتنع	*iqtana3a*	be satisfied
اقتاد	*iqtāda*	lead
اكتسب	*iktasaba*	acquire
اكتسح	*iktasaɧa*	sweep
اكتشف	*iktašafa*	discover
اكتظ	*iktaʐʐa*	become overcrowded
اكتمل	*iktamala*	be finished
التحق	*iltaɧaqa*	join
التزم	*iltazama*	be obligated
التفت	*iltafata*	turn
التقط	*iltaqaʈa*	receive
التمس	*iltamasa*	request
التهب	*iltahaba*	become inflamed
التهم	*iltahama*	devour
امتحن	*imtaɧana*	test
امتعض	*imta3aɖa*	resent
امتلك	*imtalaka*	have
امتنع	*imtana3a*	refrain
انتبه	*intabaha*	beware
انتحب	*intaɧaba*	weep
انتحر	*intaɧara*	commit suicide
انتخب	*intaxaba*	elect
انتزع	*intaza3a*	snatch
انتسب	*intasaba*	belong
انتشر	*intašara*	spread
انتصر	*ʔintaʂara*	triumph
انتصف	*intaʂafa*	be halfway over
انتظر	*intaʐara*	wait
انتظم	*intaʐama*	become arranged
انتفخ	*intafaxa*	swell up
انتفض	*intafaɖa*	shake
انتفع	*intafa3a*	benefit
انتقب	*intaqaba*	wear a veil
انتقد	*intaqada*	criticize
انتقل	*intaqala*	move
انتقم	*intaqama*	get revenge
انتكس	*intakasa*	relapse
انتهز	*intahaza*	exploit
انتهك	*intahaka*	violate

8s(a)

ائتلف	*iʔtalafa*	form a coalition
ائتمر	*iʔtamara*	confer
ائتمن	*iʔtamana*	entrust

8s(b)

اكتأب	*iktaʔaba*	become depressed

8s(c)

ابتدأ	*ibtadaʔa*	begin
اختبأ	*ixtabaʔa*	hide
امتلأ	*imtalaʔa*	be filled

8g1

ابتز	*ibtazza*	blackmail
اجتث	*ijtatta*	uproot
احتج	*iħtajja*	protest
احتر	*iħtarra*	become warm
احتك	*iħtakka*	be in contact
احتل	*iħtalla*	occupy
اختص	*ixtaṣṣa*	be marked
ارتج	*irtajja*	jar
ارتد	*irtadda*	reverse
اشتد	*ištadda*	become stronger
اشتم	*ištamma*	smell
اعتد	*i3tadda*	become proud
اعتل	*i3talla*	be weak
التف	*iltaffa*	intertwine
امتد	*imtadda*	extend
امتص	*imtaṣṣa*	absorb
امتن	*imtanna*	bestow
اهتز	*ihtazza*	shake
اهتم	*ihtamma*	be interested

8g2

اضطر	*iḍṭarra*	force sb to (do)

8a1

اتخذ	*ittaxađa*	take up
اتبع	*ittaba3a*	pursue
اتجر	*ittajara*	deal
اتجه	*ittajaha*	turn
اتحد	*ittaħada*	become united
اتزن	*ittazana*	be weighed
اتسخ	*ittasaxa*	become dirty
اتسع	*ittasa3a*	expand
اتسق	*ittasaqa*	be uniform
اتشح	*ittašaħa*	don
اتصف	*ittaṣafa*	be characterized
اتصل	*ittaṣala*	call
اتضح	*ittaḍaħa*	become clear
اتفق	*ittafaqa*	come to pass
اتكل	*ittakala*	rely
اتهم	*ittahama*	accuse

8a1(a)

اتكأ	*ittakaʔa*	lean

8a2

ادخر	*iddaxara*	store

8a3

اطلع	*iṭṭala3*	become acquainted

8a4

ازدحم	*izdaħama*	be crowded
ازدهر	*izdahara*	flourish
ازدوج	*izdawaja*	be doubled

8a5

اصطحب	*iṣṭaħaba*	accompany
اصطدم	*iṣṭadama*	collide
اصطلح	*iṣṭalaħa*	agree

8a6

اضطرب	*iḍṭaraba*	be disturbed

8h1

اجتاح	*ijtāħa*	strike
اجتاز	*ijtāza*	cross
احتاج	*iħtāja*	need
احتاط	*iħtāṭa*	be cautious
احتال	*iħtāla*	trick
احتار	*iħtāra*	be confused
اختار	*ixtāra*	choose
ارتاح	*irtāħa*	take a break
ارتاد	*irtāda*	frequent
ارتاب	*irtāba*	mistrust
اشتاق	*ištāqa*	long
اعتاد	*i3tāda*	get used
اغتال	*iɣtāla*	assassinate
اغتاظ	*iɣtāẓa*	become furious
اقتات	*iqtāta*	feed
امتاز	*imtāza*	be distinguished
انتاب	*intāba*	befall

8h1(a)

استاء	*istāʔa*	be displeased

8h2

ازداد	*izdāda*	increase

8h3

اصطاد	*iṣṭāda*	hunt
اصطاف	*iṣṭāfa*	spend the summer

8d1

ابتغى	*ibtaɣā*	strive
احتذى	*iħtađā*	emulate
احتفى	*iħtafā*	celebrate
احتمى	*iħtamā*	protect oneself
احتوى	*iħtawā*	contain
اختفى	*ixtafā*	hide
ارتدى	*irtadā*	wear
ارتشى	*irtašā*	take bribes
ارتقى	*irtaqā*	ascend
استوى	*istawā*	be even
اشترى	*ištarā*	buy
اشتكى	*ištakā*	complain
اشتهى	*ištahā*	desire
اعتدى	*i3tadā*	trespass
اعتلى	*i3talā*	climb
اعتنى	*i3tanā*	take care
افتدى	*iftadā*	sacrifice
اقتضى	*iqtaḍā*	require
اكتسى	*iktasā*	be covered
اكتفى	*iktafā*	be content
التقى	*iltaqā*	meet
التوى	*iltawā*	be bent
انتدى	*intadā*	gather
انتقى	*intaqā*	select
انتمى	*intamā*	be affiliated
انتهى	*intahā*	end
اهتدى	*ihtadā*	be guided

8d2

اتقى	*ittaqā*	beware

8d3

ادعى	*idda3ā*	allege

8d4

اصطفى	*iṣṭafā*	choose

9s

ابيض	*ibyaḍḍa*	become white
احمر	*iħmarra*	turn red
اخضر	*ixḍarra*	turn green
ازرق	*izraqqa*	turn blue
اسمر	*ismarra*	turn brown
اسود	*iswadda*	turn black
اشقر	*išqarra*	turn golden brown
اصفر	*iṣfarra*	turn yellow

10s

استبدل	*istabdala*	exchange
استبشر	*istabšara*	rejoice
استبعد	*istab3ada*	deem unlikely
استثمر	*istaṯmara*	invest
استجوب	*istajwaba*	interrogate
استحسن	*istaħsana*	recommend
استحضر	*istaħḍara*	send
استخبر	*istaxbara*	ask
استخدم	*istaxdama*	use
استخرج	*istaxraja*	mine
استخلف	*istaxlafa*	appoint as successor
استدرك	*istadraka*	rectify
استذكر	*istađkara*	memorize
استرجع	*istarja3a*	retrieve
استسلم	*istaslama*	surrender
مستشرق	*mustašriq*	orientalist
استشعر	*istaš3ara*	perceive
استشهد	*istašhada*	martyr
استصدر	*istaṣdara*	issue
استصرخ	*istaṣraxa*	cry for help
استصعب	*istaṣ3aba*	consider difficult
استصلح	*istaṣlaħa*	consider useful
استطرد	*istaṭrada*	go on
استطلع	*istaṭla3a*	investigate
استعبد	*ista3bada*	enslave
استعجل	*ista3jala*	hurry
استعرض	*ista3raḍa*	study
استعلم	*ista3lama*	inquire
استعمر	*ista3mara*	settle
استعمل	*ista3mala*	use
استغرب	*istaɣraba*	be surprised
استغرق	*istaɣraqa*	take
استغفر	*istaɣfara*	ask (God) for forgiveness

استفرغ	*istafraɣa*	vomit
استفهم	*istafhama*	ask
استقبل	*istaqbala*	receive
استقدم	*istaqdama*	summon
استقطب	*istaqṭaba*	attract
استكبر	*istakbara*	become arrogant
استكشف	*istakšafa*	explore
استكمل	*istakmala*	complete
استلزم	*istalzama*	require
استلهم	*istalhama*	seek inspiration
استمتع	*istamta3a*	enjoy
استمطر	*istamṭara*	pray for rain
استنتج	*istantaja*	infer
استنجد	*istanjada*	call out for the help
استنشق	*istanšaqa*	inhale
استنفد	*istanfada*	deplete
استنفر	*istanfara*	alert
استنقع	*istanqa3a*	become stagnant
استنكر	*istankara*	disapprove
استنكر	*istankara*	condemn
استهجن	*istahjana*	disapprove
استهدف	*istahdafa*	have in mind
استهلك	*istahlaka*	consume
استوجب	*istawjaba*	require
استودع	*istawda3a*	entrust
استورد	*istawrada*	import
استوصف	*istawṣafa*	consult
استوضح	*istawḍaħa*	ask for clarification
استوطن	*istawṭana*	settle
استوعب	*istaw3aba*	absorb
استوقد	*istawqada*	ignite
استوقف	*istawqafa*	ask sb to stop
استيقظ	*istayqaẓa*	wake up

10s(a)

استأجر	*istaʔjara*	rent
استأذن	*istaʔđana*	ask permission
استأنف	*istaʔnafa*	resume
استأهل	*istaʔhala*	be worthy

10s(b)

استرأف	*istarʔafa*	beg for mercy

10s(c)

استقرأ	*istaqraʔa*	investigate
استهزأ	*istahzaʔa*	make fun

10g

استبد	*istabadda*	overpower
استجد	*istajadda*	be new
استجم	*istajamma*	take a break
استحق	*istaħaqqa*	deserve
استحم	*istaħamma*	bathe
استخف	*istaxaffa*	look down
استرد	*istaradda*	retrieve
استعد	*ista3adda*	get ready
استغل	*istaɣalla*	exploit
استفز	*istafazza*	provoke
استقر	*istaqarra*	stabilize
استقل	*istaqalla*	become independent
استمد	*istamadda*	derive
استمر	*istamarra*	
استهل	*istahalla*	start

10h

استجاب	*istajāba*	respond
استجار	*istajāra*	seek refuge
استحال	*istaħāla*	be impossible
استدار	*istadāra*	turn
استدام	*istadāma*	continue
استراح	*istarāħa*	relax
استساغ	*istasāɣa*	approve
استشار	*istašāra*	consult
استشاط	*istašāṭa*	become angry
استضاف	*istaḍāfa*	host
استطاع	*istaṭā3a*	be able to (do)
استطال	*istaṭāla*	become long
استعاد	*ista3āda*	retrieve
استعاذ	*ista3āđa*	take refuge
استعار	*ista3āra*	borrow
استعان	*ista3āna*	seek help
استغاث	*istaɣāta*	ask for help
استفاد	*istafāda*	benefit
استقام	*istaqāma*	stand upright
استقال	*istaqāla*	resign
استكان	*istakāna*	resign oneself
استلام	*istalāma*	deserve blame
استمات	*istamāta*	risk one's life

استنار	*istanāra*	be enlightened
استهان	*istahāna*	consider easy

10h(a)

استضاء	*istaḍāʔa*	be enlightened

10d

استبقى	*istabqā*	retain
استثنى	*istaŧnā*	make an exception
استحيا	*istaħyā*	let live
استدعى	*istad3ā*	summon
استرخى	*istarxā*	become loose
استشفى	*istašfā*	seek medical treatment
استعدى	*ista3dā*	ask sb for help
استعلى	*ista3lā*	rise
استغنى	*istaɣnā*	not need
استفتى	*istaftā*	ask sb's opinion
استلقى	*istalqā*	lie down
استمنى	*istamnā*	masturbate
استوفى	*istawfā*	receive
استولى	*istawlā*	seize

Quadriliteral Verbs

11s

برعم	*bar3ama*	bud
برمج	*barmaja*	program
برهن	*barhana*	prove
بستن	*bastana*	garden
بسمل	*basmala*	say " In the name of God, the Most Gracious, the Most Merciful"
بعثر	*ba3ŧara*	scatter
بقبق	*baqbaqa*	bubble
ترجم	*tarjama*	translate
تكتك	*taktaka*	tick
تلفز	*talfaza*	televise
تلفن	*talfana*	telephone
ثرثر	*ŧarŧara*	chatter
جدول	*jadwala*	catalog
جرجر	*jarjara*	drag
حمحم	*ħamħama*	whinny
حوقل	*ħawqala*	say " There is no power nor strength except in God."
خربش	*xarbaša*	scratch
خرخر	*xarxara*	purr
خشخش	*xašxaša*	rattle
خصخص	*xaṣxaṣa*	privatize
دردش	*dardaša*	chat
دغدغ	*daɣdaɣa*	tickle
دهور	*dahwara*	cause to deteriorate
رفرف	*rafrafa*	flutter
رومن	*rawmana*	Romanize
زحزح	*zaħzaħa*	displace
زحلق	*zaħlaqa*	make slip
زخرف	*zaxrafa*	decorate
زركش	*zarkaša*	adorn
زعزع	*za3za3a*	shake
زغرد	*zaɣrada*	ululate
زقزق	*zaqzaqa*	chirp
زلزل	*zalzala*	shake
سلسل	*salsala*	sequence
سيطر	*sayṭara*	dominate
شعشع	*ša3ša3a*	dilute
ضعضع	*ḍa3ḍa3a*	undermine
عرقل	*3arqala*	hamper
عنون	*3anwana*	address
عولم	*3awlama*	globalize
غطرس	*ɣaṭrasa*	be arrogant
فرقع	*farqa3a*	bang
فرمل	*farmala*	brake
فلسف	*falsafa*	philosophize
فلفل	*falfala*	pepper
فهرس	*fahrasa*	index
قرفص	*qarfaṣa*	squat
قنبل	*qanbala*	bomb
كهرب	*kahraba*	electrify
لجلج	*lajlaja*	stammer

مركز	*markaza*	centralize
ململ	*malmala*	hurry
نمنم	*namnama*	miniaturize
هرول	*harwala*	rush
هلوس	*halwasa*	hallucinate
همهم	*hamhama*	mumble
هندس	*handasa*	engineer
هيمن	*haymana*	keep an eye
وسوس	*waswasa*	whisper

11s(a)

أقلم	*ʔaqlama*	acclimatize
أمرك	*ʔamraka*	Americanize

11s(b)

طمأن	*ṭamʔana*	reassure

12s

تبلور	*tabalwara*	crystalize
تحرشف	*taḫaršafa*	be scaly
تدهور	*tadahwara*	deteriorate
تذبذب	*tađabđaba*	fluctuate
تزحلق	*tazaḫlaqa*	slip
تزعزع	*taza3za3a*	shake
تسلسل	*tasalsala*	follow in order
تضعضع	*taḍa3ḍa3a*	become dilapidated
تغرغر	*taɣarɣara*	gargle
تغطرس	*taɣaṭrasa*	be arrogant
تكهرب	*takahraba*	become electrified
تمركز	*tamarkaza*	focus
تململ	*tamalmala*	be restless

12s(a)

تأرجح	*taʔarjaḫa*	rock
تأقلم	*taʔaqlama*	acclimatize oneself
تأمرك	*taʔamraka*	become Americanized

13s

اضمحل	*iḍmaḫalla*	fade away
اقشعر	*iqša3arra*	shiver

13s(a)

اشرأب	*išraʔabba*	crane one's neck
اشمأز	*išmaʔazza*	be disgusted
اطمأن	*iṭmaʔanna*	be calm

	و	ي	ء	*other*
R^1				
R^2				
R^3				

perfect

	singular	dual	plural
1			
2m			
2f			
3m			
3f			

indicative

	singular	dual	plural
1			
2m			
2f			
3m			
3f			

subjunctive

	singular	dual	plural
1			
2m			
2f			
3m			
3f			

jussive

	singular	dual	plural
1			
2m			
2f			
3m			
3f			

imperative

	singular	dual	plural
2m			
2f			

participles

active	passive

passive

perfect	imperfect

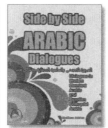

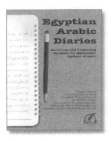

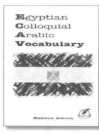

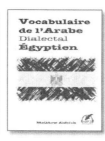

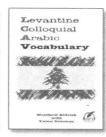

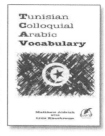

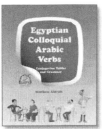

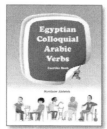

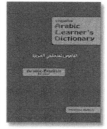

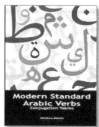

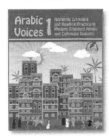

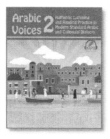

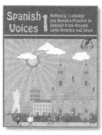

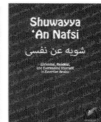

Printed in Great Britain
by Amazon

30199821R00101